S0-CTX-257

Social Class, the Nominal Group and Verbal Strategies

Primary Socialization, Language and Education
Edited by Basil Bernstein
University of London Institute of Education
Sociological Research Unit

I *Social Class, Language and Communication*
W. Brandis & D. Henderson

II *A Linguistic Description and Computer Program for Children's Speech*
G. J. Turner & B. A. Mohan

III *Talk Reform*
D. M. & G. A. Gahagan

IV *Class, Codes and Control*
Volume 1 *Theoretical Studies towards a Sociology of Language*
Volume 2 *Applied Studies towards a Sociology of Language*
Volume 3 *Towards a Theory of Educational Transmissions*
B. Bernstein

V *A Question of Answers (2 vols)*
W. P. Robinson & S. J. Rackstraw

VI *Social Control and Socialization*
J. Cook-Gumperz

VII *Selection and Control*
W. Brandis & B. Bernstein

VIII *Social Class, the Nominal Group and Verbal Strategies*
P. R. Hawkins

IX *Code in Context*
Diana S. Adlam

A catalogue of other series of Social Science books published by Routledge & Kegan Paul will be found at the end of this volume.

Social Class, the Nominal Group and Verbal Strategies

P. R. Hawkins

Department of English
Victoria University of Wellington
New Zealand

ROUTLEDGE & KEGAN PAUL
London, Henley and Boston

First published in 1977
by Routledge & Kegan Paul Ltd
39 Store Street
London WC1E 7DD,
Broadway House,
Newtown Road,
Henley-on-Thames,
Oxon RG9 1EN, and
9 Park Street,
Boston, Mass. 02108, USA
Filmset in 'Monophoto' Times 10 on 11 pt by
Richard Clay (The Chaucer Press), Ltd, Bungay, Suffolk
and printed in Great Britain by
Fletcher & Son Ltd, Norwich

ISBN 0 7100 8375 0

Contents

Foreword

Basil Bernstein

Professor in the Sociology of Education
Head of the Sociological Research Unit,
University of London Institute of Education

In this monograph, Hawkins analyses aspects of children's speech elicited by a structured interview. He focusses upon the nominal group, reference and the underlying verbal strategies which he considers account for the class differences which his analysis reveals. In general, he finds that these differences relate more to the social class position of the families of the children than to their 'intelligence' test scores. Hawkins's analysis shows the importance of carrying out a close contextual study of the children's speech. Indeed, the various situations which made up the original interview of the children at five years of age and at seven years of age made possible such an examination. Hawkins argues, and, in the context of this specific study, appropriately, that such class differences as he finds can best be understood in terms of differences between the children in their selection of verbal strategies. These differences in verbal strategies are then to be related to differences in verbal strategies in the family and community. Hawkins argues that strategies can be derived from underlying speech functions and dialect from underlying syntactic structures. In this way he considers that the difference between Labov and the theoretical perspective of the SRU is that the former focusses upon social dialect and the latter focusses upon the functions of language in different contexts, that is, upon verbal strategies. Hawkins sees a similarity between his concept of verbal strategy and my concept of speech variant and he stresses that there is less chance of over-generalising if analyses are carried out in terms of differences in verbal strategies. He argues, and I agree with him, that one can only use the concept of code if it is possible to show that there is an underlying regulation on the selection of verbal strategies across a range of different contexts or situations. In the next SRU monograph (*Code in Context* by Diana S. Adlam, Routledge & Kegan Paul, 1977) there is an attempt to inquire into whether there is such an underlying regulation. Hawkins indicates the problems of such an analysis.

One of the difficulties of the publication policy of the SRU is that often each monograph tends to be seen as a specialised study rather than as one of a related number of studies. It is important to see this study in relation to previous monographs, and in relation to the ones to follow: otherwise there is a danger that our focus will appear to be entirely confined to forms of implicitness and explicitness realised by the nominal group. The reader should also bear in mind that the children in this study are five years of age, whereas in other studies and monographs the children are seven years of age.

It might be appropriate to comment yet again on the effect of the eliciting context on the speech of children from the different social classes (middle-class and lower-working-class). In general (and particularly when the children were seven years of age) the middle-class and working-class children respond to the interview situation very differently. As we have pointed out many times, there is no difference between the children in the *amount* of speech, indeed in some situations lower-working-class children talk more than the middle-class children. Many people have argued that the class differences between the children when they were talking about the Trotin card pictures can be explained in terms of the fact that researcher and child were *both* looking at the pictures. However, as Hawkins points out, this does not explain why the middle-class children's speech at five is relatively more explicit or why at seven the class differences between the children are stronger. Further, in other situations in the interview, this shared perspective was *not present*, yet class differences in the children's orientations were found.

If we take the Trotin situation, or the picture series, the children were given no guide as to how to talk about the pictures. Second, in the situation where the child was asked to explain the rules of a game to a child who did not know how to play, no guide was given to direct the child towards any one form of explanation.

In an experiment to be published later, middle-class children and lower-working-class children were asked to group photographs of food (bread, cheese, meat, milk, vegetables, etc.). *Initially* middle-class children gave rationales for their grouping in terms of a context-independent principle, whereas the working-class children gave rationales in terms of food in the cultural context of use. The children constructed meals of various kinds. Again, the initial instruction to the children was open. The children could sort the photographs in any way they wished.

What accounts for differences in the strategies adopted by the children in these various situations? These very different situations have one feature in common. The eliciting instruction does not specify the form the response should take. Yet the middle-class children translate this open request into a request for a particular type of response. We know that this translation is independent of the 'measured intelligence' of the children, and that the translation is made in very different situations within a structured context. The translation of an open eliciting question which implicitly or explicitly says 'do it any way you want' into a very specialised response, where the meanings and realisations are less related to the child's everyday experience, makes the response of the child highly context-specific. In some way, the child believes that what is required is that his/her response is not to be based upon the meanings and realisations of everyday informal interactions. The interview context (adult–task–child–response–adult evaluation) appears to be seen by the middle-class child as calling for a specialised response irrespective of a question which appears to offer the child a variety of ways of responding. Indeed, the child translates or rather re-codes an open question into a closed question. The child re-codes a weak classification and weak framing request implicitly 'do it any way you want, and talk about it how you wish' into a strongly classified and strongly framed request 'do it one way and talk about it one particular way'. How does a child come to understand that this is what is required, this is what is to be assessed? How does the child come to hold this expectation of an adult? Further, how does the child acquire the performance rule whereby he/she constructs the appropriate text? Thus there are two interrelated questions. In Hawkins's terms, possessing the verbal strategy which constructs a specific text *and* recognising that the strategy is appropriate to a given context.

Neither middle-class nor working-class parents are constantly talking to their children in specialised ways, nor requiring that their children talk to them in equally specialised ways. Parents ask open-ended questions which are no more than that. However, it may well be that certain contexts imbedded in the flow of parent–child communication are especially marked by the social relationships, their content and their realisations. And in these contexts questions and answers, explanations and descriptions, expansions, qualifications take a very context-specific form. Their format, their inter-actional structure is different from that associated with everyday local affairs. A different pressure is exerted on the child to produce and receive a different structure of meanings and their appropriate realisations. In these contexts the meanings and realisations are less imbedded in – although they may arise out of – local social relationships, local practices, local activities. To this extent, the meanings are less directly tied to a *specific* material basis. We would argue that here the meanings, the principles which generate them, become specialised objects in their own right, and the social relationships through which they are realised become specially marked. Indeed, an open question in this context may be used by the parent to test whether the child can produce 'spontaneously' the appropriate reply. The child learns to distinguish between open questions – according to their context the child learns which open questions are in fact *testing* rather than eliciting questions, the child learns the nature of the response expected, the child learns how to select and structure his/her meanings, the child learns the appropriate form of their realisation, the child learns the confidence to manage a social relationship where the pre-suppositions of everyday relationships are temporarily suspended. The analogy with future educational contents is not too difficult to draw. From this point of view, we should distinguish between recognising when a verbal strategy is contextually relevant, possessing the strategy and using it. Because of the correspondence between features of middle-class familial transmissions and formal educational transmissions, middle-class children have the means to appropriate such transmissions and their experience is legitimated by the school, which in turn enables the child to *legitimate the school* irrespective of the immediate relevance of what is to be acquired or the level of the child's performance. What happens when this correspondence is not present? The mutual legitimising of the child of the school and the school of the child is less likely. It is not a mutually validating experience. In this situation, the school is likely to discount the experience of the child to be followed eventually by the child discounting the experience of the school.

Further, *to say the least*, the sequencing rules of educational transmissions, the pacing of the transmission (the rate of expected acquisition), its future relevance and its immediate irrelevance are based upon performance rules which the middle-class child embryonically possesses. Class regulates the elaborated codes of education and in the family. However, if we start from the view that all children possess common competences, are eager to find out about their world and control it, we might come to understand the social basis of differences in children's *performances*, how performances are socially constituted, how and why some are legitimised and others not, which might then create conditions for change, at least in education.

General introduction

The aim of this monograph is to present some of the differences which have been found in the use of language by children drawn from different social backgrounds. The results which will be given arise, in the first place, from a grammatical analysis of the children's speech which was carried out with the aid of a computer program. This grammatical analysis, the computer program, and the analysis of the results given by the program, form part of the research work that is being carried out in the Sociological Research Unit into the linguistic and sociological basis of differences in children's use of language.

In this monograph I hope to present some of the linguistic differences which have been found, and to explain them in as clear and straightforward a manner as possible, using non-technical language if appropriate and giving some explanation for the technical terms which must necessarily be used throughout the description. I do this because there may be specialists and research workers in related fields, other than linguistics, who are unfamiliar with linguistic terminology but who may nevertheless require access to the results reported here.

The monograph will be divided into two parts. Part I is concerned mainly with the results which were taken directly from the figures given by the computer analysis. It also introduces the particular grammatical area with which we shall be concerned throughout, namely, the nominal group and its constituent categories. Part II presents the findings which resulted from a more detailed and extended investigation of the nominal group. This extended research into one particular area was motivated by the results given by the computer analysis, which are presented in Part I. These results suggested that a further investigation of the data would be worthwhile, taking first a larger sample of children, and second, more finely differentiated linguistic categories. It is from the extended research, therefore, that the differences in language usage between different groups of children emerge most clearly, and they will be presented and discussed in Part II.

Part I is thus mainly concerned with putting the research into its historical perspective, and showing how the subsequent investigation developed from the earlier results. The reader might therefore wish to go straight to Part II, or to the summary at the end of Part I. It is recommended, however, that readers unfamiliar with the linguistic categories of the nominal group should consult Part I, since it contains an introduction to these categories, which in turn form the basis of the categories used in Part II.

On the whole, the results presented in Part I are superseded by those given in Part II, because as the research progressed the linguistic categories were re-defined to take account of new insights. Some categories had to be sub-divided, while others were amalgamated.

To give one example: when modifying adjectives were taken as a formal category, the frequency count performed by the computer revealed no statistically significant differences between middle- and working-class children. Yet when adjectives were sub-classified according to type and function, considerable and significant differences were found for certain types, as will be shown in the relevant sections in Part II.

I shall not be concerned in any detail with problems of language acquisition as such, and the development of phonological and grammatical competence; I shall assume that by the age of five, which is when our speech sample was collected, most of the basic phonological and grammatical structure has already been acquired, together with a substantial vocabulary. We shall thus be concerned with differences in the *use* of language by children from different social backgrounds and of different verbal ability.

The theory which forms the foundation of the research being undertaken by the S.R.U. is that developed by Bernstein (cf. especially 1962b, 1965, 1971, 1972). Discussions of the theory, and empirical results based on it, are also to be found in several works, such as Robinson (1965), Lawton (1968), and others. I shall therefore assume that the reader is to some extent familiar with the concept of restricted and elaborated codes.

The framework upon which the research is based means that we shall be primarily concerned, in this study, with differences in language usage between children of middle- and working-class origin. There are other parameters, however, which may determine differences in language behaviour, and these too must be taken into consideration. In particular, we shall investigate the effects of measured verbal ability, or IQ, on the children's performance, and also the effects of sex-difference. A further measure to be considered is a 'communication index', which was devised by members of the S.R.U. on the basis of a questionnaire given to the children's mothers, the purpose of which was to estimate the extent to which the mother encourages her child to communicate through language, by talking to the child, answering its questions, and so on. More details of this index will be given later (page 63ff.). It is of particular interest, however, in that it enables language differences to be related to a measure of the type of communication within the family, rather than to a difference purely of social class, though there is, of course, a strong correlation between social class and the communication index.

Full details of the collection of the speech samples from five-year-old children may be found in the first monograph of this series (Brandis and Henderson, 1970), and they will therefore only be summarised here.

The sample of children was chosen from two geographically separate areas of London, one containing a predominantly working-class population, the other middle-class. The children were interviewed individually after they had been at school for three weeks. Their mothers had also been interviewed in the summer before the children went to school. The social position of the family was determined in terms of the educational and occupational status of the mother and of the father.

The total sample consisted of 291 working-class children and 148 middle-class. Each interview with the children lasted about half an hour, during which they were asked to perform six different 'tasks', each designed to elicit different kinds of speech and to involve language in a variety of situations. This monograph will be concerned with the speech from only two of these six tasks, but they are the two which produced the greatest quantity of speech.

The interviews with the children were tape-recorded and subsequently transcribed. The transcriptions are in traditional orthography, but represent the spoken utterances as accurately as possible; that is to say, they are unedited, and include all interruptions to the flow of speech such as 'um' and 'er', repeated words, and incompleted phrases.

Part I

Introduction

The first part of the monograph will be devoted mainly to presenting the grammatical categories which constitute the nominal group, and differences in the frequency with which different groups of children use these categories. The data here is derived from the output of the computer program [1] which was written to analyse and count all the grammatical categories. These categories were established in the first place by a linguistic analysis of the children's speech, and then a program was written so that the categories could be handled by the computer.

As a very simple example of this procedure, consider the clause

the boys kicked the ball

Our linguistic analysis (based on 'systemic' grammar, see p. 9) will describe this as a clause containing a Subject (*the boys*), a Predicator (*kicked*), and a Complement (*the ball*). We can use the letters S, P, C, to represent these structural elements. The Subject can then be further sub-divided into a 'modifier' (*the*) and a 'head' (*boys*). Similarly, we can sub-divide the Complement, and the Predicator may be broken down into (verb) + (tense), and so on. If we use a single letter to represent each grammatical category, we can re-write the clause as:

SMH PVT CMH

A computer program can then be written which will read in the clause, coded in this way, and either simply count each category, or perform more complex operations, counting, for example, all modifiers (M) occurring at Complement (C), if it is decided that such information is required.

The grammatical analysis, and the computer program written to handle it, are described in full in Turner and Mohan (1970). The categories of the nominal group, at least those to be described in this part, are those which were established by Turner and Mohan.[2] I shall therefore only summarise the structure of the nominal group (p. 9) sufficiently for the subsequent account of the categories to be comprehensible.

The sample

Not all of the children from whom speech was collected were used for the computer analysis of speech. A carefully controlled sub-sample of children was selected, so that the children were matched for social class, measured verbal ability (or IQ), sex, and the communication index rating of the mothers. The following distinctions were recognised:

Social class	middle, working
IQ	high, medium, low
Sex	boys, girls
Communication index	high, low

This arrangement gives us $2 \times 3 \times 2 \times 2 = 24$ groups or 'cells' of children, and if we assign five children to each cell we shall obtain a sample of 120 children. It was, however, impossible to find any middle-class children who had both low IQ and low CI scores, and the design was therefore short of two cells (one for boys and one for girls). The sub-sample thus consisted of 110 children who were matched on all the four variables listed above, except for the two cells just mentioned.

This kind of design, which matches children on a number of variables or 'factors', is known as a 'factorial design'. Its advantage is that the effect of each variable may be estimated independently, since the others have been 'controlled'. One is able to estimate the effect of social class, for example, without its being confounded by differences in the measured ability of the children, or their sex and so on; and, similarly, the effect of IQ differences, independently of social class, sex or CI effects. The test used to measure the independent effect of each variable is known as 'analysis of variance'.

The tasks

The speech schedule which was given to each child in the interview contained six different tasks, each designed to bring out different uses of language in different situations (Brandis and Henderson, 1970, pp. 22 ff). We are considering here the results on two of these tasks, the second, which is known as the 'picture stories', and the third, which is known as 'the Trotin cards'. Task 2 consisted of three stories, told in a series of pictures (without captions); Task 3 consisted of three post-card reproductions of paintings by Hector Trotin. The children were asked to tell the stories, in the first case, and to describe the pictures in the second. Further details of these tasks, including the pictures themselves, may be found in Part II.

The nominal group

The nominal group is a feature of the 'system-structure' grammar[3] devised and developed by the post-Firthian group of linguists, in particular by Halliday. The description to be given here is a general one, which derives from the terms used by these linguists, but the grammatical categories which were used in the computer analysis were those established by Turner and Mohan, and although most of the terms they use are also to be found in general use, certain differences in terminology may arise. Turner and Mohan did base their categories on those of system-structure grammar, but made some selections, modifications and extensions to suit their immediate purpose, viz. the analysis of a large quantity of children's speech. I shall be using both the general terms, and some of the particular categories devised by Turner and Mohan. All terms will be briefly explained as they occur.[4]

The nominal group, then, as defined within system-structure grammar, usually operates as Subject or Complement within the clause, and consists of three elements, two of which are optional (modification and qualification) and one obligatory (head). Any word or words occurring within the group and *before* the 'head' are known as 'modifiers', while those occurring *after* the 'head' are called 'qualifiers'. The basic sequence is thus,

(m) h (q)

The head of a nominal group is usually a word of the class 'noun' or 'pronoun', though it may be a word of almost any class (see p. 11). A description of each of these three elements, with examples, now follows.

(i) **Qualifier**

Qualifiers may consist of either one word, or a prepositional group, or a clause. Examples of h and different kinds of q will make this clear:

he wanted something *else*
h q (one-word)

they *all* went shopping
h q (one-word)
I'll smack you *both*
h q (one-word)
A piece *of glass*
h q (adverbial group)
The mint *with the hole*
h q (adverbial group)
That one *over there*
h q (adverbial group)
She's the lady *who's getting married*
h q (clause)
They're looking for something *to eat*
h q (clause)

(ii) **Modifier**

Whereas anything in the nominal group which occurs *after* the head must (by definition) be a qualifier, anything that occurs *before* it is known as a modifier, as we have already noted. Modifiers are sub-divided into different kinds of words which are defined according to their position of occurrence [5]—deictics (mainly determiners—words like *a*, *the*, *some*, *any*, *no*, *this*, *that*), ordinatives (*one*, *two*, *three*, *first*, *second*, *next*, *last*), epithets (*little*, *big*, *black*, *green*, *nice*, *naughty*), and nominals (nouns functioning as 'adjectives', like *stone* in *a stone wall*).[6] Any head may have one or more modifiers before it. Usually there is only one, a determiner as in: *a boy*, *the fish*, *some people*.

If there is more than one, the sequence

d o e n h

is maintained, eg.

the two little red motor cars
d o e e n h

A type of sub-modifier known as the 'intensifier' (words like *very*, *too*) may be inserted into this sequence, eg.

A very good breakfast
d i e h
Too many people
i o h

(iii) **Head**

The head of the nominal group is usually realised by a noun or pronoun, but it may be a word of another class, for example an adjective like *hungry* in

he was hungry

which of course may be preceded by an intensifier like *very*. Altogether, ten types of 'head' were recognised for the computer analysis. These types, and examples to illustrate them, will now be given.

	Categories at 'head'	*Example*
1	Determiners (except those in categories 6 and 7)	I want *some*
2	Ordinators	*Two* came
3	Adjectives	It's *lovely*
4	Nouns	The *bus* came
5	Pronouns	*It* came
6	This, these	*This* came
7	That, those	*Those* came
8	Question-words	*Who* came?
9	Missing element	the —
10	'Rankshifted' clause	I think *they came*

Category 9, missing element, occurred only in interrupted utterances and need not concern us further. The concept of 'rankshift', however, which appears in category 10, requires further explanation.

Rankshift

'Rankshift' (also frequently referred to as 'embedding' in some contexts) takes place when an element is realised not by units of the rank below it, as is usual, but by other units at the same or higher rank than itself. Clause-elements like S and C, for example, are usually realised by a nominal group (*clause* being the rank above *group*), but they may instead be realised by another clause – which is in that case called a 'rankshifted' clause, eg.

S	P	C
they	did	their duty (C realised by nominal group)
they	did	what was necessary (C realised by rankshifted clause)
what was needed	was	a rest (S realised by rankshifted clause)

Similarly, rankshifting can occur at the modifier or qualifier within the nominal group, such that a qualifier may be realised not by a word, like *all* in *they all*, but by a group, as in

the people *with red hats*
m h q (q realised by rankshifted group —a 'group within a group')

or even by a clause, as in

the people *who were here*
q (realised by rankshifted clause)

(see also the previous examples of qualifiers, on pp. 9–10).

Within the modifier, it is possible to have rankshifted groups, but rankshifted clauses are rare. An example like

the sailor's trousers

is treated as one group (*the sailor*) rankshifted within another group (*the trousers*). An example of a rankshifted clause in this position might be

a going-to-the-shops picture

(Note how such examples are generally written with hyphens in English, to make the structure clear.)

Rankshifted clauses may, as we have seen, occur as qualifiers but they usually realise the position of 'head', and are generally found at the Complement within the clause. Further examples of this type of structure are:

she saw *them running away*
he thought *it was a fish*
I wonder *what he's doing*

A nominal group, then, may appear at any position within the clause, except as a 'Predicator' (or 'verb'). The clause

they broke the window with a ball

contains three nominal groups, *they*, *the window*, *a ball*.

Linguists have found it necessary to introduce these new terms, or give new meanings to old terms, in order to base their definitions on formal, or structural criteria. The traditional terms which they replace were founded on a rather imprecise mixture of semantic (or 'notional') and structural criteria (cf. footnote 5, p. 47).

We shall observe a distinction between the terms 'modification' and 'modifier'. Each 'modification' of a single head may contain any number of 'modifiers' (but at least one). Thus the great big black (whale)

is one modification which contains four modifiers.

For the purposes of the computer analysis, therefore, the nominal group was first divided into its three components, modification, head, and qualification. To put this another way, we can say that these three components are 'values' realising the (more general) category 'nominal group'.

'Modification' was sub-divided, and realised by the five 'values' deictic, ordinative, epithet, nominal and intensifier.

The computer counted the number of occurrences of each 'value' (or grammatical category) and gave the total number for each child on each task. We were thus able to see how many times each grammatical category was used by each child in any particular task, and to calculate, for example, what percentage of the heads were modified. The scores for all the children were collected, and totals for each 'cell' of five children on each value were calculated.

The results which are to be given here are taken from only 80 of the 110 children, that is, 40 high IQ and 40 medium IQ children. Low IQ children were not included because the cells were incomplete (see p. 8). The results for each task will be presented separately. In general, we shall present first the numerical information for several categories together, including the results of any statistical tests, while the interpretation of these figures will be reserved for the discussion at the end.

Hypotheses

Frequency of occurrence is, in itself, mainly of value in presenting a broad and generalised picture of differences which may be present in the usage of children from the different groups. It serves as a basis for the selection of particular categories for more detailed investigation; if, for example, one group is found to use rankshifted clauses significantly more frequently, one can then consider (a) subdividing this category according to functional criteria, and/or (b) ascertaining whether the difference occurs throughout the speech schedule (i.e. in all sections of both tasks) or whether it is confined to particular sections.

The tasks in the schedule are such as to provide a fairly tightly controlled speech situation: given this identical situation,[7] we can ask whether the linguistic options taken up by the children differ from group to group. The null hypothesis is that social class, IQ, sex and CI rating are irrelevant in determining the options which are taken up, hence no differences, other than random ones, in usage-frequency will be found. On the basis, however, of Bernstein's theoretical formulation of the existence of language codes related to social class (see for example Bernstein, 1965) and on the basis of empirical work carried out by Bernstein (1962), Lawton (1964) and others, we may suggest the following predictions in relation to the present study.

(a) That differences in usage-frequency will be found, and that social class will prove to discriminate the options taken up, more powerfully than any of the other independent variables (sex, IQ and CI).[8] Bernstein has shown, for example, that social class, independent of IQ, reveals differences in the performance of 15-year-old boys on certain linguistic categories.

(b) As far as social class differences are concerned, the number of specific predictions, involving nominal group categories, which may be derived from previous work, is rather small; thus, Bernstein (1962) found that the middle-class boys he studied, used a higher proportion of 'total adjectives' and 'uncommon adjectives'. We may on this basis make a prediction about 'total' adjectives, but 'uncommon' adjectives were not taken as a linguistic category in the computer analysis, there being no formal criteria for deciding what is 'common' or 'uncommon'. The personal pronoun *I*, for which Bernstein found differences in usage, is dealt with in detail in Part II, as are *you* and *they*. Such predictions must however be tentative, bearing in mind the difference in age between Bernstein's and Lawton's experimental groups (15- and 12-year-olds) and the 5-year-olds of our present study.

(c) More generally, we may note the following:

> The codes [restricted and elaborated] are defined in terms of the probability of predicting which structural elements will be selected for the organization of meaning. The structural elements are highly predictable in the case of a restricted code and much less so in the case of an elaborated code. It is considered that an elaborated code facilitates the verbal elaboration of intent whilst a restricted code limits the verbal explication of intent (Bernstein, 1962b).

If we apply this observation to the nominal group, we may predict that an elaborated code will tend to select *nouns* at head while a restricted code will select *pronouns*. There are two reasons for this: (a) because pronouns belong to what is called by the neo-Firthian linguists a 'closed system' with a small number of members and hence higher predictability, whereas nouns belong to an 'open set' with a very large number of members each having relatively low predictability; (b) because nouns present a wide range of opportunity for modification and qualification and hence a greater chance to make one's intentions verbally explicit, whereas pronouns present a very narrow range of opportunity here: pronouns may normally take only a small number of one-word qualifiers, like *all* or *both*, as in *they all*, *them both*, etc.

Broadly, then, if middle-class speakers move towards an elaborated code, we should expect more nouns, and more frequent use of the options available from using nouns, viz. modifiers such as ordinatives, adjectives, and nominals, and qualifiers of various kinds. From restricted code speakers we should expect a shift towards pronouns at head and a lesser tendency to use modifiers and qualifiers.

Statistical treatment

The grammatical categories can be roughly divided into 'frequent' and 'infrequent' in occurrence. For those which were frequent, statistical tests such as the analysis of variance or the t-test could be carried out. For the infrequent categories, however, the totals were relatively small, and there were several children out of the eighty who did not use the category at all. In this case, a χ^2 test was more appropriate.[9] For each category, tables will be presented giving the number of occurrences for each group of children, and for the infrequent categories, a table of the number of children *not* using the category at all will also be given. The categories will be designated 'infrequent', 'rather infrequent', 'frequent', 'very frequent'. Statistical tests were only carried out where there was a possibility that significant differences would be revealed. Significant differences are taken to be those for which the probability that the two sets of scores differ by chance is less than one in twenty (represented as $p < 0{\cdot}05$). Differences in which the probability is less than one in a hundred ($p < 0{\cdot}01$) will be regarded as 'highly significant'.

Total output of speech

Fluctuations in the total output of speech from each child will of course have an effect on the frequency of occurrence of individual categories, particularly on 'frequent' categories like nouns and pronouns. In order to make allowance for this, some analyses of variance are based on percentages (of the total) instead of, or in addition to, the 'raw' scores. For further discussion of the effect of total output, see Part II (p. 70).

The results are presented for each task separately, (a) because the computer was not programmed to sum the scores for the two tasks,

(b) so that we shall be able to see which differences occur in both tasks and which are confined to one task only.

RESULTS: TASK 2 (PICTURE STORIES)

1 Modifiers and qualifiers

(a) **Qualifiers**

Occurrence: infrequent.

Table 1 Number of children with zero scores (n = 80)

	Class		*Sex*		*IQ*		*CI*
Middle	16	Girls	18	High	21	High	15
Working	19	Boys	17	Medium	14	Medium	20
Total	35		35		35		35

Table 2 Number of qualifiers

	Class		*Sex*		*IQ*		*CI*
Middle	63	Girls	49	High	39	High	51
Working	34	Boys	48	Medium	58	Low	46
Total	97		97		97		97

The biggest difference in Table 2 lies between the social classes, the middle class producing nearly twice as many qualifiers. When the scores were compared by a t-test, this difference was significant ($p < 0{\cdot}05$).

(b) **Modifiers**

(i) *Ordinatives*
Occurrence: infrequent.

Table 3 Children with zero scores (n = 80)

	Class		*Sex*		*IQ*		*CI*
Middle	23	Girls	25	High	21	High	25
Working	31	Boys	29	Medium	33	Low	29
Total	54		54		54		54

The table indicates that more middle-class and high IQ children use ordinatives. Seventeen out of 40 middle-class children used them, compared with 9 out of 40 in the working-class. This difference when tested by χ^2 was 'tentative' ($\chi^2 = 2{\cdot}78$, $p = 0{\cdot}10$). Nineteen high IQ children but only 7 medium IQ (out of 40) used this category, the difference being significant ($\chi^2 = 6{\cdot}9$, $p < 0{\cdot}01$).

Table 4 Number of ordinatives

Class		*Sex*		*IQ*		*CI*	
Middle	39	Girls	33	High	39	High	27
Working	11	Boys	17	Medium	11	Low	23
Total	50		50		50		50

Middle-class and high IQ children clearly produce more ordinatives. The difference was in each case the same, both being significant on a t-test ($t = 2{\cdot}56$, $p < 0{\cdot}02$). It is in fact children who are both middle-class and of high IQ who utter the most ordinatives. This group produced 31 out of the 39 ordinatives (see Table 4), and only 7 out of 20 children in the group did not use the category, compared with 14, 16 and 17 children in the other three groups.

(ii) *Adjectives*

Occurrence: rather infrequent.

Table 5 Children with zero scores (n = 80)

Class		*Sex*		*IQ*		*CI*	
Middle	11	Girls	12	High	14	High	13
Working	19	Boys	18	Medium	16	Low	17
Total	30		30		30		30

The difference between middle and working class was not significant ($\chi^2 = 2{\cdot}62$, p = n.s.).

Table 6 Number of adjectives

Class		*Sex*		*IQ*		*CI*	
Middle	70	Girls	71	High	55	High	65
Working	46	Boys	45	Medium	61	Low	51
Total	116		116		116		116

An analysis of variance was carried out on these scores, to ascertain the extent of the difference attributable to each variable. Results are shown in Table 7.

Table 7 Analysis of variance—adjectives

	d.f.	*V.*	*F.*	*p.*
Class	1	7·20	2·26	n.s.
Sex	1	8·45	2·66	n.s.
IQ	1	0·45	0·14	n.s.
CI	1	2·45	0·77	n.s.
CI with sex	1	24·20	7·61	0·01
Within-scores	64	3·18		

With four main variables, as we have here, six combinations of first-order interaction are possible, four combinations of second-order and one combination of third-order. In this analysis, only one of these interactions was significant, the first-order interaction of CI with sex. The numerical values for the other interactions have therefore been omitted. None of the main variables was significant, as can be seen in Table 7.

The absence of significance in all the main variables is due to the size of the 'within-scores' variance, which provides the denominator in working out the F-ratio (i.e. $F = \frac{V}{3{\cdot}18}$). This large within-scores variance indicates a wide range of scores from the 80 children. More than one-third of the children did not use the category, while others had up to seven or eight adjectives.

(iii) *Nominals, and* (iv) *Intensifiers*

These were used so infrequently that statistical testing would be unreliable.

(v) *All modifiers*

The five values of modifier (determiner, ordinative, adjective, nominal, intensifier) were added together to be considered as a total category. We have already seen that the scores on the last four of these are relatively small. Determiners, in fact, constitute 87 per cent of all modifiers. The inclusion of determiners makes 'all modifiers' a frequent category, there being no zero scores. An analysis of variance was based on the totals shown in Table 8.

None of the interactions was significant. The largest of them is given in Table 9. Social class is the only main variable to reach the level of significance. It indicates that middle-class children gave more modifiers than working-class children.

Table 8 Number of modifiers

	Class		*Sex*		*IQ*		*CI*
Middle	1002	Girls	973	High	972	High	889
Working	798	Boys	827	Medium	828	Low	911
Total	1800		1800		1800		1800

Table 9 Analysis of variance—all modifiers

	d.f.	*V.*	*F.*	*p.*
Class	1	520·2	4·95	< 0·05
Sex	1	266·5	2·54	n.s.
IQ	1	259·2	2·47	n.s.
CI	1	6·1	0·06	n.s.
Class with IQ (interaction)	1	115·2	1·10	n.s.
Within-scores	64	105·1		

(c) **Modification**

The distinction between 'modification' and individual 'modifiers' has already been noted; thus, each modification of a noun-head may contain any number of modifiers. We must note here that the total number of nominal groups (measured by the total heads) was smaller for the working class than the middle class (by about 4 per cent), so that to make a true comparison, the number of modifications must be expressed as a *percentage* of the heads, not compared as 'raw' scores. For each child, therefore, the number of modifications was calculated as a percentage of the heads, and it was these figures which were used for the analysis of variance. The results are shown in Table 10.

Table 10 Average percentages of modified heads

	Class		*Sex*		*IQ*		*CI*
Middle	36·7	Girls	35·8	High	35·6	High	35·8
Working	31·9	Boys	32·8	Medium	33·1	Low	32·8

An analysis of variance was carried out to estimate the extent of these differences. The results are given in Table 11.

Table 11 Analysis of variance—modification

	d.f.	*V.*	*F.*	*p.*
Class	1	465·6	6·61	< 0·02
Sex	1	177·0	2·52	n.s.
IQ	1	122·5	1·74	n.s.
CI	1	171·1	2·43	n.s.
Class with sex *	1	112·9	1·60	n.s.
Within-scores	64	70·5		

* None of the interactions was significant.

Discussion

The results so far support the prediction that social class would prove a stronger discriminator of usage than any other variable. Sex and CI appeared only once, as an interaction effect among adjectives. IQ gave a significant result for ordinatives, but this occurred in conjunction with a class difference. Social class on the other hand was a significant factor among qualifiers, ordinatives, 'all modifiers' and modification.

These results also provide some evidence that middle-class children tend to take up available options to a greater extent than working-class children. They gave more qualifiers, more ordinatives, more 'all modifiers', and modified a greater proportion of heads than the working class. The result for adjectives was not significant but at least moved in the same direction, fewer middle-class children having zero scores, and the total occurrences being greater (Tables 5 and 6).

Balanced against these findings is the fact that the potentially interesting categories such as qualifiers, ordinatives and adjectives all turned out to be infrequent in occurrence, so that the class-differences, although significant, are not on such a scale that we could claim major differences in orientation. Total adjectives, for example, are only 116, an average of 1·5 per child, and representing 6·5 per cent of all modifiers.

The class-difference in the use of 'all modifiers', however, is interesting, since it suggests a middle-class orientation towards nouns. Taking this result in conjunction with the one for modification, we may ask the following question: do the middle-class children use more modifiers because they have more nouns available to be modified, or because each modification is 'richer' in modifiers? If the former is true, we should expect more modifications from the middle class; if the latter, there will be no difference in the number of modifications. Table 11 tells us that we have more, rather than 'richer', modifications; obviously, the differences we found for ordinatives were on too small a scale to make the modifications appear significantly 'richer'. The fact that they use more modifications indicates a greater use of nouns at head, since nouns, which together with pronouns constitute the majority of heads, can be modified, pronouns cannot.

We shall now go on, therefore, to present and discuss differences in the use of the various types of 'head', with particular reference to the noun and pronoun.

2 Heads

The types of head which were recognized in the computer analysis are listed on page 11. Some of these categories of head occurred very infrequently. Table 12 shows what percentage of all heads was accounted for by each category.

Table 12 Percentage distribution of 'head' categories

	n	%
Determiners	22	0·6
Ordinators	18	0·5
Adjectives	61	1·7
Nouns	1273	35·5
Pronouns	1833	51·0
This/these	8	0·2
That/those	81	2·2
Question-words	96	2·7
Missing element	77	2·1
Rankshifted clause	122	3·4
Total	3591	99·9

The category 'missing element' was not considered, because it was used only to denote a place in the structure where a head-word was expected, but could not be identified because of a noise on the tape, or an interruption, or the child's pronunciation.

Determiners, ordinators and this/these were used too infrequently to make any comparisons reliable (see Table 12).

The results for the remaining categories were as follows:

(a) **That/those**

Occurrence: infrequent.

Table 13 Children with zero scores (n = 80)

	Class		*Sex*		*IQ*		*CI*
Middle	19	Girls	21	High	20	High	21
Working	22	Boys	20	Medium	21	Low	20
Total	41		41		41		41

Table 14 Number of occurrences

	Class		*Sex*		*IQ*		*CI*
Middle	39	Girls	37	High	45	High	38
Working	42	Boys	44	Medium	36	Low	43
Total	81		81		81		81

No differences between any of the groups were significant.

(b) **Question-words**

Occurrence: infrequent. The table of children with zero scores showed no differences and is therefore not given, except for the variable social class:

Middle class	13
Working class	18
Total	31 (n = 80)

This difference was due to the high IQ children, for whom the distribution was:

Middle class	5
Working class	11
Total	16 (n = 40)

This difference was however not significant ($\chi^2 = 2{\cdot}60$, $p = 0{\cdot}12$).

Table 15 Number of question-words

	Class		*Sex*		*IQ*		*CI*
Middle	57	Girls	44	High	48	High	46
Working	39	Boys	52	Medium	48	Low	50
Total	96		96		96		96

The overall difference for class was not significant when the scores were compared by a t-test ($t = 1{\cdot}49$, $p = 0{\cdot}15$). When high IQ children were taken separately, the scores were:

Middle class	35
Working class	13
Total	48

This difference was significant ($p < 0{\cdot}01$). Middle-class children of high IQ therefore use more question-words than high IQ working-class children.

(c) **Rankshifted clauses**

Occurrence: rather infrequent.

Table 16 Children with zero scores (n = 80)

	Class		*Sex*		*IQ*		*CI*
Middle	13	Girls	18	High	15	High	21
Working	21	Boys	16	Medium	19	Low	13
Total	34		34		34		34

The difference between the class and CI groups was not significant ($\chi^2 = 2{\cdot}50$). There was, however, again a wider difference between the high IQ children of each social class than between the medium IQ children.

The distribution for these high IQ children was

Middle class	4
Working class	11
Total	15 (n = 40)

This difference was significant—$\chi^2 = 3{\cdot}84$, $p = 0{\cdot}05$. Since these are children with zero scores, we may convert the scores and present them as follows: 16 (out of 20) middle-class high IQ children used rankshifted clauses, compared with only 9 (out of 20) working-class high IQ.

Table 17 Number of rankshifted clauses

	Class		*Sex*		*IQ*		*CI*
Middle	67	Girls	70	High	71	High	46
Working	55	Boys	52	Medium	51	Low	76
Total	122		122		122		122

No overall differences were significant. When high IQ children were considered separately, the scores were:

Middle class	48
Working class	23
Total	71

This difference was, surprisingly, not significant ($t = 1{\cdot}82$, $p = 0{\cdot}08$), the reason being the wide variation between individual scores.

(d) **Adjectives**

Occurrence: infrequent.

Table 18 Children with zero scores (n = 80)

	Class		*Sex*		*IQ*		*CI*
Middle	23	Girls	24	High	25	High	27
Working	28	Boys	27	Medium	26	Low	24
Total	51		51		51		51

Table 19 Number of adjectives

	Class		*Sex*		*IQ*		*CI*
Middle	45	Girls	39	High	29	High	29
Working	16	Boys	22	Medium	32	Low	32
Total	61		61		61		61

T-tests were performed to estimate the variance for class and sex. The difference was significant for social class ($p < 0{\cdot}02$) but not for sex ($p = 0{\cdot}15$).

The scores for each of the four groups of children involved here are as follows:

Middle-class girls	28
Middle-class boys	17
Working-class girls	11
Working-class boys	5
Total	61

(e) **Nouns**

Since nouns account for 35 per cent of all heads, it was thought necessary to consider first the total number of heads given by each group of children, since fluctuations in this total could affect the quantity of nouns directly. Table 20 thus presents the total heads for each group.

Table 20 Total number of heads for each group

	Class		*Sex*		*IQ*		*CI*
Middle	1835	Girls	1847	High	1859	High	1716
Working	1756	Boys	1744	Medium	1732	Low	1875
Total	3591		3591		3591		3591

Clearly the differences in total heads from one group to another are not very great. The social class difference amounts to only 4 per cent. The biggest difference, that between high and low CI children, was estimated by a t-test and found to be non-significant ($t = 1{\cdot}02$, $p = $ n.s.). Because there is little difference in the total number of heads (which incidentally is a reliable estimate of the total amount of speech, since nominal groups account for almost everything within the clause except predicators and conjunctions), we are justified in taking the 'raw' scores to perform an analysis of variance for the number of nouns. As a further check, however, each noun score was expressed as a percentage of the total 'heads' for each child, and the percentages were then compared (by a t-test, taking the social class variable only).

Scores for each group, and the results of the analysis of variance performed on them, were as shown in Table 21.

Table 21 Number of nouns

Class		*Sex*		*IQ*		*CI*	
Middle	688	Girls	673	High	669	High	642
Working	585	Boys	600	Medium	604	Low	631
Total	1273		1273		1273		1273

Table 22 Analysis of variance: nouns

	d.f.	*V.*	*F.*	*p.*
Class	1	132·6	2·94	0·10
Sex	1	66·6	1·47	n.s.
IQ	1	52·8	1·17	n.s.
CI	1	1·5	0·03	n.s.
Class with CI	1	70·3	1·56	n.s.
Within-scores	64	45·1		

All the interactions were non-significant; the strongest of them is given in Table 22.

The variance for social class was then estimated, by a t-test, on the basis of percentage scores instead of 'raw' scores. The result was similar: t = 1·71, p = 0·10.

(f) **Pronouns**

Pronouns in Task 2 account for 51 per cent of all heads and are therefore the most frequent category. In the computer analysis they were sub-classified into nine different types, and since these types are rather different in function, it will be necessary to specify them before they can be considered further.

The sub-categories numbered 1, 2, 3, 5, 6 and 7 represented the three persons, singular and plural, respectively, in the role of Subject (viz. I, you, he, we, you, they). No. 4 was the 'impersonal' *it* and No. 8 was the 'weak' (unstressed) *there* as in

there's a boy in the water.

No. 9 included all other pronouns and any pronoun occurring at the Complement, regardless of person (i.e. me, you, him, it, us, them, etc.).[10]

No. 8 will not be included in our study, as it does not belong to the set of 'personal' pronouns. The other categories are treated individually in Part II, so the results for each of them are not presented here. Instead, the categories are combined to create a division between first/second person pronouns on the one hand, third person on the other.

That there is an overall class difference in the use of pronouns is clear from Table 23.

Table 23 Differential use of all pronouns

	Middle class	*Working class*
Total heads	1835	1756
Number of pronouns	867	966
Pronouns as % of total heads	47·2	55·0

If we are interested, however, in the question of a choice, within the nominal group, between a noun at head and a pronoun at head, then it is the third-person pronouns to which we must direct our attention. Only third-person pronouns can be said to substitute for or replace a noun; there is no noun equivalent for first- and second-person pronouns, in the same sense as there is an equivalent for third-person pronouns. We may therefore divide pronouns accordingly, to see what proportion of them are in the third person.

In Table 24, value 9 has been counted as third person, although it does include some first- and second-person pronouns. This is because the vast majority of its constituents were in fact third person. In Part II, third person will be treated as a separate category. 'Others' includes values 4 and 8.

Table 24 Division of pronouns

	Middle class	*Working class*
1st and 2nd person	127	101
3rd person	669	790
Others	71	75
Total	867	966

It is clear from this table that the difference in the use of pronouns is accounted for entirely by third-person pronouns. Indeed, the working class use rather fewer first- and second-person pronouns. We therefore decided to carry out an analysis of variance for third-person pronouns only. Scores were expressed as a percentage of the total heads for each child, in order to take account of fluctuation in the total quantity of speech produced.[11] The results are shown in Table 25.

Table 25 Analysis of variance: third-person pronouns

	d.f.	*V.*	*F.*	*p.*
Class	1	1540·0	21·50	0·001
Sex	1	25·3	0·35	n.s.
IQ	1	46·5	0·65	n.s.
CI	1	221·1	3·08	n.s.
Class with IQ	1	324·1	4·52	0·05
Sex with CI	1	262·9	3·67	n.s.
Within-scores	64	71·77		

All the other interactions were non-significant. The result shows an overwhelming difference between middle and working class, and one significant interaction between class and IQ.

Discussion

Once again, social class has revealed greater differences between the linguistic categories than any other variable. IQ, sex and CI feature occasionally, and always in conjunction with social class, as for example in rankshifted clauses where the IQ difference only appears in connection with a class difference.

For the individual categories of head, infrequency of occurrence has again been a problem, but on the limited data available the predictions that middle-class children would use a wider range of heads, and would use particular categories like adjectives more frequently, are generally borne out. The most interesting results are those for nouns and pronouns, but before discussing these the minor categories will be considered briefly.

No differences were found in the use of *that/those*. This is rather surprising in view of the differences which we shall show in Part II for this category, with a larger sample of children. It is possible that the differences are obscured here because the *that* occurring in the terminator sequence 'that's all' or 'that's all I can think of' was included, whereas in Part II we shall exclude this use as 'meta-task' speech (see p. 59).

There is evidence of social class differences for high IQ children only, in the categories 'question-word' and 'rankshifted clause'. Question-words here include only those which may occur as Subject or Complement, that is, *who*, *which* and *what* (adjunctival question-words like *how*, *where* and *when* belong outside the nominal group). The questions may be either 'direct' or 'indirect' but the latter are more frequent.

Since 'indirect' questions are treated as rankshifted clauses, the category 'question-word' and 'rankshifted clause' are to some extent related. In an example like

I wonder what they're doing

we have an instance of both categories; *what they're doing* is a rankshifted clause, a constituent element of the larger clause; *what* is a question-word.

There are two reasons why middle-class children might be expected to use more rankshifted clauses. The first is because these clauses indicate some degree of structural complexity (though this is open to argument), and the second is because they often occur after 'I think', 'I wonder' and other verbs which are considered to indicate 'tentativeness'. Bernstein has suggested that the middle class, as users of an elaborated code, will put forward their individual view in a tentative, 'hypothetical' way; linguistic structures which express this tentativeness are therefore more likely to be used by middle-class children. These structures are dealt with in greater detail in Part II. Here we may simply note that high IQ middle-class children used both question-words and rankshifted clauses more frequently, which is in the direction of our predictions.

In the category 'adjective' we found class and, to a lesser extent, sex differences. The significant class-difference here reinforces what was only a tentative result for adjectives within the modifier. We may note here that adjectives which occur at head are more likely to be of the evaluative kind than are modifying adjectives.[12] Thus, an evaluative adjective like *naughty* can occur freely in both positions, whereas the modifier position is frequently filled by less informative words such as *little*, *big*, which are almost never found in the head position (the boy is *little*, the fish is *big*). *Little* in particular was frequent as a modifier but its information value is minimal—in phrases like *the little boy/girl* it is never used contrastively (the *little*, as opposed to the *big*, boy), but is reduced to a verbal formula rather like the 'Homeric' epithet (for further discussion of this, see Part II, ch. 6). A class difference among adjectives at head may therefore be of greater significance than a difference in modifying adjectives. Clearly, we need to sub-divide adjectives into different types, and this will be done in Part II.

The results of the two major categories of head-word, nouns and pronouns, are of greater interest because of their high frequency of occurrence. Nouns and pronouns between them account for 86 per cent of all the words at head, i.e. about half the nominal groups are (unmodified) pronouns and over a third contain a noun. We have already seen that middle-class children use 'modification' more frequently, and it was suggested that this is because they use more nouns and fewer pronouns at head. Now we find that these middle-class children do in fact have a strong tendency to use more nouns, on the one hand, and the working class more pronouns, on the other. The wider implications of this finding will be discussed at the beginning of Part II; here, we shall only make reference to the numerical results which have just been given.

The prediction that middle-class children would move towards the noun, and working-class children towards the pronoun, is given strong support. The difference in the use of nouns was only tentatively significant ($p = 0{\cdot}10$—see Table 22) but the class-difference was the one which accounted for more of the variance than any other parameter. We have also seen already that the middle class use more adjectives at head, and, among the high IQ children, more question-words and rankshifted clauses. It is possible that this differentiation of variety in the type of heads produced may result in the difference for nouns themselves, taken as a category on their own, being not great enough to reach significance.

When we turn to consider pronouns, there is no doubt about the fact that working-class children use more of them than middle-class children. In order to make a direct comparison between nouns and the type of pronouns which can replace them, it was necessary to re-group the pronouns and consider those referring to the third person separately from the first and second pronouns. We found a highly significant social class difference here, and a significant interaction between class and IQ. The main variable CI was also of considerable magnitude ($F = 3{\cdot}08$); this means that the children of high-communicating mothers are less likely to use pronouns than children of low-communicating mothers.

To understand the interaction between class and IQ (Table 25) we must consider the summed percentages for each of the four groups involved. They are as shown in Table 26. The interaction is caused by the fact that medium IQ, middle-class children have higher percentages of pronouns (849) than the corresponding high IQ group (738), while in the working class the relationship is the other way round. It seems that the difference within the working class is small, and may be due to chance, but within the middle class the difference is greater. It was estimated by a t-test and was

Table 26

	Middle class	*Working class*
High IQ	738	994
Medium IQ	849	944

nearly significant (t = 1·98, p = 0·06). We may conclude from this that IQ does have some effect in discriminating use of pronouns within the middle class, but not within the working class. It is however clear that, although medium IQ middle-class children use more pronouns than the high IQ, there is still a considerable gap between them and the working-class scores.

A summary of the significant results for the nominal group categories within Task 2 is given in Table 27.

Table 27 Summary of significant results (Task 2)

		Test	*Group*	*Level of significance*
1 Qualifiers		t	MC	0·05
2 Modifiers	(a) Ordinatives	χ^2	High IQ	0·01
		t	High IQ	0·02
		t	MC	0·02
	(b) Adjectives	A/V	CI with sex	0·01
	(c) All modifiers	A/V	MC	0·05
	(d) Modification	A/V	MC	0·02
3 Heads	(a) Question-words	t	MC, high IQ	0·01
	(b) Rankshifted clauses	χ^2	MC, high IQ	0·05
	(c) Adjectives	t	MC	0·02
	(d) Nouns	A/V	MC	0·10
	(e) Third-person pronouns	A/V	WC	0·001
		A/V	Class with IQ	0·05

RESULTS: TASK 3 (TROTIN CARDS)

We now present the results for the nominal group categories in Task 3, in the same order as before.

1 Modifiers and qualifiers

(a) **Qualifiers**

Occurrence: rather infrequent. The category was, however, used by

86 per cent of the children, and χ^2 tests of users/non-users are thus not required. The distribution of scores is given in Table 28.

Table 28 Number of qualifiers

	Class		*Sex*		*IQ*		*CI*
Middle	138	Girls	136	High	152	High	134
Working	114	Boys	116	Medium	100	Low	118
Total	252		252		252		252

A t-test to compare the group which differs most, IQ, gave a nearly significant difference between high and medium IQ ($t = 1{\cdot}97$, $p = 0{\cdot}06$). No other differences were significant.

(b) **Modifiers**

(i) *Ordinatives*
Occurrence: infrequent. Neither the zero scores nor the quantity scores showed differences between any of the groups. The tables are given in Appendix I (see Table 2).

(ii) *Adjectives*
Occurrence: rather more frequent than in Task 2; they were used by 80 per cent of the children, and the zero scores show no differences. Table 29 shows the distribution of quantities.

Table 29 Number of adjectives

	Class		*Sex*		*IQ*		*CI*
Middle	129	Girls	123	High	131	High	108
Working	99	Boys	105	Medium	97	Low	120
Total	228		228		228		228

An analysis of variance was performed, based on these scores. The results were as shown in Table 30.

Table 30 Analysis of variance: adjectives

	d.f.	*V.*	*F.*	*p.*
Class	1	11·25	1·23	n.s.
Sex	1	4·05	0·44	n.s.
IQ	1	14·45	1·58	n.s.
CI	1	1·80	0·20	n.s.
Class with CI	1	54·45	5·94	0·02
Within-scores	64	9·17		

None of the main variables is significant. One interaction, of class with CI, was significant at the 0·02 level.

(iii) *All modifiers*
This category includes the determiners and is therefore 'frequent' (Table 31).

Table 31 Number of 'all modifiers'

	Class		*Sex*		*IQ*		*CI*
Middle	1613	Girls	1446	High	1479	High	1619
Working	1335	Boys	1502	Medium	1469	Low	1329
Total	2948		2948		2948		2948

The apparently considerable differences within the social class and CI groups proved not to be significant, because of the wide range of individual scores. Since this wide range might have been caused by fluctuations in the total amount of speech among individuals, the modifiers were expressed as a percentage of total heads for each child.

This procedure, however, revealed smaller differences between the groups than the 'raw' scores did, and no analysis of variance was carried out. The table of percentage scores is given in Appendix I (Table 3).

(c) **Modification**

Occurrence: frequent.

Social class is the group with the greatest divergence here. The difference, however, when estimated by a t-test, was not significant.

This again suggests a wide variation in individual scores, which might be related to variations in the total output of speech. It was

Table 32 Number of modifications

Class		*Sex*		*IQ*		*CI*	
Middle	1059	Girls	953	High	954	High	1044
Working	888	Boys	994	Medium	993	Low	903
Total	1947		1947		1947		1947

therefore decided that an analysis of variance should be based on the percentage scores (see Table 33).

Table 33 Analysis of variance: modification

	d.f.	*V.*	*F.*	*p.*
Class	1	208·0	2·02	n.s.
Sex	1	324·0	3·15	n.s.
IQ	1	241·5	2·35	n.s.
CI	1	117·6	1·14	n.s.
Sex with IQ	1	127·6	1·24	n.s.
Class with sex with IQ	1	864·4	8.40	< 0·01
Within-scores	64	102·9		

Once again, none of the main variables gave significant differences. One interaction, however, of class with sex with IQ, reached significance at the 0·01 level.

Discussion

The results given for the nominal group categories of qualifier and modifier have not been as decisive as they were on the previous task. There has been no consistent pattern of class-differences as was found before, nor have the other variables shown significant differences. Our predictions, therefore, have not been upheld so far in the speech given in this task. This may be partly due to differences in the total amount of speech produced by individual children, but also, I think, to the different kinds of speech which were elicited, there being more room for variation in the type of answer given than there was in the previous task.

The differences which have been found on this task are as follows: first, a difference between high and medium IQ children in the use of qualifiers, which was in fact not quite significant. As it has not been supported by differences between the IQ groups elsewhere, on this task, we cannot make any definite claims about it.

Second, the analysis of variance for adjectives indicated a significant interaction between social class and CI. In order to interpret this result, it is necessary to consult the scores for each of the four groups involved (the table can be seen in Appendix I, No. 4). We find that in the middle class, high CI children, especially girls, produce more adjectives than the low CI children—this is as would be expected, and as has been found elsewhere by Henderson (Brandis and Henderson, 1970, pp. 39, 51). But in the working class, it seems that the low CI children produce more adjectives than the high—69 compared with 30. A closer inspection of the figures, however, reveals that this is due almost entirely to two children with high scores of 10 and 15 adjectives respectively. Since the frequency of adjectives is small, random variances such as this are likely to occur from time to time, and it is not thought that this result has any wider significance. The result is also not supported by any similar findings elsewhere.

Thus, the analysis of variance for adjectives showed no differences between the main variables. It will be remembered that similar results were found in Task 2. We shall see in Part II that the range of adjectives in Task 3 is wider than in Task 2, and that it includes a heterogeneous collection of different types of words; so it is not until we reach a finer classification of adjectives that differences between the main variables begin to appear.

Ordinatives proved to be a very rare category in this task. This appears to be due to the nature of the picture-material, there being few items in the pictures which can be readily counted and yet do not exceed four or five (five being a likely threshold of counting for most 5-year-olds). The number of people in each picture exceeds twenty, and few children bother to count them up.

With 'all modifiers' and modification we failed to show any differences between the main variables, either by taking the 'raw' scores or percentages. This is somewhat surprising, in view of the fact that in the next section we shall once again find a difference in the use of nouns. It is however possible, first, that a considerable proportion of the nouns are unmodified because they are plural in form, especially those referring to humans—*men*, *ladies*, *people*—which occur frequently. Second, although the figures are not significant, the total modifications (Table 32) and modifiers (Table 31) was greater for middle-class than for working-class children, which indicates at least that the results are in the predicted direction. If one considers determiners alone (the commonest type of modifier), the difference between middle and working class on the 'raw' scores then approaches significance. A t-test to compare the high IQ children gave $t = 1{\cdot}70$, $p < 0{\cdot}10$, and for high and medium IQ together, $t = 1{\cdot}67$, $p = 0{\cdot}10$. There is thus some support to be found among the modifiers, particularly the determiners, for the difference in the use of nouns to be presented below.

The second-order interaction between class, sex and IQ may again be interpreted by considering the scores for each constituent group individually. To do this we need a more detailed table than the type usually given (see Appendix I, Table 5). The interaction expresses the difference between middle-class, high IQ girls who use far more than the average percentage modification, and working-class, medium IQ boys who use far less. The summed percentages (from the table) are, respectively, 266 and 274 (total, 540, for middle-class high IQ girls), compared with 180 and 187 (total, 367, for working-class medium IQ boys). This difference is in the predicted direction, and supports Henderson's finding (loc. cit.).

We shall now go on to consider the categories of nominal group at the 'head', with particular reference to nouns and pronouns.

2 Heads

The types which were recognised in the computer analysis were originally given on page 11, and the relative frequencies of each category for Task 2 were presented in Table 12 (p. 21). The percentage frequencies of each of these categories for Task 3 are as shown in Table 34.

If we compare this table with the similar table for Task 2 (Table 12, p. 21), we notice first, that the amount of speech in Task 3 is rather greater, about 20 per cent more; second, a remarkable reversal in the relative frequencies of the two main categories, nouns and pronouns. Pronouns were more common than nouns in Task 2, but less common in Task 3. This is caused by the different nature of the two tasks. Where narrative is required, pronouns are the easiest and most usual way to obtain cohesion from one clause to the next—

three boys saw a window and *they* broke *it*.

Where the speech is not narrative but descriptive, the clauses will tend not to be connected in this way, and there will be a relatively greater number of nouns, performing their traditional function—the naming of persons, places and things.

Table 34 Percentage distribution of 'head' categories

	n	%
Determiners	66	1·5
Ordinators	49	1·1
Adjectives	57	1·3
Nouns	2343	53·2
Pronouns	1325	30·1
This/these	19	0·4
That/those	226	5·1
Question-words	96	2·2
Missing element	105	2·4
Rankshifted clause	119	2·7
Total	4405	100·0

The only other category whose proportion differs from one task to the other is *that/those*, which accounted for 5 per cent of the heads in Task 3 but only 2·2 per cent in Task 2. The difference is probably due to the greater use of the naming function, in clauses such as

that's a ...., those are ....

We shall see in Part II how this usage can be of great interest for social class differences.

The categories 'missing element', determiner, ordinator, and this/these were again not considered for the reasons offered previously (see p. 21). The results for the remaining categories are as follows:

(a) **That/those**

Occurrence: rather infrequent.

Table 35 Children with zero scores (n = 80)

Class		*Sex*		*IQ*		*CI*	
Middle	6	Girls	10	High	12	High	7
Working	9	Boys	5	Medium	3	Low	8
Total	15		15		15		15

The greatest difference here is between high and medium IQ children. Tested by χ^2, the result was significant ($\chi^2 = 5{\cdot}25$, $p = 0{\cdot}03$); fewer high IQ children use this category.

Table 36 Number of 'that/those'

	Class		*Sex*		*IQ*		*CI*
Middle	127	Girls	92	High	108	High	112
Working	99	Boys	134	Medium	118	Low	114
Total	226		226		226		226

The difference between girls and boys was estimated by a t-test, and gave a 'tentative' result ($t = 1{\cdot}76$, $p = 0{\cdot}10$).

(b) **Question-words**

Occurrence: infrequent. Neither the table of zero scores nor the table of quantities revealed differences between any of the groups. The middle-class total (57) was rather higher than the working-class (39), but this difference was not significant.

(c) **Rankshifted clauses**

This category was also infrequent, and again showed no differences between any of the groups either for zero scores or for total scores. An apparent difference between middle-class high IQ (41) and working-class high IQ (14) was in fact mainly due to one middle-class boy with a score of 20.

(d) **Adjectives**

An infrequent category, with, again, no differences between the major variables either in total scores or in the number of children who used the category. A tendency for girls to produce more (36) than boys (21) was not significant ($t = 1{\cdot}56$, $p = 0{\cdot}15$).

(e) **Nouns**

At this stage, as we come to deal with the 'frequent' categories *nouns* and *pronouns*, it becomes necessary to take account of the total output of speech, as we did at the same stage in Task 2 (p. 25), since fluctuations in the total could have a direct effect on the number of nouns. The distribution of total heads may be taken as an approximate index of total speech, and the data is given in Table 37.

Table 37 Total heads (Task 3)

Class		*Sex*		*IQ*		*CI*	
Middle	2389	Girls	2094	High	2173	High	2282
Working	2016	Boys	2311	Medium	2232	Low	2123
Total	4405		4405		4405		4405

An analysis of variance, based on these scores, was carried out. None of the main variables or the interactions was significant (see Appendix I, Table 1). We therefore assumed that a consideration of the 'raw' scores was justified in the case of the 'infrequent' categories where it would not be suitable to take percentage scores. For the very frequent categories *nouns* and *pronouns* at head, however, percentage scores were used in addition to raw scores, for two reasons: (a) because although the variance was not significant, the middle-class total output is still 16 per cent greater than the working-class, and the output of boys 10 per cent greater than that of girls (see Table 37); (b) because there may be great fluctuations in the output of individual children, the effect of which can be reduced by taking percentages. That such fluctuation does occur is indicated by the extremely high within-scores value in the analysis of variance (Appendix I, Table 1)—compare this value (729·3) with those in Tables 9, 11, 22, 38, etc.

There is a further statistical problem here: if one can see that the total amount of speech is affecting the quantity produced in a particular category, is one justified in taking percentage scores, when the category itself constitutes a large proportion of the total amount of speech? Nouns, for example, comprise 50 per cent of the total heads (which is the basis of the total amount of speech), so that the number of nouns is affecting not only the percentage nouns/total but also the total itself. There is, apparently, nothing in the literature which deals with this kind of statistical problem, and the only solution is to try both raw and percentage scores, and compare the difference.[13] This then is the procedure adopted here.

An analysis of variance for nouns was carried out, using first the raw scores (see Table 38).

Table 38 Analysis of variance—nouns ('raw' scores)

	d.f.	*V.*	*F.*	*p.*
Class	1	1102·6	4·30	0·04
Sex	1	10·5	0·04	n.s.
IQ	1	13·6	0·05	n.s.
CI	1	137·8	0·54	n.s.
Class with sex	1	365·5	1·42	n.s.
Within-scores	64	256·8		

None of the interactions was significant, the largest of them being given in the table. For purposes of comparison, another analysis of variance was then performed, this time using the percentage scores (Table 39).

Table 39 Analysis of variance—nouns (percentage scores)

	d.f.	*V.*	*F.*	*p.*
Class	1	931·6	5·18	0·03
Sex	1	332·1	1·84	n.s.
IQ	1	556·5	3·10	n.s.
CI	1	3·6	0·02	n.s.
Class with sex with IQ	1	340·2	1·89	n.s.
Within-scores	64	179·8		

None of the interactions was significant.

The results of each A/V are approximately the same: in each case we have social class as the only variable to give a significant difference; in each case the results go in the same direction (M.C. children use more nouns); and in each case the magnitude of the probability is about the same—$p < 0{\cdot}04$ from the raw scores, $p < 0{\cdot}03$ from the percentages. The higher significance is achieved because the within-scores value has been reduced from 256·8 to 179·8, showing that the percentage scores have in fact ironed out some of the fluctuation in individual scores. We may conclude that middle-class children use significantly more nouns than working-class children in this task, whereas the other variables, sex, IQ and CI, produce no differences.

(f) **Pronouns**

In this task pronouns account for 30 per cent of all nominal groups. By considering pronouns as a whole as we did at first in Task 2, we can show a difference between the two social classes (Table 40).

Table 40 Differential use of all pronouns

	Middle class	*Working class*
Total heads	2389	2016
Total pronouns	656	669
Pronouns %	27·4	33·2

Pronouns were sub-classified in the same way as before, so that third-person pronouns could be separated in order to obtain a true comparison with nouns (Table 41).

Table 41 Division of pronouns

	Middle class	*Working class*
1st and 2nd person	121	68
3rd person	349	433
Others	186	168
Total	656	669

This table shows, that, again, it is third-person pronouns which the working-class children use more frequently. It appears, indeed, that they use the other pronouns rather less frequently than the middle class. To estimate the extent of the difference in the use of third-person pronouns, two analyses of variance were carried out, the first using 'raw' scores, the second percentages. The results are shown in Tables 42 and 43.

The two analyses of variance for pronouns give similar results in that they go in the same direction, but the percentage scores bring out a far greater class-difference, which is achieved in spite of an increase in the within-scores value. A likely explanation for this is the fact that middle-class children use more nouns, which is increasing the total number of heads; thus when pronouns are expressed absolutely, the quantities may differ only slightly, but when ex-

Table 42 Analysis of variance—third-person pronouns ('raw' scores)

	d.f.	*V.*	*F.*	*p.*
Class	1	88·20	1·66	n.s.
Sex	1	0·05	0·00	n.s.
IQ	1	14·45	0·27	n.s.
CI	1	0·80	0·02	n.s.
Sex with IQ	1	162·45	3·06	n.s.
Within-scores	64	53·14		

Table 43 Analysis of variance—third-person pronouns (percentages of total heads)

	d.f.	*V.*	*F.*	*p.*
Class	1	1140·05	10·87	0·003
Sex	1	57·85	0·55	n.s.
IQ	1	18·05	0·17	n.s.
CI	1	8·45	0·08	n.s.
Sex with IQ	1	319·95	3·04	n.s.
Within-scores	64	104·95		

pressed as percentages relative to nouns, middle-class children have a much lower ratio of pronouns. Table 41 shows that the difference between the raw score totals for third-person pronouns is rather small (349 and 433) but when these are calculated as a percentage of total heads, the difference is considerable—for the middle-class, 14·6 per cent, for the working-class, 21·4 per cent.

Discussion

The infrequent categories of head-word have, like the infrequent modifiers and qualifiers, failed to reveal differences between the groups on this task. Since the categories are so infrequent, it may be that a larger sample of children would give clearer results, and we shall see in Part II that differences in some of the categories are evident from the larger sample. The only significant difference found was that fewer high than medium IQ children use the category *that/those*. This is interesting in view of the exophoric referential function of this category (see Part II), but the difference in *frequency* of use between high and medium IQ groups is small (see Table 36).

The most interesting result here, as in Task 2, is the differential use of nouns and pronouns as determined by social class. Whichever analysis of variance one takes, there is clearly a class-difference in the use of nouns, and class is the only variable to reach significance. The percentage analysis also indicates a tendency for high IQ children to use more nouns. This is in the predicted direction, but not statistically significant. The result, then, reinforces what was found in Task 2, where the difference was not quite as strong.

Pronouns, too, show considerable differences on the basis of a percentage score analysis. The variance for class was the only significant one, and the probability is high—$p = 0{\cdot}003$. Working-class children thus use more third-person pronouns as a percentage of their total speech than middle-class children, though it is likely that the greater use of nouns by the middle-class children has some effect on the statistical procedures involved here.

Task 3 is rather different in kind from Task 2. The picture stories sought to elicit a narrative type of speech in which clauses would be linked cohesively one with another to form a continuous sequence. The Trotin cards, on the other hand, aimed at a more descriptive type of speech. The pictures were not linked in series; the child was required to comment upon one picture at a time. There was thus less possibility that the description would appear as a cohesive narrative and more likelihood of a series of independent, unconnected clauses.

There was also a possibility that children would put names to the people and things they could see, without connecting them, thus producing 'lists' of simple nouns. The effect of 'listing' was minimised by the probes which the interviewer gave, the emphasis being on activity. Most of the probes contained the words 'going on' or 'happening'—'what's happening in this picture?', 'what else is going on?', 'what are the people doing?'. But this possibility of lists of nouns prompts two further questions.

(1) If the middle-class children use more nouns, is it simply because they give lists of the phenomena in the pictures? If so, then those nouns are not comparable with pronouns and we cannot treat the situation as one of choice between noun or pronoun. Thus, parallel with a sentence like

a man's pushing a bicycle

we have

he's pushing it (or, he's pushing that)

whereas, parallel with

there's an aeroplane, a cart and a little girl

we cannot have

there's it, it, and her

(although

there's that, that, and her

is, I suppose, possible, if rather unlikely).

If the middle-class children's nouns are mainly lists, therefore, the significance (in the non-statistical sense) of the difference is greatly reduced. In Part II, list nouns are counted separately from nouns which fulfil a variety of roles in the clause, in order to provide an answer to this question.

(2) The slight increase in the working-class frequency of pronouns could be because some of them interpret the task differently; if they construct a narrative story around the events, then pronouns could be used quite normally and appropriately to provide cohesion, and there would be no question of nouns being a preferable option in such a situation; thus

an aeroplane's in the sky and *it's* coming to fetch the people

is preferable to a repetition of *aeroplane*. This possibility is also investigated in Part II by considering pronoun-function in greater detail.

A summary of the significant results obtained for the nominal group categories within Task 3 (Trotin cards) is given in Table 44.

Table 44 Summary of significant results (Trotin cards)

		Stat. test	*Group*	*Level of significance*
1 Qualifiers		t	High IQ	0·06
2 Modifiers	(a) Adjectives	A/v	Class with CI (interaction)	0·02
	(b) Modification	A/v	Class with sex with IQ (interaction)	0·01
	(c) Determiners	t	Middle class	0·10
3 Heads	(a) That/those	χ^2	Medium IQ	0·03
	(b) Nouns	A/v	Middle class	0·03
	(c) Pronouns (%)	A/v	Working class	0·003

Summary of Part I

A sample of eighty 5-year-old children divided into equally matched groups according to social class, sex, verbal ability and the maternal index of communication (CI) were given (individually) a number of tasks designed to elicit different types of speech. Task 2 (picture stories) and Task 3 (Trotin cards) gave the greatest output of speech and were used as the basis of the present study. The sentences were analysed into a number of linguistic categories and a frequency count of the occurrence of each category was made with the aid of a computer. The present study is concerned only with categories comprising the nominal group.

The differences in total output of speech between the groups were small, and shown to be statistically non-significant. Nevertheless, 'frequent' categories like nouns and pronouns were treated both as raw scores and as percentages of total heads.

Following the empirical work of Bernstein (1959, 1962), Lawton (1964) and others, and the theoretical outline of restricted and elaborated codes proposed by Bernstein (eg. 1961, 1965) it was predicted that social class would account for more variance between the groups than any other factor. More specific predictions concerning the individual linguistic categories were that in the middle-class group the proportion of nouns relative to pronouns would be higher than in the working-class, since middle-class children would prefer the wider range of options opened up by the use of nouns; in system-structure terms, the category *noun* is the entry condition to a greater number of systems than the category *pronoun*. Thus, nouns may be extensively modified and qualified; pronouns normally take a limited range of one-word qualifiers only. It was also predicted that the middle class would take up some of the wider options made available, by using more modifiers and qualifiers of various kinds.

The predictions that social class would account for more variance than the other factors was substantially upheld. Neither sex nor IQ nor CI gave regular or consistent significant differences within the linguistic categories.

The wider options made available by the use of a noun at head (i.e. modifiers and qualifiers) were infrequently used by all children in both tasks and the results did not give strong confirmation to our predictions. Nevertheless, middle-class children were found to use more qualifiers, more ordinatives, more modifiers taken as a whole, and more modifications, than the working-class, in Task 2. In this task they were also found to use more adjectives at head, and the middle-class high IQ group used more question-words and rankshifted clauses. There is thus some evidence that some of the wider options are being taken up. Comparable results were not found in Task 3, however.

The most consistent and significant result achieved in both tasks was the differential use of nouns and pronouns. Middle-class children relative to the working-class used more nouns and fewer pronouns in both tasks, in each case at high levels of significance (see Table 45). Since nouns and pronouns together account for more than 80 per cent of all nominal groups, this can be considered a major finding.

Table 45 Significance levels of results

	Task 2	*Task 3*
Pronouns	0·001	0·003
Nouns	0·10	0·03

An explanation for the fact that the more promising results found in Task 2 were not upheld in Task 3 is thought to lie partly in the different nature of the two tasks. The picture stories were designed to obtain cohesive narrative speech and it is likely that the responses here were more homogeneous than in Task 3. Provided the child responded at all (and more than 95 per cent of them did), a narrative type of speech was almost inevitable, whereas in the other task a variety of responses was possible, ranging from cohesive narrative (if the child saw the picture as telling a story) through descriptive (separate and largely unconnected clauses detailing the events and visible objects in each part of the card, eg. *the train's stopped at the station and there's a man selling apples*) to simple lists of people and objects (eg. *there's a man, a lady, a horse, a bike, a car*). Since the categories of modifier, qualifier and heads other than nouns and pronouns were infrequent anyway, it is likely that the diversity of responses in Task 3 obscured any possible differences in frequency of use.

The difference in the use of nouns and pronouns in Task 3 can be given a more meaningful interpretation if we know how and when they are being used. Thus, we need to know whether the middle class are using nouns simply to provide lists of the visible objects, or whether they select them in preference to pronouns in order to make their language more explicit and potentially more 'elaborated'. Similarly, we can ask whether the working class are selecting pronouns because they have opted for a cohesive narrative type of speech in this task, in which pronouns would be quite appropriate, or whether such usage is indeed a symptom of less explicit communication involving a narrower range of options. Some answers to these questions will be offered in the more detailed investigation of the nominal group pursued in Part II.

Notes to Part I

[1] The 'American' spelling of 'program' is the generally accepted one, in the context 'computer program'.

[2] The grammatical analysis was applied to the speech of a selected sample of 110 children (see p. 8).

[3] System-structure grammar developed out of the earlier 'scale and category' model which was essentially a surface-structure grammar. The more recent 'systemic' approach overcomes many of the disadvantages of a surface grammar (cf. Hudson, 1971), but by 1965 when the computer program was written, only certain areas of the grammar had been 'converted' to the systemic model, for example determiners, and tenses (Turner and Mohan, 1970, pp. 74 ff, 93 ff). In the present study, the surface nature of some of the grammatical description will be apparent. From the practical point of view, however, the theoretical deficiencies of the grammar have not proved critical, since in each case we have moved as far as possible towards more refined function-based categories from either broader functional ones or from purely formal ones. The theoretical framework, therefore, should be regarded as simply a convenient basis for establishing an initial range of grammatical categories.

[4] Turner and Mohan (1970) contains a concise account of system-structure grammar as well as a description of their own categories.

[5] Position of occurrence is a crucial feature of scale and category theory. In part this is an attempt to overcome the deficiencies of a traditional grammar in which 'nouns', for example, could be (used as) 'nouns' or 'adjectives', and in which the terms were defined according to a variety of criteria. In scale and category terms, structures are set up and positions within them are then *realised by* words of different categories. Thus the position h (head) in a nominal group may be realised by a noun, or a pronoun, or some other class of word. *Motor* in *motor car* is not a noun 'used as an adjective' but a noun realising the structural position n (nominal, or classifier). In this way, the class-membership of a word is clearly separated and kept apart from the function performed by that word in the structure. Hence may arise a dual terminology for what traditionally had a single label, eg. e (epithet) is a *position*, realised usually by the *word-class* adjective; d (deictic) refers to the position, *determiner* to a class of words that often fill that position, and so on. Thus the term *adjective* as we use it is to be taken in its narrower sense; it does not include ordinatives or nominals, which were sometimes called 'adjectives' in traditional grammar.

[6] Another, perhaps less ambiguous, term for 'nominal' is 'classifier'.

[7] It will be argued by some that such a situation, where middle-class interviewers confront both middle- and working-class children, is *not* identical. This issue will be discussed in the final chapter of Part II.

[8] The capacity of the communication index to predict differences is unknown, but we must note that the version of the CI used in Part I is an earlier one, based on only two out of five schedules which were given in the mothers' questionnaire to assess the extent of her 'communication' towards the child. A more elaborate index based on five schedules was constructed later, and is used for the further research reported in Part II. The earlier CI was in fact found to be rather less reliable than the later one; Henderson's work on form-class differences (Brandis and Henderson, 1970, ch. 1) shows that it was not as powerful as social class in predicting differences.

[9] Readers unfamiliar with these tests may consult Lindquist (1940) or Moroney (1956). χ^2 tests compare the number of children in the sample who use or do not use the category at all (users/non-users). T-test and analysis of variance compare the number of occurrences of the category, based on the scores for each child; they are only reliable if the category is used by most of the children in the sample.

[10] For the rationale behind this method of sub-dividing pronouns, see Turner and Mohan (1970, pp. 75–7).

[11] This procedure was not adopted for nouns, but the findings given there (see p. 26) suggested that either procedure (raw scores or percentages) gives similar results.

[12] Colour adjectives, which can occur at 'head', were not found in this task because the picture stories were black-and-white drawings.

[13] I am indebted to W. Brandis of the SRU for advice and help with statistical procedures.

Part II

Introduction to Part II

As a consequence of the positive results (reported in Part I) given by the categories of the nominal group, in differentiating middle- and working-class speech, it was decided to examine nominal group categories over a wider sample of children, including the 80 children of the factorial design but adding to them about 200 more children. At the same time, it also seemed desirable to modify the categories themselves, in the light of the knowledge we had already gained, and as a result of new insights into the functioning of certain categories. The purpose of the re-classification was to examine some of the categories in greater detail than the computer analysis had given, testing particular hypotheses which we had been able to formulate on the basis of our experience, and, in particular, moving away from the formal definitions in which some of the language categories had been framed towards a more functional approach, i.e. taking into account the context and functions in which the categories were actually used, as well as their frequency of occurrence.

Thirty-seven linguistic categories have been selected, all of them related in some way to the nominal group.[1] The numerical frequency of occurrence of each category will be correlated with a range of 'sociological' variables based on information about the subjects and their background, including social class, measured intelligence, sex and other factors, in order to ascertain the relationship between the latter ('sociological') and the former (linguistic) variables.

The arrangement to be followed in Part II is as follows: chapter 1 is introductory; it presents details of the extended sample of subjects, the sociological variables, the speech schedule, and the statistical treatment of the data. Each subsequent chapter except the last is devoted to a particular group of linguistic categories: chapter 2 to the 'reference' categories, chapter 3 to nouns, chapter 4 to modifiers, etc. The format of these chapters is as follows: each chapter begins with a description of the categories and an outline of the hypotheses we are testing; this is followed by the results, which sometimes lead to a further investigation of particular categories; then there is a section in which the results are discussed. No summary for each chapter is given, since the discussion section itself constitutes essentially a summary of the chapter as a whole. The last chapter, however, begins with a brief résumé of all the results, followed by an overview of the aims and background of this research, and its relationship to the work of others in the field.

Note

[1] In some cases, the treatment of particular nominal group categories has led us to consider categories which are strictly speaking beyond the nominal group itself; if the function of a category was found to be closely related to some wider grammatical structure, that structure was also included; for example, pronouns in tag clauses (*isn't it*, *aren't they*, *won't he*, etc.) are to be distinguished in function from pronouns occurring elsewhere. Hence a separate category of *tag clause* was established.

Chapter 1 Framework of the research

Sources of the data

The data are taken from the same two tasks of the six-task speech schedule as in Part I, namely, from Task 2 (the picture stories) and Task 3 (the Trotin cards). Details of these tasks are given in a later section of this chapter (pp. 55ff.).

The sample

The results given in Part I were based on a sample of 80 children selected from the total of 450 who were interviewed. This sample was arranged in a factorial design with four main variables, social class, sex, IQ and communication index, which gave 16 'cells', with five children allotted to each 'cell'.

The advantage of a factorial design is that it enables one to control each variable independently, and the differences attributable to each can be estimated by analysis of variance. Factorial designs, however, depend on the selection, from a large sample, of a small and carefully controlled sub-sample in which the subjects are matched for each of the variables. An alternative method is to compare one set of variables with another by means of correlations: in our case, we would be comparing use of the linguistic variables with indices of social class, IQ, etc. One advantage of the correlation method is that data becomes available from a much larger proportion of the total sample; in this study, for example, we shall observe the behaviour of 312 children, instead of the 80 in the factorial design. Another advantage is that the 'background' variables can sometimes be quantified more precisely; for example, for social class, the correlations are based on a ten-point scale, whereas the factorial design requires a bipartite division into two discrete groups, working and middle class.[1]

The sample we have used in this study was devised as follows: the total number of children interviewed was 439, of whom 148 were from schools in the 'middle-class' area, and the remaining 291 from schools in the working-class area (of London).[2] In order to make the samples from each area approximately equal in size, we reduced the group from the WC area from 291 to 180 by a process of random selection.[3] This gave a total sample of 328, which was subsequently reduced to 312 (for the picture stories task) and 299 (for Trotin) for two reasons.

(1) The amount of speech given by a few of the children did not reach the required minimum of 20 nominal groups. The choice of this figure as a lower limit was, in part, arbitrary: it was clear that some limit was necessary, since children with very few nominal groups were scarcely organising their speech beyond a monosyllabic answer to the probes, and their speech was therefore different in kind, as well as in quantity, from those who were more fluent. Twenty was taken as the very lowest limit allowable; since each task was divided into three sections, this meant an average of only 7 nominal groups per section.

This limitation excluded seven children from Task 2 (4 working-class, 3 middle-class) and twenty children (15 working, 5 middle) from Task 3.

(2) Nine more children had to be excluded from the sample because relevant information about their social background or IQ was missing.

The number of children in the final sample which was used for the correlation programme was therefore:

Task 2	312 children
Task 3	299 children

One problem associated with the use of the correlation method arises when certain of the language categories are found to be used by only a small proportion of all the children, i.e. when the scores for these particular categories are 'skewed' towards zero. For statistical reasons the correlations based on infrequent categories are likely to be unreliable, and we therefore wished to support the correlational results in these categories with χ^2 tests, which compare the number of children who use the category at all (rather than the *frequency* of the category itself). To carry out χ^2 tests, however, requires a sample in which each group is as homogeneous as possible in its composition, and we therefore had to divide our sample in such a way as to create discrete working-class and middle-class groups.

We did this by excluding, for the χ^2 sample only, all marginally middle-class or marginally working-class children. This meant the exclusion of all children of class 5 and above in the working-class area from our 'working-class' sample, and the exclusion of all those of class 6 and below in the middle-class area from our 'middle-class' sample. We shall call these excluded children (for want of a better term) the 'marginal' group.

The χ^2 sample is therefore constituted as shown in Tables 1.1 and 1.2.

Table 1.1

	Task 2
MC	124
WC	139
Total	263
Marginal group	49
	312

Table 1.2

	Task 3
MC	124
WC	130
Total	254
Marginal group	45
	299

This sample can be further subdivided into boys and girls.[4] When the sex-division is included, the χ^2 sample appears as shown in Table 1.3.

Table 1.3

	Task 2	*Task 3*
MC boys	65	65
MC girls	59	59
WC boys	59	54
WC girls	80	76
Total	263	254

It will be observed that the correlation sample includes more than 300 children, and the χ^2 sample more than 250. The size of this sample enables the results achieved to be regarded with greater confidence than small-scale studies can provide.[5]

The speech schedule

The nature of the two tasks, the picture stories and Trotin cards, and the kinds of speech they gave rise to, narrative and (in the main) descriptive, were mentioned in Part I. Here, two of the series of picture cards are given in full, so that the reader will understand the context of the discussion on linguistic categories which will follow in chapters 2–8.

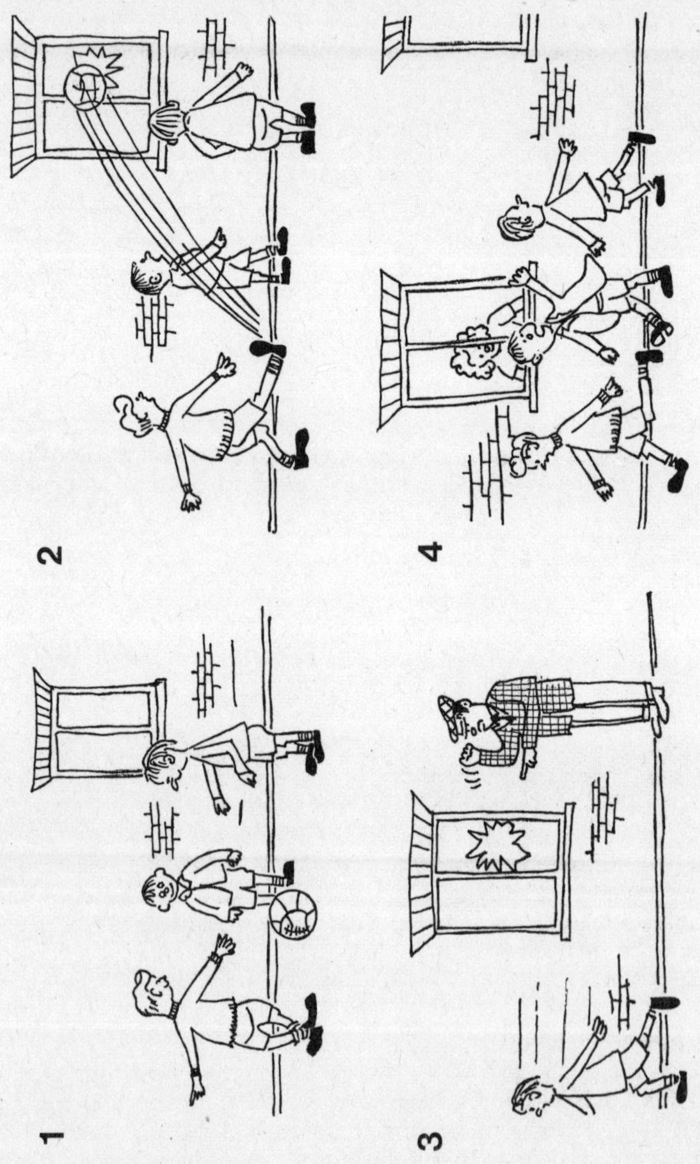
1
2
3
4

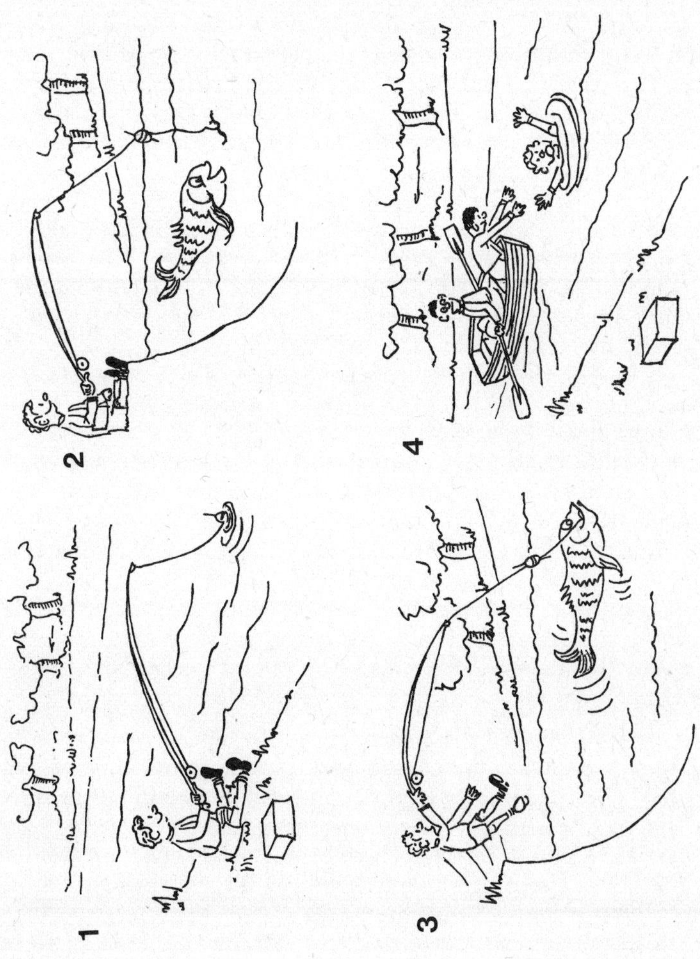
1
2
3
4

The introduction and probes given by the interviewer were as follows.

Task 2 (picture stories)

> Introduction: 'I've got some pictures that tell a story. I'm going to show them to you and I want you to tell me the story.' (Lays cards down slowly.) 'This is a story about some boys playing football. The ball breaks a window. The story starts here' (points to card 1).
>
> If child stops after first card, interviewer says 'What happens next?' and repeats this if necessary. When the child has told his story, interviewer gives Probe 1: (points to card 3) 'What's the man saying?' Then Probe 2: (points to card 4) 'What about the lady?' If child says 'I don't know' to either of these: 'What do you think he/she *might* be saying?'
>
> Interviewer then moves to second series: 'These pictures tell another story. This is a story about a boy fishing. What's happening in the story?'
>
> The probes are 1: (points to card 4) 'What do they say to the boy in the water?' 2: 'What does the boy in the water say?' And again, for a refusal: 'What do you think they/he *might* be saying?'
>
> For the third series: 'This is a story about a cat and some fish. What's happening in this story?'
>
> The probes are 1: (points to card 4) 'What are they saying' (If reply is inadequate) 'What is the lady saying?' 'What is the boy saying?' And again, 'What do you think they *might* be saying?'

We note here that each series is introduced by saying something *about* the story—'This is a story about . . .' and that the probes in each case ask what the characters are saying, inviting 'role-play' speech. The child's reply to these probes could be in either 'direct' or 'indirect' speech, preceded or not preceded by *they're/he's/she's saying* or by simply *saying*. These distinctions were not taken into account, being regarded as determined by the probe and not as part of the child's spontaneous utterance.

Each series of pictures in this task therefore comprises two sections: the *narrative* speech as the child told the story, and the *role-play* speech in response to the probes *what is X saying?* This role-play speech has the function of *social control* (see ch. 4, p. 117) in the first and third series of cards. A distinction between the narrative and role-play types of speech will be necessary in the investigation of certain categories.

Task 3 (Trotin cards)

> Introduction: 'Now I've got some more pictures. These are nice coloured ones.' (Gives child the first picture.) 'What's going on/happening in this picture?'
>
> If the child says very little, add: 'Tell me what you can see.' 'What are the people/they doing?' 'What else is going on/happening?'
>
> Finally (the 'naming' probe)—'What shall we call this picture? What name shall we give it?'
>
> 'Now I'll show you another picture.' (Gives child second picture.) 'What's going on . . .' etc., as for first picture, and repeat again for third picture.

Note here (1) that the probes are action-oriented—thc verbs are *going on*, *happening*, and *doing*. (2) Not all the children were given the probe 'tell me what you can see' which might produce a 'list' of items in the picture as a reply. (3) The interviewer has to decide whether the child has said 'very little', in deciding whether to give him further probes or not. There are further comments on these points in chapter 3. (4) The 'naming' probe generally elicited very little further speech. The response to this probe was usually a single nominal group, e.g. *train* or *train picture*, the clause structure being latent and based on the question form, i.e. [we'll call it a] *train picture*. These short responses were not included with the main body of descriptive speech so as to keep the latter homogeneous.

'Meta-task' speech

Not all the child's speech that occurred between the beginning and end of the task was analysed, because some utterances were clearly not part of the task. Those utterances which were judged to be unconnected with the task were said to constitute *non-task* speech, and they were given separate treatment in the computer analysis. They included statements about the child's own experiences, or his family, or questions to the interviewer, for example:

(3, i)[6] I know of another station East Croydon that's the one we have to go to when I see my nanna.
(3, i) Not very interesting are they?
(3, ii) Have you got a table as big as that at your house?

In the extended analysis of the nominal group we decided to exclude other utterances which were considered not to be directly relevant to the performance of the task, but which had not been excluded previously in the computer analysis. We called this 'meta-task' speech.

The reason for excluding certain categories of utterance in this way was to achieve a speech sample which was as homogeneous as possible. Task 2 was designed to elicit a narrative section (subject tells the story) and a role-play section (subject responds to the probes); Task 3 was designed mainly for its descriptive section (subject describes the pictures). We wanted to exclude any utterances which fell outside these particular objectives, since in comparing the performance of a large number of children, it is essential to control for the speech situation(s) as far as possible, otherwise the data may simply not be comparable.

There is always some difficulty in deciding exactly what is and what is not 'directly relevant' to the task. Even the classification of non-task speech posed difficulties, as one can see from the second example, above, which could be taken as a comment about the pictures themselves and therefore to be included as task-relevant speech. (It was excluded in that instance because it was not directly part of the description of the picture.)

Meta-task speech can be regarded as an extension of the principle of non-task speech rather than as a distinct category on its own. The general criterion on which it was based was: does the utterance contribute to a description of the pictures (or narrative of the story)? Does it add any further information to them? If not, then it should be regarded as meta-task, even if it arises as a direct result of the pictorial material in front of the child. Since the coding of the speech was done by two of us, we had to obtain some measure of agreement on what should be excluded as 'meta-task'. From a preliminary inspection of the data, and on the basis of our previous experience, we were able to outline the following categories of meta-task speech. This is not a complete classification but it covers about 90 per cent of the cases. Utterances not covered by these categories, but which might be regarded as meta-task, were submitted for joint consultation, and the decision was used as a precedent for any similar examples.

1 'Terminator' sequences
That's all
That's all I can see
That's all I can think of
Can't think of anything else
2 'Refusal' sequence
(I) don't know
(I) don't know what that is
(I) don't know what they're saying
(I) can't think
3 'Early' comments (before interviewer has introduced the task)

The cat's eaten the fish

4 'Sequence' comments
Is this the last one?
In the first one . . .
That's number two

5 Questions addressed to interviewer
What's that?
How did those cats get up on the roof?
Is that train going?
Have I got to tell all that?
You have to have a lot of boys don't you?

6 General comments about the pictures
Aren't they funny
This is nicer
I want them to be interesting
In the other picture it wasn't there

One can see that the analysis of meta-task speech itself might produce some interesting results. All the instances were collected but there has so far been no opportunity to analyse them. They actually constituted a very small proportion of the total speech output. Once the meta-task speech was excluded, we were reasonably confident that we had achieved a fairly homogeneous, and hence comparable, collection of data.

The sociological (or 'background') variables

In Part I, four variables were considered—social class, sex, IQ and CI (maternal index of communication). For Part II we extended the range of indices available for each variable, and added some new variables: for example, we used three indices of social class and three of IQ instead of one for each, and we included the five separate components of the new communication index as well as the combined index. In this way we hoped to identify the significant factors which influence the use of the linguistic categories. Our use of correlations instead of a factorial design made these extensions possible.

All the 'sociological' information was collected by other members of the Research Unit and the author is indebted to them for being able to include these variables with his linguistic data. The account of the variables which follows will be taken from their material, and will be as brief as is compatible with comprehensibility. For full details, the reader should consult, in particular, Brandis and Henderson (1970, ch. 3 and the Appendices).

The main variables are as follows.

(i) **Social class**

The scale from 0 to 9 which measures social class has already been mentioned (p. 53). It was devised by members of the Research Unit (Brandis and Henderson, 1970, Appendix I) and is based not only on the occupational status of the father as is the Hall-Jones Scale, but also on the occupational status of the mother (with reference to 'whatever job she has held that occupies the highest position on the Hall-Jones scale'), and on the educational status of *both the mother and the father*.

For the purpose of the present study, two further indices of social class were derived from this ten-point scale. Since it is a long scale, it was thought that correlations with the linguistic variables (particularly the infrequent ones) might respond better to an abbreviated scale with only three divisions which could be called middle-, intermediate- and working-class. This is based on the assumption that 'middle' and 'working' class exist as strata within the ten-point scale, such that the intervals at the top and bottom ends of the scale between, let us say, 0 and 1, are smaller than the interval between 3 and 4 or between 5 and 6, which represent points of change from one stratum to the next. The ten-point scale was therefore divided in two different ways to give the two new indices.

(a) New Social Class Index I (NSC I): The original scale was divided straightforwardly as follows:

		n[7]
Middle class	= 0 – 2	81
Intermediate	= 3 – 5	76
Working class	= 6 – 9	155
	Total	312

(b) New Social Class Index II (NSC II): The areas from which the sample was drawn are also taken into account. Let us call the predominantly middle-class area B, and the working-class area H. The division is then:

		n
Middle class	= 0 – 3, from B	100
Intermediate	= 4 – 9, from B	73
	0 – 5, from H	
Working class	= 6 – 9, from H	139
	Total	312

The latter index has the advantage that area is taken into account in the division, excluding from 'middle class' those children who, although of high social class, live in the working-class area, and from 'working class' those who, although of low social class, came from the middle-class area (the 'intermediate' group here thus corresponds to the 'marginal' group referred to previously in connection with the χ^2 sample). Another advantage is the greater similarity in the relative size of the middle- and working-class samples; there is a difference of 74 in the first index (81 MC, 155 WC) but of only 39 in the second (100 MC, 139 WC).

(ii) **Sex**

Boys *v.* girls. No new divisions are proposed here.

(iii) **IQ**

The children were given, after three weeks in the infant school, three kinds of IQ tests to ascertain their verbal and non-verbal ability. First, they were given Raven's Progressive Matrices, which are essentially tests of performance (non verbal); second, the Crichton Vocabulary Scale, which is a test of verbal ability, and, more specifically, tests the child's *active* vocabulary by asking him to give definitions; third, they were given the English version of the Peabody Picture Vocabulary Test (EPVT), which is essentially a test of *passive* vocabulary, the child being asked to point to a named object in a picture.

The children's scores on each of these three tests were included as variables to be correlated. Of the three, we might expect the Matrices to correlate the least with our linguistic categories, because they test non-verbal ability; the Crichton scale might be expected to correlate the most strongly with linguistic categories, because it tests not only verbal ability, but active rather than passive vocabulary.

(iv) **Communication index**

This index, is, as mentioned previously, based on interviews given to the children's mothers. In brief, it is an attempt to measure the extent to which mothers are willing to promote verbal exchanges with their children, by answering their questions, encouraging them to ask questions, explaining unusual things to them, etc.

From the questionnaire the mothers were given, four schedules were chosen as the basis for the index. Three of these schedules were 'closed', the other one 'open'.[8] The 'old' communication index which was used, in Part I, to select children for the factorial design, was based only on scores from two of the closed schedules. The new index which will be used here is based on scores from all four schedules. A full account of the construction of the index is to be found in Brandis and Henderson (1970) Appendix II, from which the information, in the summary which follows here, is taken.

Schedule I ('Avoidance') 'samples the universe of responses available to the mother when the child asks difficult questions' (Brandis and Henderson, 1970). The mother was asked what she would mostly do when children 'ask about things which are difficult to explain to a child'. High scores were given to mothers who were disposed to answer difficult questions ('tell them a little bit until they ask again' or 'tell them as much as you can'), low scores to mothers who were disposed to *avoid* answering the questions ('try and change the subject', 'make up something until they are older', and 'tell them to ask daddy').[9] The series of scores thus derived was known as the 'Avoidance' scale.

The second schedule ('Verbal Interaction') measures the extent to which mothers are prepared to talk to their children when otherwise occupied. Seven situations were given, and for each one the mother was asked to tick which of the following she would usually do: (i) tell the child to stop, (ii) tell him to wait, (iii) give him a quick answer, (iv) chat with him. Mothers who regularly gave responses (iii) or (iv) would obtain high scores, those giving (i) or (ii) low scores. The seven situations were: working around the house; walking along the street; trying to relax; talking to the husband; in a shop; in a bus or tube; at meal-times. The scale, derived from summing the scores for each response, is known as the 'Verbal Interaction' scale; it 'measures the mother's disposition to continue a verbal interaction initiated by the child' (*ibid.*). This and the 'Avoidance' schedule just described formed the basis of the old communication index, whereas they form only part of the new one.

The third schedule 'samples behavioural problem situations initiated by the child, and asks the mother to relate what her response to the child would be' (*ibid.*). The mother is asked, apropos of six different situations, what she would say or do if her child did something wrong, for example if he (or she) refused to go to bed because he wanted to watch something on TV, or if he brought his mother some flowers but she found out that he had got them from a neighbour's garden. The responses to this schedule were open, in the sense that the mother was free to say what she liked—no specified alternative answers were given.

The classifying and coding of 'open' responses like these is complex,[10] but from the data given two separate indices were initially constructed[11]—a 'Punishment' index which measures the extent to which the mother will resort to punishment, physical or verbal (including the 'categoric' statements like 'I'd make him do it'); and a child-oriented reasoning index, measuring the extent to which the mother would give reasons of a certain kind to the child, for his behaviour being wrong. The index was based only on the *child*-oriented appeals, that is, those reasons which mentioned the consequences *for the child* of his behaviour, e.g. 'if you stay up late, you'll be tired in the morning' (Brandis and Henderson, 1970, ch. 3).

From this 'open' schedule, then, were derived the two indices of the mother's behaviour, the 'Punishment' index and what we shall call the 'Reasoning' index.

The fourth schedule ('Toys') is a closed schedule, in which the mothers were asked about the functions they thought toys should perform. Six different functions were given, and the mothers were asked to rank them in importance.

Function C ('so that the children can find out about things') and Functions D and F ('to free the mother so that she can do other things', 'to show that mother cares when she has been away') were considered the most important functions as reflections of the mother's attitude, and the index was constructed such that the highest score would be given to mothers who ranked C at the top of the scale of importance, F and D at the bottom. Deviations from this order of ranking would merit correspondingly lower index scores. (Brandis and Henderson, 1970.)

These five indices, based on responses to four different schedules in the mothers' interviews, were then combined to form an overall 'communication index', which we shall call the 'new' index to distinguish it from the 'old' one used for the computer analysis (see Part I).

The 'background' variables, then, based on class, sex, IQ and CI are as follows:

1 Social class (ten-point scale)
2 NSC I (three-point scale, middle, intermediate and working class)
3 NSC II (three-point scale, also taking area into account middle, marginal, and working class)
4 Sex
5 Matrices (test of non-verbal ability)
6 Crichton (verbal ability—active vocabulary)
7 EPVT (verbal ability—passive vocabulary)
8 Avoidance
9 Verbal interaction

10 (Child-oriented) reasoning
11 Punishment
12 Toys
13 New Communication Index (combined index based on all four schedules, i.e. on 8–12 above)

To these can be added
14 Area. A straightforward division into (1) the predominantly middle-class area (B) and (2) the predominantly working-class area (H).

This variable was included to see whether area of residence could be held to play a significant part in linguistic development, in addition to measures of social class. In this case, B and H were separate not only geographically, but also socially, the correlation between area and social class being as high as 0·74. There is a possibility that working-class children in B might behave linguistically more like the middle-class children who are in the majority in that area, and, conversely, middle-class children in H might adopt working-class speech patterns. In this case, the correlations of the linguistic variables with *area* would be higher than the correlations of the same variables with social class.

A number of other sociological variables were originally included, namely, an index of family size, an index of the child's ordinal position in the family, and a series of teachers' ratings which evaluated the child's performance in school. As the study progressed, however, it became clear that some limitation on the quantity of data was necessary, and these variables were dropped.

Statistical treatment

We have now established a total of 51 independent variable factors, 37 of them being linguistic categories, the other 14 sociological. Clearly we are interested principally in correlations between the linguistic variables on the one hand and the sociological ones on the other, and not in correlations between one linguistic variable and another or one sociological factor and another.[12]

It was necessary to perform more than one series of correlations to account for all the data we had prepared. First, we obtained a matrix for Task 2 and Task 3 separately; then the scores for both tasks were combined, to give a further matrix for Combined Tasks 2 + 3.

The reason for combining the scores thus was to give a larger sample of speech over which to observe any category which was very infrequent in each task separately. This combination is only meaningful if the category concerned has a similar function in both tasks and if there appears to be no inherent reason why the scores for both tasks should not be combined. In many cases the functions *were* different; in these instances the Combined Tasks results can be ignored.

These three matrices (Task 2, Task 3, and Combined Tasks) will be taken as the basic information for which we shall report results, together with the χ^2 tests for the infrequent variables. But we shall derive supplementary information from a number of other matrices which were also generated from the data.

First, we wanted to know the relative influence of sex, IQ and communication index *within* each social class, since there is evidence that CI at least has a greater effect in one class than in the other. Brandis (Brandis and Henderson, 1970, Appendix III) writes:

> Clearly, the social class affects the mother's orientation towards communication and control in the working-class area much more dramatically than in the middle-class area. . . . It seems reasonable to suggest that [this] orientation clearly differentiates working-class strata, but fails to discriminate very adequately between middle-class strata. Indeed, the relative homogeneity of the mother's orientation towards communication and control in the middle-class area indicates that its power to discriminate between anything at all within the middle class is considerably reduced.

We therefore split the total sample into three groups, middle, marginal, and working class, in accordance with the NSC II division (see p. 62) and obtained correlations for each group separately, both for Task 2 and Task 3 and the Combined Tasks. The disadvantage of this division is the reduction of the sample size from about 300 to only just over 100 for the middle- and working-class groups, which affects the reliability of the correlations.

Second, one of the most obvious findings from our original matrices was the high correlation of each linguistic variable with 'total nominal group heads', i.e. the total amount of speech.[13] This was only to be expected, since clearly it is those who talk the most who are likely to use any particular category more frequently, irrespective of their social class, sex, IQ or other factors. To make allowances for this, and to reduce the effect of total speech as much as possible, a different kind of computer program was used, which divided the sample into four groups according to the total speech produced, and then performed correlations for each group separately. The division of the sample was based on the distribution curve for total heads, the cut-off points for each group being located in such a way as to get (a) a reasonable sample size within each group and (b) the narrowest range possible for the most important groups. Thus, the average number of 'total heads' in Task 2 was 53·6, but the highest went to 186. By placing cut-points at 40 and 60, we obtained two groups with fairly narrow ranges of scores (20–40 and 41–60) which contained within them 95 and 129 children respectively, that is, 72 per cent of the total sample. This enabled us to control for the 'length' variable while still observing the effects of social class, IQ, etc. The disadvantage of this procedure was, again, the reduction of the sample size, so that the information given by these correlations will again be regarded as supplementary, rather than basic. Further discussion of the influence of total speech on the results is given below (pp. 70ff.).

The matrices obtained may thus be represented as shown in Table 1.4.

Table 1.4

		Task 2	*Task 3*	*Combined Tasks*
Basic: whole sample		+	+	+
Supplementary:	middle class only	+	+	+
	intermediate only	+	+	+
	working class only	+	+	+
	20–40 heads only	+	+	
	41–60 heads only	+	+	
	61–85* heads only	+	+	
	86* + heads only	+	+	

* = 95 and 96, respectively, for Task 3. The distribution of scores suggested that different cut-points for each task would be advantageous; hence the scores were cut at 85 in Task 2, 95 in Task 3.

For all the matrices except those where the 'length' factor was controlled, the computer also gave the statistical probabilities of any correlation for which the probability was smaller than 10 per cent.[14] In the tables accompanying our results (Tables 2.1 ff.) we shall show these probabilities symbolically rather than numerically, alongside the numerical value of the correlation, as this method of presentation has the advantage of being easier to read. The precise probability can be obtained by referring to the summaries in Appendix II. The system of marking probabilities symbolically will be as follows:

/ $p < 0{\cdot}05$—significant
// $p < 0{\cdot}01$—highly significant
/// $p < 0{\cdot}001$—very highly significant

Because the sample is large, a correlation does not have to be very high to reach the level of significance. In the matrices based on the total sample of 300, a correlation of $\pm$ 0·112 is enough to be significant at 5 per cent, while a correlation of $\pm$ 0·150 is significant at 1 per cent.

In the tables accompanying the results, we give the correlations between the linguistic category under consideration and the principal sociological factors, namely, social class, two measures of verbal IQ, the New Communication Index, and sex. The individual indices on which the NCI is based ('Avoidance', 'Verbal Interaction', etc.—see p. 64) are not examined in detail in this study; on the whole we found that none of them, on their own, correlated very strongly with the linguistic categories, but in combination (i.e. as the NCI) they performed much better. The tables thus give the figures for the whole index and not for its individual components.

The *sign* of the correlation (positive/negative) tells us which social group a linguistic variable is associated with. A positive correlation between a linguistic variable and social class means that the variable is used more frequently by lower-class children; a negative correlation indicates a middle-class feature.

For IQ and CI correlations, a positive sign indicates that the variable is associated with high IQ and high CI children, a negative sign with low IQ or low CI children. In general, therefore, correlations which are positive for class will be negative for IQ and CI, there being a tendency for working-class children to be in the lower IQ and CI ranges.

For correlations with sex, a positive sign indicates a feature used more frequently by *girls*, a negative sign means *boys*.

For the infrequent variables, the χ^2 test, which compares the number of children using the variable at all rather than the total scores, is likely to be more reliable than the correlations. For this reason, Tables 2.1 ff. also include χ^2 results, where these were obtained. The χ^2 sample was divided into four groups, working-class boys and girls and middle-class boys and girls (see p. 55). This gives six possible permutations[15] for testing by χ^2, but in general the sex differences are small and unless there is a possibility of a large difference, the tests between boys and girls within each social class will not be reported. We shall therefore present just the overall class-difference, the class-difference for boys and girls separately, and the overall sex difference.

Frequency ratings

At the beginning of the results for each category we shall give the percentage of users for each task, and a general estimate of how frequently this category occurred. A four-point scale of frequency was devised, based on the data given in Appendix III. The scale is as follows:

	Rating
Very frequent (c. 2000 or more occurrences)[16]	4
Relatively frequent (c. 500–1000 occurrences)	3
Relatively infrequent (c. 100–500 occurrences)	2
Very infrequent (below c. 100 occurrences)	1

Total speech

It is important to consider the total amount of speech produced by each child, and by each group, since fluctuations from one group to another could result in categories being used more or less frequently by one group of children simply because that group produced more or less speech than the others. As already noted, we have assumed that total output of nominal groups is representative of the total amount of speech and we shall therefore use this as our index.

For the correlation program, the factor of total speech was minimised by dividing the sample into four divisions according to the amount produced, the lowest division being those with between 20 and 40 nominal groups, the next 40 to 60 and so on. Nevertheless, this was a useful procedure only for the categories which were used frequently, like nouns and third-person pronouns. The less frequent categories could not give reliable correlations when the sample was sub-divided. We therefore need to know to what extent total speech varies from one group to another, according to social class, IQ, sex etc.

We can ascertain this first by observing the correlations of the variable 'total heads' with the sociological variables, and second by comparing the means of the four groups of children (working-class boys and girls, middle-class boys and girls), into which the sample was divided for χ^2 tests.

The correlations of 'total heads' may be seen in Table 1.5. None of them is significant, and we may therefore assume that there are no variations in the total amount of speech, other than would occur by chance, for any of the major sociological variables. In other words they give no evidence that children of any particular sex, or social class, IQ or CI grouping are uttering a greater quantity of speech in these two tasks than any other groups.

Table 1.5 Correlations of 'total heads' with social class, IQ, etc.

Correlations		*Task 2* *r*	*p*	*Task 3* *r*	*p*	*Combined Tasks* *r*	*p*
Class	SC	0·006		0·027		0·019	
	NSC I	0·010		0·058		0·043	
	NSC II	0·009		0·052		0·043	
Sex		0·036		0·046		0·039	
IQ	Crichton	0·079		0·066		0·073	
	EPVT	−0·087		−0·043		−0·072	
New CI		−0·074		−0·020		−0·066	

All probabilities are non-significant.

Second, we must consider the means of the four groups for which χ^2 tests were calculated. Table 1.6 gives the number of children, the mean number of nominal groups uttered in Task 2, and the standard deviation, for each group of children; Table 1.7 does the same for Task 3.

Table 1.6 Total heads, Task 2

	n	*Mean*	*SD*
WC boys	59	51·2	21·0
WC girls	80	57·1	28·2
MC boys	65	53·3	28·7
MC girls	59	52·8	16·5

Table 1.7 Total heads, Task 3

	n	*Mean*	*SD*
WC boys	54	60·3	36·1
WC girls	76	67·2	39·2
MC boys	65	60·3	29·7
MC girls	59	57·1	25·7

We observe that the differences between the means in Task 2 are small in comparison with the standard deviations, which indicates that the distributions of scores do not differ significantly, and that the frequencies of individual linguistic categories will not be substantially affected by fluctuations from group to group in the quantity of speech. The greatest difference (in Task 2) is between the means of working-class girls (57·1) and working-class boys (51·2); but this is accompanied by a larger SD for the girls, which suggests that a small number of girls have a high output, eg. more than 100 nominal groups each, and not that girls as a whole are uttering more speech than boys.

In Task 3, however, there is a considerable difference between the mean of working-class girls (67·2) and that of middle-class girls (57·1). This is the biggest difference throughout the two tasks, and it was thought necessary to compare the two groups of scores by a t-test. The result showed this difference was not significant ($t = 1{\cdot}69$, $p = 0{\cdot}10$), and we therefore decided not to alter the sample by cutting out children with high scores or taking only part of their utterances. The difference, nevertheless, is of some magnitude, as is shown by the level of probability (0·10), and cannot be entirely discounted, but it was felt that the categories which would be most affected by this difference were nouns and third-person pronouns, ie. the highly frequent categories; and we could control for the differences here by splitting the sample according to quantity. The difference in means is not very likely to affect the use of infrequent categories which we shall test on the basis of users *versus* non-users (ie. by χ^2). If a category has not appeared in the course of 57 nominal groups (the average for middle-class girls) it is not much more likely to appear in the course of 67 (the average for working-class girls).

Notes

[1] The principles and methods of correlations are outlined in Moroney (1956, ch. 16). A correlation may vary from $+1$ (complete positive relationship between two sets of scores) to -1 (complete negative relationship), a correlation of zero indicating no relationship at all.

[2] The terms *lower-class* (LC) and *working-class* (WC) will be used interchangeably. Neither term is quite satisfactory; working-class is the traditional one but implies a dichotomy (working/middle) which we wish partly to avoid because we are using a *scale* of social class with *upper* and *lower* ends. The upper end will be referred to as *middle-class* (MC), which is also in some ways an unsatisfactory term. Our avoidance of the dichotomy is only partial, because we do recognise separate middle- and working-class groups in our χ^2 sample (see below).

[3] I am again indebted to W. Brandis for his advice in the selection of the sample.

[4] The sample cannot be divided into IQ and CI groups, for reasons given earlier—any division yielding discrete groups based on IQ and CI as well as social class would reduce the sample to the size of the factorial design, viz.

to about 80. We must therefore rely on the correlations alone to give us differences between children of high or low IQ and CI respectively.

[5] The analysis of the speech was carried out by two people, the author and Richard Pickvance, at that time research assistant at the Sociological Research Unit.

[6] These numbers refer to the task (Task 3, in this case) and the section (card 1, 'The train', in this case).

[7] Only the N for the Task 2 sample are given here. Those for Task 3 would be correspondingly a little smaller.

[8] In a 'closed' schedule, the subject is asked to tick one of a limited number of possible responses, which are specified. In an 'open' schedule, the subject answers a question in her own words.

[9] This is of course a simplified account. The scoring of responses to a schedule such as this requires some fairly complex statistical procedures.

[10] The coding frame for this schedule was constructed by Bernstein and Cook.

[11] The results of the classification, and a full discussion of the mothers' replies, are in Cook-Gumperz (1973).

[12] The computer program takes all the variables and correlates everything with everything else, giving a matrix of $\frac{50 \times 51}{2} = 1{,}275$ correlations (each correlation is given only once in the matrix).

[13] Total nominal group heads had previously been found to be a reliable index of the total output of speech.

[14] A probability of 0·03 would be given as 3·000, i.e. the figures are taken to three decimal places. Such precision is not required for our purposes. To avoid confusion, the probabilities mentioned in the text will be written as they are normally, eg. $p < 0{\cdot}05$, $p < 0{\cdot}01$, etc. But in the correlation summaries in Appendix II the significance levels are expressed as the computer gave them, to three decimal places; thus a probability of (eg.) 1·562 means, in the more usual notation, $p = 0{\cdot}01562$, i.e. $p < 0{\cdot}02$.

[15] I.e. LC boys with LC girls
LC boys with MC boys
LC boys with MC girls, etc.

In addition we can have class-differences irrespective of sex (overall class) and sex-differences irrespective of class (overall sex).

[16] The numbers here refer to total occurrences for the whole sample of 312 children; thus, a category with 2000 occurrences has an average of about 7 occurrences per child.

Chapter 2 The reference categories

In this chapter and the following chapter on nouns we shall be dealing with the linguistic variables which involve a choice of reference; in particular we shall be concerned with nouns and third-person pronouns (P3), but also with a number of less frequent variables which present the same choice.

Description of the categories

In the factorial sample of 80 children studied in Part I, one of the major findings was the greater use of P3 (third-person pronouns) by working-class and nouns by middle-class children. It was suggested that, linguistically, P3 are more restricted than nouns because (a) they contain less information and are therefore more predictable than a noun, and (b) they are not open to a wide range of modification and qualification; modifiers (eg. adjectives) and qualifiers hardly ever occur in association with pronouns at H and the range of possibilities here is very limited. A more frequent use of nouns thus means the possibility of expansion on a much wider scale, whereas the use of the pronoun entails considerable restriction.

We have already seen that these opportunities are to some extent taken up by the middle-class children, particularly in Task 2 where there was evidence that they used more modifiers as a whole, and more qualifiers.

Other researchers have found evidence of differences between middle- and working-class children in this area of the nominal group. Bernstein, in studies of adolescents of similar measured ability aged fifteen, found class-differences in the use of a number of grammatical categories, including adjectives, 'uncommon' adjectives, and the personal pronoun *I*, which are used more frequently by the middle class, and the personal pronouns *you* and *they* which are preferred by the working class. In interpreting the latter, Bernstein suggested that the use of *you* and *they* indicated a 'lack of specification', which 'also implies that there is possibly some implicit agreement about the referent such that the elaboration is redundant'.

In a study conducted on the same material as is used in this report, namely Tasks 2 and 3 and one other task of the speech schedule, Henderson counted types and tokens of (among other things) nouns and adjectives, and found that middle-class children use significantly more different (i.e. type) adjectives, more nouns, and more type nouns, than the working class (Brandis and Henderson, 1970, ch. 1). The importance of a difference in type nouns is discussed below (pp. 76, 96).

These results, and the ones derived from our present study, are thus consonant with the predictions obtained from Bernstein's theory of restricted and elaborated codes. In terms of these codes, one would expect the middle-class children to show relatively greater flexibility in their choices within the nominal group, and their groups to be more elaborated. We have already found a certain amount of evidence in this direction.

Let us now take the discussion of noun/P3 usage a stage further.

We have seen class-differences in the frequencies with which nouns and P3 are used, but we need to know how and where these two types of head are being used, to illuminate the real meaning of this finding. It could be the case, for example, that the middle class use more nouns simply because they repeat a noun in places where a P3 could have equally well, perhaps better, been substituted, eg.

The boy kicked the ball and the ball broke the window

In an example like this, the substitution of *it* for the second occurrence of *the ball* would be an improvement, if anything. At the other extreme, the excessive use of P3 can lead to completely inadequate communication. Compare these two (somewhat exaggerated) versions[1] of the same story (based on the first picture story; see drawings, pp. 56–7).

1 Three boys are playing football   and one boy kicks the ball and it goes through the window   the ball breaks the window   and the boys are looking at it   and a man comes out   and shouts at them   because they've broken the window   so they run away and then that lady looks out of her window   and she tells the boys off.
No. of nouns: 13   No. of P3s: 6

2 They're playing football   and he kicks it   and it goes through there   it breaks that   and they're looking at it   and he comes out   and shouts at them   because they've

broken it so they run away and then she looks out and she tells them off.

No. of nouns: 1 No. of P3s: 14

These two versions are parallel in clause structure, but in the first the nominal groups are realised mainly by nouns, in the second mainly by P3s. One can see that the difference between them lies not only in the amount of elaboration, actual or potential, of the nominal group, but also in the amount of information communicated. The first version explicitly states *who* performed the various actions and *what* objects or persons were affected by them. It is a version which can be immediately understood and interpreted, even without reference to the pictures themselves.

The second of the versions makes great demands on the listener. It means that the context (in this case the series of pictures) must be present if the listener is to understand who and what is being referred to. It assumes that the listener can *see* the pictures the speaker is describing, or knows enough about them not to need the relevant information about the characters and objects involved. Bernstein suggests that this kind of assumption is typical of a speaker using a restricted code. He (the speaker) feels no compulsion to make his meaning more explicit; the social relationship existing between himself and the listener is such that further elaboration would be felt redundant (cf. Bernstein, 1965).

Is it possible to demonstrate that the working class, who as we know produce more P3s, actually use these pronouns in this way? One indication that the middle class are not simply repeating their nouns, in situations where a P3 would do equally well, is the fact that they use significantly more *type* (as opposed to *token*) nouns, as has been shown by Henderson (Brandis and Henderson, 1970, pp. 29–30, 68). If they were only using more 'token' nouns (that is, more nouns altogether, irrespective of whether they were different nouns or not), we might have suspected that some nouns were being repeated more frequently than was necessary. But the class-difference in the use of *type*-nouns demonstrates otherwise.

The other way to show this kind of difference is to look at the P3s themselves, and in particular to distinguish different types of pronoun reference. These reference types will now be briefly presented.

Pronoun reference

At about the same time as our study of pronoun-usage began, there appeared a paper on grammatical cohesion and reference by

R. Hasan (1968). It is concerned with reference and cohesion within and between clauses and sentences in English, in which P3s play an important part. Briefly, narrative cohesion is usually achieved by the use of grammatical items which refer either backwards (to something already mentioned) or forwards (to something about to be mentioned). 'Backward' reference is known as anaphoric reference, 'forward' as cataphoric. Examples of their use are:

1 Anaphoric: The boy kicked the ball and it broke the window (where *it* refers backwards to *the ball*).
2 Cataphoric: It was difficult not to break the window (where *it* refers forwards to *not to break the window*).

Anaphoric reference is much more common than cataphoric, and may be applied to a variety of grammatical categories, principally to pronouns, but also to deictics like *this*, *that*. There is, however, a third possibility, and that is the reference type known as 'exophoric', or reference 'outwards' to the 'context of situation'. In this case, the pronoun or other grammatical item refers not to something already or about to be *mentioned*, but to something in the environment of the speaker. If, for example, one is standing on the edge of a football field and the players are clustered round the goal, one might say 'they've scored!' and there would be no doubt who *they* referred to.

If we apply these reference categories 'anaphoric' and 'exophoric' to the two versions of the story given above (p. 75), we can clearly see that the six P3s in the first all have referents within the text itself—they refer backwards to things or people already mentioned, such as the ball, the window, the boys; they are therefore *anaphoric* in reference. Most of the P3s in the second version, however, are quite different. They refer 'outwards' to items in the pictures which the listener is supposed to be aware of. The first 'they', for example, refers to 'the three boys you can (presumably) see in Card 1'; 'he' refers to 'the boy in the picture with his foot raised'; 'it' refers to the football there; and so on. This kind of reference is *exophoric* in nature; the pronouns have what is called a deictic, or 'pointing', function.

We mentioned earlier that pronouns were relatively restricted *linguistically* in comparison with nouns; we can now see that pronouns may be limited *contextually*, if they are used exophorically—they mark a use of language which is tied very closely to the immediate visual and situational context; they make assumptions about the prior knowledge held by the addressee, and they impose on him an extra burden of interpretation in so far as he has to retrieve the referents from the given context of situation. The use of nouns, by contrast, makes the referent explicit, in other words the speaker himself has taken on a greater share of the burden of communication, and made the interpretation relatively easier for the listener.

Our hypothesis is, then, as follows: Bernstein suggests that a social group which has developed strong communal bonds as a result of its common occupational function and social status, will communicate via a particular kind of code, one which makes use of the closely shared identifications and the common expectations held by the speakers (1972, p. 472). We have seen that the extensive use of exophoric pronouns makes the assumption that the addressee shares in the speaker's knowledge, which accordingly does not need to be made verbally explicit. Hence, we may predict that working-class speakers will tend to use exophoric items in a situation where a choice is possible between the explicit formulation (with a noun) and a less explicit mode (with exophorics); while middle-class speakers, who do not participate in a social structure of the same kind, will tend to prefer the more explicit forms.

The two tasks of our speech schedule do offer choices of this kind to the speakers: in narrating the stories (Task 2) or describing the cards (Task 3) there are many opportunities for choosing either a noun or an exophoric item. If we observe the frequency of nouns and exophorics in the speech offered, we shall expect to find lower-class speakers using exophorics more frequently than middle-class speakers, and the latter using nouns more frequently.

Exophoric reference is conveyed mainly through the use of P3 but there are a number of other grammatical categories in which a choice of reference type is possible. It is important that these should also be included in our investigation. The categories involved are as follows.

(1) The demonstratives *this/these*, *that/those* at H. These forms may be used either anaphorically, eg.

'go away', *that*'s what she said (*that* refers back to the utterance 'go away')

or exophorically, eg.

that's a little boy (reference to the picture-card)

(2) *This/these*, *that/those* at M may also be used either anaphorically,[2] eg.

the boy broke the window, so the lady told *that* boy off

or exophorically, eg.

these boys were playing football

(3) *Here*, *there* at H after a preposition, eg. *on here*, *up there*, *along there* are always exophoric.

These three categories were therefore included in our analysis in addition to P3.

It could be argued that occurrences of *here*, *there* alone, as adverbs not preceded by a preposition (eg. 'a man's selling apples there'), are also exophoric in reference and should therefore be included in our investigation of the reference categories. The reason why they were not included is because their degree of 'exophoricness', i.e. the extent to which they depend on the extra-verbal context, is much less than for *here*, *there* after a preposition. If the speaker says

the train goes through there

the addressee is directed to the picture to find out what or where the train goes through, and the exact location is in this case important. But an utterance like

a man's selling apples there,

with *there* unstressed, gives us information about an event without directing us to a particular point in the picture—the exact location is not important. The difference amounts to this: when *here*, *there* follow a preposition, they replace a noun and thus represent a choice between explicit (speaker-given) reference and implicit (addressee-supplied) reference; compare *through the bridge* (explicit) with *through there* (implicit). But when *here*, *there* are used adverbially without a preposition, no alternative with a noun is involved.

For this reason, then, *here*, *there* as adverbs were not included in our present study.

The coding of reference pronouns

The distinction between anaphoric and exophoric is theoretically a clear one, the deciding factor being whether the reference of the pronoun has previously occurred within the text (i.e. has been uttered) or not. But in practice there are some difficulties. The commonest of these is when the referent *has* occurred previously as a noun, but so much text has intervened that the referent is no longer retrievable, except from the 'context of situation', which then classifies the pronoun as 'exophoric'. An example may clarify:

(2, i) ('The first story's about some boys playing football. The ball breaks a window. That's the first story. Can you tell me what's happening? This is where it starts.') They're (1)

> kicking it (2) and it (3) broke the window and the man told them (4) off and they're (5) running away ('What about the lady?') She's (6) shouting ('What's she shouting?') Why they (7) broke the window ('What's the man saying?') Get out of it (8).
>
> (Working-class boy)

(The interviewer's speech is given in brackets.) *They* (1) and *it* (2) in the first clause are recoverable from the interviewer's speech, to refer to *boys* and *ball*; but four clauses of interviewer's speech have intervened, including nouns like *window* and *story*. We can scarcely retrieve the referents of *they* and *it* without recourse to the 'context of situation', which in this case includes the linguistic item *kicking*.

Granted that we have established referents for (1) and (2), we can assume that *it* (3) has the same referent as *it* (2), and classify it as 'anaphoric'. Similarly, (4) *them* and (5) *they*, being plural, can be assumed to refer to the previous plural form, *they* (1). *She* (6) refers anaphorically to the interviewer's *lady*, but with *they* (7) we are again faced with the problem of a distant referent, either *they* (5) which is now four clauses away or, ultimately, *boys* which is now twelve clauses away.

Not always, then, does there exist a clear-cut division between anaphoric and exophoric reference. We decided that pronouns occurring right at the beginning of a section should be counted as exophoric, even if the referent(s) were ultimately retrievable from the interviewer's introduction. That would distinguish the child who specified the characters right from the start, from those who assumed their identity and used *they* and *it*, as in the example above. But after the beginning, a pronoun was classified 'anaphoric' even if its referent was several clauses away, *so long as no ambiguity arose*. Thus *they* (7) above is unambiguous because only one plural referent has so far been mentioned—*the boys*. But if the child had said 'why *he* broke the window', *he* would be ambiguous (and hence 'exophoric') because it could refer either to one of the boys, or to *the man* who 'told them off'.

It (8) in the clause *get out of it* is not really a referential pronoun at all, because one cannot suggest a likely referent for it either from the text or from the situation. We cannot meaningfully ask 'get out of what?' (except humorously).

Our classification of the pronouns in the above example was therefore:

1, 2 exophoric
3, 4, 5, 6, 7 anaphoric
8 non-referential

Another example will show how purely pronominal reference can be highly ambiguous:

(2, ii) ('Let's see what happens in this story. That's where it starts.') He (1) going fishing   and he (2) catching a fish and [it] he (3) got hold of [the] that (4) and pulled him (5) in the water   and then they (6) got in a boat and saving him (7).

(Working-class boy)

(Words in square-brackets are 'false-starts', where the child changed his mind and substituted a different item.) *He* (1) must be exophoric; even the interviewer provides no possible referent. The second *he* refers anaphorically to *he* (1) (for which we have to supply some noun like *a boy*) but we have to assume from the context that *he* (3) must refer to the fish in the water, not the boy on the bank, whereas *him* (5) again refers back to an assumed *boy*. Notice an exophoric *that* (4) referring presumably to the fishing hook, and a further exophoric *they* (6) referring to the two boys in the boat. We can allow *him* (7) to be anaphoric, after *him* (5), the one who has been pulled in the water.

We can see from these two actual examples of speech that our fabricated versions comparing nouns and pronouns in a text (p. 75) were perhaps not so fanciful after all.

One suggestion for a way of telling exophoric from anaphoric pronouns is a possible difference in intonation patterns. Without going into technical details, we might expect exophoric pronouns to carry a certain amount of stress, whereas an anaphoric pronoun would normally be unstressed. In the following examples, words which receive stress are italicized:

(i) the boy's got a *line* and he's going *fishing* (*he* unstressed, because anaphoric)
(ii) *he*'s going *fishing* (*he* stressed, because exophoric) and *that* came *up* (*that* stressed, because exophoric) and *pulled* him in the *water* (*him* unstressed, because anaphoric) and *they came* (*they* exophoric) and *saved* him (*him* anaphoric)

It is likely that an adult speaker who used exophoric reference in this way would put additional word-stress on the exophoric items, but this does not seem to happen with children. The fact is that to vary one's intonation pattern from the norm in this way, probably requires some sort of implicit acknowledgment on the part of the speaker that the reference *is* exophoric; but if the speaker assumes that the addressee *knows* what is referred to, then he would not even be aware of the exophoricness of his references—and would therefore make no attempt to show this by changing the stress pattern. Intonation, therefore, cannot be relied on as a distinguishing criterion between exophoric and anaphoric reference.

The reference categories to be considered in this chapter can now be summarised as follows:

(a) Exophoric

(1) S/T exoph.[3] (demonstratives at H):	*that*'s a little boy
(2) D2 (demonstratives at M):[4]	*those* boys
(3) Adverb at H (*here*, *there* after preposition):	over *there*
(4) P3 exoph. (third-person pronouns):	*they*'re playing

(b) Anaphoric

(5) S/T anaph. (demonstratives at H):	a new toy—*that*'s nice
(6) P3 anaph. (third-person pronouns):	the boys . . . and *they* . . .

Results

We shall take the categories in the order given in the summary above.

(1) **Exophoric demonstratives at H**

This category was used by 46 per cent of the sample in Task 2 and by 68 per cent in Task 3. Occurrences in Task 3 were relatively frequent (rating: 3)[5] and the distribution of users and occurrences is such as to give both the χ^2 tests and the correlations a considerable degree of reliability. The results are given in Table 2.1.

The χ^2 tests indicate a significant social class difference, in the direction of the working class, in Task 2 ($\chi^2 = 5.61$, $p = 0{\cdot}02$). This difference is supported by the correlations with the social class variables,[6] which are positive in sign (i.e. in the working-class direction) and significant on all three scales ($r = 0{\cdot}177$, $p = 0{\cdot}002$). Strong relationships are also found with IQ and CI in this task, indicating that low IQ and low CI children use exophoric demonstratives more frequently.

The class-differences found in Task 2 do not reappear in Task 3. χ^2 tests and correlations are low in value, though the latter are positive which indicates working-class direction. The correlations with IQ and CI are still significant, however, though at a lower level of confidence.

In order to ascertain why the differences which appeared in one task were not repeated in the other, we decided to investigate the

Table 2.1 Variable: S/T Exophoric (this, that at head)

χ^2 tests	Task 2 χ^2	Task 2 p	Task 3 χ^2	Task 3 p
Class	5·61	0·02	0·02	n.s.
Class (boys only)	3·81	0·05	0·05	n.s.
Class (girls only)	1·61	n.s.	0·22	n.s.
Sex	0·13	n.s.	2·53	n.s.

Correlations	Task 2 r	Task 2 p	Task 3 r	Task 3 p	Combined Tasks r	Combined Tasks p
Class	0·177	//	0·100		0·139	/
Sex	−0·023		−0·120	/	−0·110	
IQ Crichton	−0·136	/	−0·105		−0·138	/
IQ EPVT	−0·211	///	−0·155	//	−0·199	///
New CI	−0·193	//	−0·122	/	−0·174	//

Notes

For social class	Positive	r = working class
	Negative	r = middle class
For sex	Positive	r = girls
	Negative	r = boys
For IQ, CI	Positive	r = high IQ, or high CI
	Negative	r = low IQ, or low CI

/ = significant ($p < 0{\cdot}05$) // = highly significant ($p < 0{\cdot}01$) /// = very highly significant ($p < 0{\cdot}001$)

occurrences of this category in greater detail. It seemed to us that the function of S/T exophoric may in fact differ according to the kind of linguistic environment in which it finds itself, and this in turn may affect the degree of 'exophoricness', i.e. the degree of dependence on the external context for interpretation.

Consider the following types:

A (i) That's a man who's selling apples
 (ii) This looks like a house
 (iii) That's where the train's standing in the station
 (iv) That's a lady and she's got a dog
B (i) That's a man
 (ii) Those are trees
 (iii) That's a house
C (i) A boy's left that
 (ii) That's going that way
 (iii) I can see that and that and that
 (iv) That's flying
D (i) (What's the lady saying?) 'Who's done that?'
 (ii) (What's the lady saying?) 'How did that happen?'

The kind of information which is conveyed differs greatly from one type to another. In type A, the initial S/T at Head is fully elaborated afterwards; although, strictly speaking, the S/T word is exophoric in reference, the listener does not need to rely on the presence of the picture to understand the sentence as a whole, because the referents are made fully explicit, linguistically, in the latter part of the sentence.

Type C, on the other hand, tells the addressee virtually nothing unless he can see the details in the picture; it is highly exophoric because the addressee has to move beyond the verbal context for interpretation and refers directly to the picture; otherwise he would be forced to ask for the referent to be identified, eg. by '*what*'s flying?' in response to 'that's flying', 'what's going where?' to understand 'that's going that way', etc.

Type B is closer to type A because an 'equational' (identifying) noun follows the verb *be*, and this at least identifies the referent, though the utterance is otherwise low in informative or cognitive value: it is simply putting names to a list of items.

Type D probably should not be among the exophorics at all. It only occurs in response to the probes in Task 2. We decided originally to count it as exophoric but it is a marginal case. If we assume that the lady is standing and looking at the damage (either to the window or the fish), the response 'who's done that?', where *that* refers to the damage, is quite acceptable. The exophoricness is, as it were, one stage removed from the 'direct' exophorics which refer straight to items in the picture.

The key to the difference between types A or B, and C lies in the presence or absence of the equational verb *be*, which serves to identify the referent in types A and B. Thus we can base our distinction between the four types A–D on the following formal criteria:

Type A = S/T + (be) + $\left\{\begin{array}{l}\text{`expanded' nominal group}\\ \text{rankshifted clause}\end{array}\right.$

where 'expanded' is to be taken as something more than deictic + noun.

Type B = S/T + (be) + $\left\{\begin{array}{l}\text{deictic + noun}\\ \text{noun}\end{array}\right\}$ only

Type C = Any other occurrence of S/T apart from A, B, D and

Type D = 'S/T', i.e. occurs within the response to the probe, in Task 2 only.

We may now consider the distribution of these types, both in quantity and in the number of children using each category (Tables 2.2 and 2.3).

Table 2.2 Quantity distribution of S/T exophoric types (Task 2)

Type	*WC Boys*	*WC Girls*	*MC Boys*	*MC Girls*
A	15	16	10	1
B	37*	17	4	2
C	30	29	6	7
D	22	26	28	27
Total	104	88	48	37

* One boy contributed 32 to this total.

Table 2.3 Number of children using each type (Task 2)

Type	*WC Boys* (N = 59)	*WC Girls* (N = 80)	*MC Boys* (N = 65)	*MC Girls* (N = 59)
A	8	11	8	1
B	5	10	4	2
C	18	22	5	6
D	20	18	18	18

χ^2 tests based on the data in Table 2.3 showed no overall class difference in the use of types A ($\chi^2 = 2{\cdot}20$, p = n.s.) or B ($\chi^2 = 2{\cdot}40$, p = n.s.), but more working-class children used type C, and the difference is very highly significant ($\chi^2 = 15{\cdot}4$, $p < 0{\cdot}001$). The result held both for boys and girls separately (for boys, $\chi^2 = 9{\cdot}21$, $p < 0{\cdot}005$, and for girls, $\chi^2 = 5{\cdot}32$, $p < 0{\cdot}03$).

For type D, the one we considered as a 'legitimate' exophoric, there are absolutely no differences at all, either in quantity or the number of children using the category (see Tables 2.2 and 2.3).

The results for Task 3 are as shown in Tables 2.4 and 2.5. We can see that the overall quantities (see 'totals' row, Table 2.4) do not differ enough to make the correlation significant for class (cf. Table 2.1). But when we examine the distribution of types A–C, we see that these totals are masking internal differences, since the middle class are using *fewer* of types B and C, but *more* of type A; and to some extent they are cancelling each other out.

The results given by χ^2 tests were as follows: for type A, a comparison for boys only (working-class = 17, middle-class = 28,

Table 2.4 Quantity distribution of S/T exophoric types (Task 3)

Type	*WC Boys*	*WC Girls*	*MC Boys*	*MC Girls*
A	32	28	60	20
B	97*	69	55	38
C	66	69	39	26
Total	195	166	154	84

* One boy contributed 25, and another 24, to this total.

Table 2.5 Number of children using each type (Task 3)

Type	*WC Boys* (N = 54)	*WC Girls* (N = 76)	*MC Boys* (N = 65)	*MC Girls* (N = 59)
A	17	18	28	13
B	17	27	22	19
C	27	32	23	20

Table 2.5) gave $\chi^2 = 1{\cdot}30$, p = n.s., and on type C, for boys only, $\chi^2 = 2{\cdot}02$, p = n.s. The difference in the number of all children using type C was tentative ($\chi^2 = 2{\cdot}60$, p. = 0·11 in the direction of the WC) but when the quantities of type C were compared (see Table 2.4), the result was highly significant ($t = 3{\cdot}07$, $p < 0{\cdot}005$). A test of the quantities of type A, for boys only, gave a tentative result ($t = 1{\cdot}18$, $p = 0{\cdot}25$), in the direction of the middle class. Hence, although the overall differences in the use of S/T exophoric on Task 3 are not significant, by a break-down of the category into different types we have shown that the working class use type C, the type most dependent on context, significantly more frequently, while there is a tendency, among the boys at any rate, for the middle class to use the elaborated kind more often.

(2) **Exophoric demonstratives at M**

This category was used by about two-thirds of the sample in both tasks and occurred moderately frequently (rating: 3). χ^2 tests and correlations will both be reliable. The results are given in Table 2.6.

Table 2.6 Variable D2 (exophoric)

χ^2 *tests*	*Task 2* χ^2	*p*	*Task 3* χ^2	*p*
Class	4·54	0·033	7·91	0·007
Class (boys only)	1·59	n.s.	3·92	0·05
Class (girls only)	2·74	(0·10)	2·98	(0·10)
Sex	0·16	n.s.	0·31	(0·10)

Correlations	*Task 2* *r*	*p*	*Task 3* *r*	*p*	*Combined Tasks* *r*	*p*
Class	0·027		0·139	/	0·112	/
Sex	−0·014		0·044		0·017	
IQ Crichton	−0·008		−0·000		−0·011	
IQ EPVT	−0·136	/	−0·071		−0·115	/
New CI	−0·038		−0·027		−0·045	

The χ^2 tests show that more working-class children use this category in both Task 2 and Task 3, the result for Task 3 being stronger, and highly significant (p = 0·007). The subsidiary χ^2 tests indicate that this trend applies almost equally for boys (χ^2 = 3·92, p < 0·05) and girls (χ^2 = 2·98, p < 0·10).

These results are supported by the correlations in Task 3, where significance is found only for class. There is evidence of a difference in the EPVT measure of IQ for Task 2 (r = 0·136, p < 0·02) but this is not repeated in Task 3. Otherwise, only social class appears to discriminate those who use this category more or less frequently.[7]

(3) **Adverb at H**

The category was used by 33 per cent of the sample (Task 2) and by 63 per cent (Task 3). Occurrences in Task 3 were moderately frequent (rating: 3). χ^2 tests will thus be reliable for both tasks, and correlations more reliable in Task 3. The results are given in Table 2.7.

The χ^2 tests give significant class-differences, in the direction of the working class, for both tasks: χ^2 = 6·24, p = 0·02, in Task 2, and χ^2 = 8·33, p = 0·004, in Task 3. The difference is maintained independently among both boys and girls and there are no sex-differences.

The correlations give strong support to the evidence offered by

Table 2.7 Variable: adverb at head

χ^2 *tests*	*Task 2* χ^2	*p*	*Task 3* χ^2	*p*
Class	6·24	0·02	8·33	0·004
Class (boys only)	2·93	(0·10)	3·10	(0·10)
Class (girls only)	3·11	(0·10)	5·08	0·025
Sex	0·24	n.s.	0·27	n.s.

Correlations	*Task 2* r	*p*	*Task 3* r	*p*	*Combined Tasks* r	*p*
Class	0·156	//	0·234	///	0·249	///
Sex	−0·011		0·033		0·020	
IQ Crichton	−0·053		−0·067		−0·082	
IQ EPVT	−0·120	/	−0·137	/	−0·157	//
New CI	−0·116	/	−0·223	///	−0·241	///

the χ^2 tests. For each task, highly significant positive correlations mean that this category is a feature more of working- than of middle-class speech (r = 0·234, p < 0·001). The communication index is also successful in discriminating those who will use the category frequently; children of high CI mothers produce fewer occurrences than those with low CI mothers, and the correlations are about as high as those for social class in Task 3 (r = −0·223, p < 0·001).

The correlations with IQ are only significant for the EPVT measure, and they are of smaller value than for social class or CI.

(4) **P3 exophoric**

Exophoric third-person pronouns were used by over 90 per cent of the sample in both tasks, and occurrences were relatively frequent. The correlations can therefore be expected to give highly dependable results, but χ^2 tests will not be reliable because almost all children used the category; the χ^2 results are therefore enclosed in brackets. The data are presented in Table 2.8.

The correlations with social class are highly significant, in the direction of the working class, in both tasks (Task 2, r = 0·223, p < 0·001; Task 3, r = 0·252, p < 0·001). Relationships with both measures of IQ, and with CI, are also significant, indicating that low IQ children, and children of low-communicating mothers, use exophoric pronouns more frequently. Notice that the results hold good for both tasks independently, in spite of the different nature

Table 2.8 Variable: P3 exophoric

χ^2 *tests*	*Task 2* χ^2	*p*	*Task 3* χ^2	*p*
Class	(2·05	n.s.)	(4·21	0·04)
Class (boys only)	(0·69	n.s.)	(3·24	0·10)
Class (girls only)	(0·69	n.s.)	(0·59	n.s.)
Sex	(0·00	n.s.)	(0·01	n.s.)

Correlations	*Task 2* *r*	*p*	*Task 3* *r*	*p*	*Combined Tasks* *r*	*p*
Class	0·223	///	0·252	///	0·273	///
Sex	−0·102		0·025		−0·037	
IQ Crichton	−0·203	///	−0·146	/	−0·201	///
IQ EPVT	−0·275	///	−0·271	///	−0·313	///
New CI	−0·208	///	−0·184	//	−0·235	///

of the tasks and the relatively less frequent use of pronouns in Task 3.

Results for the two anaphoric categories will now be presented.

(5) **Anaphoric demonstratives at H**

This category was used by only 16 per cent of the sample and occurrences were infrequent (rating: 1). χ^2 tests will thus be more reliable than the correlations. The results are given in Table 2.9.

Table 2.9 Variable: S/T anaphoric

χ^2 *tests*	*Task 2* χ^2	*p*	*Task 3* χ^2	*p*
Class	11·30	0·001	0·09	n.s.
Class (boys only)	1·61	n.s.	0·05	n.s.
Class (girls only)	10·33	0·002	0·31	n.s.
Sex	0·01	n.s.	0·02	n.s.

Correlations	*Task 2* *r*	*p*	*Task 3* *r*	*p*	*Combined Tasks* *r*	*p*
Class	−0·179	//	0·019		−0·113	/
Sex	−0·040		−0·025		−0·053	
IQ Crichton	0·121	/	0·152	//	0·180	//
IQ EPVT	0·084		0·051		0·091	
New CI	0·094		0·004		0·064	

The χ^2 tests show a significant class-difference, in the direction of the middle class, in Task 2 ($\chi^2 = 11{\cdot}30$, $p < 0{\cdot}001$), which appears to be due mainly to a class-difference within the girls ($\chi^2 = 10{\cdot}33$, $p < 0{\cdot}002$). The percentages of children using this category is as follows:

MC girls	25
MC boys	20
LC boys	10
LC girls	5

The significant result for girls is because middle-class girls use the category most and working-class girls least, but the percentages show that there is a clear division between the class groups as a whole.

The correlations with social class in Task 2 offer supporting evidence of greater MC usage.

In Task 3, no class-differences are apparent, either among the χ^2 tests or the correlations. A significant relationship with Crichton, however, holds across both tasks, indicating that high IQ children use this category more frequently.

The individual occurrences of this category were then collected, in order to ascertain why the differences which are evident in Task 2 did not recur in Task 3. There appeared, however, to be no satisfactory sub-classification possible with such a small number of occurrences. No typical patterns of usage emerged, each example having its own unique context. The reasons for the different pattern of results in each task are thus not clear.

The number of users and occurrences of anaphoric demonstratives is therefore too small to give conclusive results, but evidently they do not behave in the same way as exophoric demonstratives, which are a feature of working-class speech. If anything, the anaphoric items incline towards the middle-class speakers (significantly so in Task 2) and are preferred by children with high IQ scores.

(6) **P3 anaphoric**

Anaphoric third-person pronouns were used by all children in both tasks and were highly frequent in occurrence, particularly in the narratives of Task 2, as one might expect. Average occurrences were 15·1 per child in Task 2 and 7·6 per child in Task 3. Since all children were users, χ^2 tests in this category are not possible, but the correlations will be correspondingly more reliable. The results are presented in Table 2.10.

Table 2.10 Variable: P3 anaphoric

χ^2 tests	Task 2 χ^2	Task 2 p	Task 3 χ^2	Task 3 p
Class				
Class (boys only)				
Class (girls only)				
Sex				

Correlations	Task 2 r	Task 2 p	Task 3 r	Task 3 p	Combined Tasks r	Combined Tasks p
Class	0·059		0·132	/	0·107	
Sex	0·015		0·099		0·056	
IQ Crichton	0·076		0·051		0·068	
IQ EPVT	−0·082		−0·110		−0·112	
New CI	−0·114		−0·107		−0·136	/

The correlations for Task 2 give no significant results for any of the major variables in the use of this category. In Task 3, however, we find a distinct social class difference showing that working-class children use anaphoric pronouns more frequently ($r = 0{\cdot}132$, $p = 0{\cdot}02$; on the three-point class scale (NSC II) the level of confidence is higher: $r = 0{\cdot}188$, $p < 0{\cdot}002$). None of the other major variables reveal significant differences.

Since the category is a frequent one, the subsidiary correlation matrices for within-class variance and for the sub-divisions according to total speech output will have some reliability and are worth investigating. The results here are as follows.

(i) The within-class correlations measure the variance attributable to sex, IQ or CI when social class is held constant. In this case no significant differences were found, so that the pattern within the sample as a whole, which revealed no differences of any size for these variables, is confirmed in the sub-samples.

(ii) The division of the sample according to total speech output shows that, for Task 2, social class and CI differences are apparent within the middle-output groups (groups 2 and 3).[8] Here, working-class children use anaphoric pronouns more frequently; the differences are significant for both groups (group 2, $r = 0{\cdot}190$, $p = 0{\cdot}04$; group 3, $r = 0{\cdot}276$, $p = 0{\cdot}04$), and together these groups account for 191 children, or 61 per cent of the sample. These groups yielded comparable differences for CI, in the direction of low CI children.

These two middle-output groups represent children who offered from 40 to 85 nominal groups. The results from the other groups, group 1 (20–40 nominal groups) and group 4 (85 + nominal groups), are not significant but there is reason to believe that the results from these groups are less reliable. Thus, group 4 has a satisfactory output of speech (85 or more nominal groups) but includes only 26 children, which makes the sample somewhat unreliable, while group 1 contains a sufficient number of children (95) but may be unreliable for two reasons: first, the distribution of children within the group is unbalanced, since it has 47 working-class but only 25 middle-class speakers (the other 23 being of 'marginal' social class); second, the output of speech is insufficient for patterns of usage to be firmly established. This group gives an average of 9 anaphoric pronouns per child; spread over three series of story cards, this means only three pronouns per series, which is adequate for only the very barest outline of the story.

For these reasons it seems that the most reliable results can be expected from groups 2 and 3, which have both a representative sample of speakers and an adequate amount of speech output.

The within-group correlations for Task 3 reveal a similar pattern: class-differences begin to emerge as the amount of speech increases. Here, there are no differences in the first two groups (up to 60 nominal groups) but beyond this the results are significant, in the direction of the working class; for group 3, with 80 children, $r = 0{\cdot}368$, $p < 0{\cdot}001$, and for group 4 (38 children), $r = 0{\cdot}322$, $p < 0{\cdot}05$. Thus the significant result for the sample as a whole (see Table 2.10) is shown to be concentrated largely in the groups with higher speech output.

In both tasks, then, we have considerable evidence to suggest that working-class children use anaphoric pronouns more frequently than middle-class children. The data show that this trend begins to appear as the total speech increases, from about 40 nominal groups upwards.

Discussion

The general prediction, that social class would account for more of the variance than any other factor, has been strongly upheld; class-differences have proved high, and consistent in direction, for almost all the categories considered. Most of the categories also show lesser, but nevertheless strong, relationships with one or both measures of IQ; overall, IQ appears to discriminate almost as successfully as social class. A number of categories also correlated significantly with the index of communication; sex differences however were negligible.

The division of pronouns, demonstratives and other categories into anaphoric and exophoric types has thus proved very successful in exposing differences of usage according to social class and the other variables. The class differences all move in the predicted direction; among the exophoric categories, the working-class speakers consistently produced either more users or more occurrences, usually both, in both tasks of the schedule. The consistency of these results, the high levels of significance, and the implications for the orientation towards different modes of communication, combine to make this a noteworthy finding.

Before discussing the exophoric categories, we shall comment briefly on the results for the two anaphoric variables. *Anaphoric demonstratives* occurred very infrequently throughout the schedule and their influence is correspondingly small, but a significant class-difference, which indicated that more middle-class children use them, was evident in Task 2 only. This result falls into place when we bear in mind that Task 2 is designed to elicit cohesive narrative ('cohesive' in the grammatical sense), so that anaphoric pronouns and demonstratives are desirable as devices for suitable cohesion. The demonstrative *that*, in particular, is a useful device because it has a wide range of applications; it can refer back not only to a noun but also to a clause, a sentence or even an entire 'paragraph' of several sentences (for example: a lengthy explanation, followed by *so that's why he did it*, where *that* refers back to the entire explanation). Our evidence shows a tendency for middle-class children to make greater use of this particular device.

Anaphoric pronouns were widely used by all children in both tasks. In Task 2 no class-difference emerged for the whole sample, but when the sample was divided according to output of speech the correlations revealed a significant difference in the largest group of 129 children, indicating that working-class children use anaphoric pronouns more frequently ($p = < 0{\cdot}02$). A similar result in Task 3 was significant for the sample as a whole, but in both tasks we found that class-differences increased as the total output increased, so that the results became significant beyond a minimum of 40 nominal groups per child.

The finding that working-class children use anaphoric, as well as exophoric, pronouns more frequently was not expected. As far as Task 3 is concerned it is likely that a few working-class children intersperse narrative into the description of the cards (cf. ch. 7), while others refer to the people in the pictures in a non-specific way by using *they*, *them* (see below, p. 96), but this latter explanation is not possible in Task 2, because the stories necessitate reference to individual characters rather than groups of people. One possible reason[9] for the class-difference is that some middle-class children avoid anaphoric pronouns by repeating nouns unnecessarily, eg.

the boys broke the window and the boys ran away

instead of '. . . and *they* . . .'. This is unlikely, however, because such redundancy is unnatural and is not normally found anywhere in the language. It is not normal, that is to say, so long as the two clauses with the identical referent are juxtaposed, as in the foregoing example; but the further the clauses are separated from each other, the more desirable a replacement noun (rather than a pronoun) becomes. Thus, if two or three other clauses intervene, repetition of the original noun may become preferable to the use of a pronoun, though if the pronoun *were* used, it would be technically anaphoric because a referent can be found in the preceding text. In analysing our data, we sometimes found that a pronoun was, strictly speaking, anaphoric although its referent was several clauses away, and for ease of understanding a repetition of the original noun would have been an improvement—these pronouns were quasi-exophoric in that the referent was difficult to retrieve from the text (see the section on coding problems of reference pronouns, pp. 79ff.).

It is possible, then, that those working-class children who use more anaphoric pronouns are using them in this way, to refer back to a noun several clauses away. The fact that the class-difference increases as speech output increases is evidence in support of this, because the greater output enables a number of clauses to intervene between referent and pronoun whereas children in the low-output group 1 devoted no more than two or three clauses to the whole story. Thus, the working-class use of these 'quasi-exophorics' is parallel with, and similar to, their greater use of exophorics; if our analysis had not given these pronouns the benefit of the doubt, as it were, they would have been classed as exophoric rather than anaphoric. It looks as if a third category of reference, somewhere between anaphoric and exophoric, is desirable, but such a category would not be easy to define; it would depend on a fairly sophisticated analysis of textual cohesion, because the degree of separation, i.e. the distance between referent and item, and the type of text which intervenes, are critical factors in deciding whether a pronoun or a repetition of the noun is more suitable.

Exophoric demonstratives, in contrast with anaphoric ones which are appropriate for cohesion, are likely to leave the identity of the referent ambiguous and indeterminate, and to demand reference to the visual material itself for interpretation. Of the sub-types which we recognised, type A is the only one which identifies a referent satisfactorily, by means of an 'equational' verb (usually *be*) and an expanded nominal group, eg.

that's a football and the boys have kicked it
that's a whale and it's going to pull him in

Sub-type B is less acceptable (in Task 2) because it tends to isolate and focus upon individual persons or objects unrelated to anything else instead of a cohesive narrative, eg.

those are boys, that's a football

instead of

the boys are kicking a football

Sub-type C is the least acceptable since it provides no identification for the referent, which must somehow be extracted from the physical context, eg.

the boys are kicking that

or

that came along

The data of Tables 2.2 and 2.3 show us that working-class children have a clear tendency to use types B and C more frequently: 40 working-class children (out of 139) used type C at least once, compared with only 11 middle-class children (out of 124), a highly significant difference ($\chi^2 = 15{\cdot}4$, $p < 0{\cdot}001$). For type B the difference is in the same direction (15 working-class compared with 6 middle-class children) but not significant.

Exophoric pronouns will likewise lead to ambiguity of reference in Task 2, and reliance on the pictures themselves for interpretation, especially because in each series of pictures a number of discrete characters are involved (eg., in the second series, the boy on the bank, the fish, two boys in the boat) and the indiscriminate use of *he*, *him*, *it*, *them*, etc. makes interpretation difficult because there are a variety of possible referents for each pronoun.

Exophoric demonstratives at M, on the other hand, create fewer interpretational difficulties than the other exophorics because the head noun specifies the identity of the referent. Thus, in

the boys are kicking that football
that fish is coming along

we are given the referents *football*, *fish*. To the question *What football?* or *What fish?* we can answer 'the only one there is in the picture' without difficulty. A problem arises only when there is more than one of whatever noun stands at head: thus, if there are three boys in the picture, the phrase *that boy* is ambiguous—it does not specify *which* boy.

So far we have considered the incidence of the linguistic variables in Task 2 only; the occurrences of the same categories in Task 3 may have different implications because of the different nature of the task. The pictures are not intended to form the basis of a narrative (though of course it is always possible to create narrative as part of the description, as some children in fact did), so the incidence of anaphoric pronouns will be reduced; on the other hand, an orientation towards nouns becomes of greater importance, because we are directly concerned with a number of people and objects—which need to be specified, using nouns—and with the relationships between them (people-people, people-object, object-object), eg.

> there's a man pushing a cart
> the train is standing in the station
> the people are getting off the train, etc.

The incidence of anaphoric pronouns in this task is in fact much less than in Task 2, yet there is still a class-difference, in the direction of the working class, which is significant for the whole sample (see Table 2.10). The difference is due partly to a number of working-class girls, who tended to include a certain amount of narrative within the overall description (see chapter 7), but this is not the only cause; if it were, we should expect a high correlation between P3 anaphoric and sex *within* the working class. The value of r here, however, is small (0·104) and not significant, indicating that both boys and girls within the working class are responsible.

The most likely explanation for the difference in frequency is that in this task it is possible to respond without referring to the characters specifically; one begins the description with *the people* (or an exophoric *they*) and henceforth one refers (anaphorically) to an undifferentiated *they* (or *them*):

> They're at the station and they're waiting for a train and a lady's looking at them, etc.

A response like this builds up a big count of anaphoric pronouns while remaining largely unspecific. By contrast, we shall find (chapter 3) that middle-class children use more 'structured nouns' in Task 3, and there is additional evidence from Henderson's study (Brandis and Henderson, 1970, pp. 29–30) that they use more *type* nouns, i.e. a greater variety of nouns. It seems, then, that middle-class children are selecting more subjects from the pictures to talk about; in addition to what the people as a whole are doing, they may mention what some of the *individuals* are doing too, eg. a man pushing a barrow, or a lady walking with her dog, or the presence of the 'bride' and 'bridegroom'. A similar result for the use of non-specific *they* by working-class speakers was previously found by Bernstein (1962a) in his study of adolescents.

Exophoric demonstratives at H may be sub-classified for Task 3 along the same lines as for Task 2, but the sub-type B (*that's a train, those are apples*) is less objectionable in this case because the purpose is not cohesive narrative but simply description; even so, this type gives information at a rather low level and does not combine the participants in a meaningful relationship. We found no class-differences in the use of type B, but type C, which is highly exophoric in this task too (because no clue is given to the identity of the referent—the addressee is left to seek it from the picture, eg. *I can see that and that*; *that's flying*) is again used more frequently by the working class ($t = 3{\cdot}07$, $p < 0{\cdot}005$).

Exophoric demonstratives at M are more likely to cause ambiguity in this task than in Task 2, because this category is most ambiguous whenever more than one of the items identified by the head-noun are present, and because there are more pluralities of people and objects in these pictures. Thus *that man*, *that lady*, etc. are inexplicit and require reference to the picture for identification, because there is more than one man, lady, etc. in the picture. The results show that more working-class children use this category (the highly significant result, $p < 0{\cdot}007$, applies to boys and girls equally) and that they use it more frequently (see the correlations, Table 2.6).

A similar result was found for *adverbs at H*, which are also highly exophoric in this task and contrast with a noun alternative; compare *on there* with *on the platform*.

In conclusion, we began this chapter by asking whether working-class children made greater use of exophoric reference than middle-class children. Each exophoric category has given us strong evidence that this is in fact so. We have come to recognise degrees of 'exophoricness' depending on the situation, but the results show that all the highly exophoric items are used more frequently by working-class children. The sociological significance of exophoric reference is discussed in chapter 9.

No predictions were made about the incidence of anaphoric pronouns but our results show a higher frequency of these too among working-class children. Possible reasons for this, related to the nature of the task in each case, have been put forward. Taken as a whole, our results point to a general working-class orientation towards pronouns, i.e. towards a type of reference which is less specific and takes for granted a greater degree of common knowledge linking speaker to addressee.

Finally, a word of caution about the interpretation of these results. We are not suggesting that there exists a large group of children who use exophoric items to the near-complete exclusion of nouns, or that there are children whose knowledge of the language excludes the use of nouns. The version of the picture story (p. 75) using pronouns only was not at all *typical* of working-class speech though there were some (a small number of) children who did approach this extreme. Working-class children in fact used almost as high a proportion of nouns as middle-class children (see ch. 3). The balance between nouns and pronouns is indicated by the average frequency of each category: for exophoric pronouns the figures are 3·51 per child (Task 2) and 3·45 (Task 3); there are the other exophoric categories to be added to this, but the average frequency of nouns, by comparison, is 17·9 per child (Task 2) and 22·6 (Task 3). Thus nouns, overall, heavily outweigh exophoric items in number. The significance of our results lies in the observation that, at certain points, working-class children have preferred an exophoric item to a noun, and that even a few such items can give a different orientation to the type of communication which takes place, since the identity of even one referent can be crucial to the interpretation of an utterance. Ambiguous or inexplicit reference forces the addressee to search the non-linguistic context for identification, and thus makes demands of him which are absent when the referents are made verbally explicit.

Notes

[1] Cited also in Hawkins (1969).

[2] Examples of demonstratives at M used anaphorically were extremely rare in our data. See footnote 4.

[3] S/T exoph., D2 etc. are the notations used in our coding-frame. For the complete list of categories, see Appendix II, III.

[4] *Anaphoric* demonstratives at M occurred only twice in the whole sample and were therefore ignored.

[5] On frequency ratings, see chapter 1, p. 70, and Appendix III.

[6] In the tables of results (eg. Table 2.1), only one of the three scales of class is given (the one based on the ten-point scale). The correlations with the other two scales (NSC I and NSC II) are given in the data summaries in Appendix II. These two scales always have correlations similar in magnitude to those of the ten-point scale, and have therefore been omitted from the accompanying tables for the sake of simplicity.

[7] Just as S/T exoph. at H can be used in relatively explicit verbal con-

texts which overcome its interpretational disadvantages, so also can demonstratives at M; eg. in *that boy with the football, that cat who has stolen the fish*, the qualifier phrases *with the football, who . . . fish* identify the head nouns *boy, cat*. But in such instances the reference of *that* would not be exophoric, but cataphoric because it refers *forward* to the qualifier. Thus, the instances we have counted as exophoric are 'truly' exophoric in that they demand reference to the extra-verbal context.

[8] For the division of the sample into speech-output groups, see chapter 1 (p. 68).

[9] Note that the differences cannot be due simply to differences in total speech output, because they appear most strongly when total speech is controlled.

Chapter 3 Nouns

This chapter will include the results of the noun categories at the head of the nominal group. The following are the three categories involved:

(1) Nouns, structured
(2) Nouns, unstructured (Task 3 only)
(3) Nouns at Adjunct

Description of the categories

Nouns at A (Adjunct) include all nouns which function as Adjuncts in the clause. Usually these nouns follow a preposition (eg. through the *window*, in *school*) but very occasionally one finds a nominal group functioning as an Adjunct without being introduced by a preposition, eg. *this morning* in the clause *it came this morning*.

Nouns, structured include all nouns other than nouns at A, in Task 2. But in Task 3 a division was made between 'structured' and 'unstructured' nouns; the latter include any nouns occurring in a simple list, eg.

there's a train, a boy, a bicycle. . . .

The former include all other nouns (except nouns at A, of course). The reason for the division into 'structured' and 'unstructured' types is given below.

Hypotheses

In Part I it was found that, in the factorial sample of 80 children, middle-class children used more nouns than working-class children in their narration of the picture stories (Task 2) and in their description of the Trotin cards (Task 3), even though the total output of speech from the children in each group was approximately the same. In Task 3 the class differences for nouns were highly significant; but the total quantity of nouns, relative to pronouns, in this task was much greater anyway, and there is a possibility that children who use more nouns are simply giving lists of visible objects, rather than bringing people and/or objects into some sort of relationship with each other by means of transitive verbs, verbs of 'action', verbs of 'equation', etc.

Compare

	there's a man, a lady, two cats . . .
or	that's a man, that's a lady, that's a cat . . . (unstructured nouns)
with	there's a man walking into a shop two cats are sitting on the roof (structured nouns or nouns at A)

The latter examples are a real attempt to answer the interviewer's probe, which was 'what's *going on* (or "what's *happening*") in this picture?' The former examples are less satisfactory as answers to the probe, and represent a low level of complexity, both linguistically and cognitively.

Following our previous findings, then, and those of others (eg. Henderson, 1970),[1] we may expect middle-class children to use more nouns, but we wish to know whether, in Task 3, these nouns occur in a 'structured' or an 'unstructured' (listing) context.

Nouns at A, which consist mainly of prepositional phrases, have been separated from other nouns in order to provide a comparison with the exophoric equivalents *here/there* (adverbs at H—see chapter 2). Since we have already found that working-class children use the latter more frequently, we may find a relatively higher proportion of nouns among the middle-class children.

Results

(1) **Nouns, structured**

This category was used by all children in the sample in both tasks, and was highly frequent in occurrence (rating: 4). Structured nouns account for 33 per cent and 37 per cent of all nominal group heads in Tasks 2 and 3 respectively. χ^2 tests of users are therefore not possible but correlations will be highly dependable. The results are given in Table 3.1.

The signs (positive/negative) of the correlations are in the predicted direction for social class in both tasks, and for the Crichton measure of IQ in both tasks. The magnitude of these correlations is, however, not sufficient to reach the level of significance except in one instance.

Table 3.1 Variable: nouns, structured

χ^2 tests	Task 2 χ^2	p	Task 3 χ^2	p
Class				
Class (boys only)				
Class (girls only)				
Sex				

Correlations	Task 2 r	p	Task 3 r	p	Combined Tasks r	p
Class	−0·058		−0·102		−0·102	
Sex	0·037		0·028		0·028	
IQ Crichton	0·066		0·129	/	0·112	(/)
IQ EPVT	−0·037		0·048		0·017	
New CI	−0·004		0·076		0·042	

As structured nouns are so frequent in occurrence, the factor of the total quantity of speech must be taken into account. The correlations of this category with 'total speech' are in fact very high (r = 0·847, Task 2, and r = 0·842, Task 3). We were able to control partly for this factor by dividing the sample into the four groups on the basis of total output (see p. 68), and then observing correlations with the sociological variables for each group separately. The data resulting from this procedure are presented in Tables 3.2 and 3.3.

Table 3.2 N. str. Division of total speech (Task 2)

Variable	Group 1 r	p	Group 2 r	p	Group 3 r	p	Group 4 r	p
Class	0·121		−0·263	//	−0·031		−0·143	
Sex	0·167		−0·075		−0·076		0·089	
IQ Crichton	0·049		−0·011		0·082		0·003	
IQ EPVT	−0·049		0·049		0·017		0·046	
New CI	0·015		0·255	//	0·000		−0·143	

Note
Group 1 20–40 heads n = 95
Group 2 41–60 heads n = 129
Group 3 61–85 heads n = 62
Group 4 86+ heads n = 26

Table 3.3 N. str. Division of total speech (Task 3)

Variable	Group 1 r	p	Group 2 r	p	Group 3 r	p	Group 4 r	p
Class	−0·226	/	−0·214	/	−0·118		−0·373	/
Sex	−0·199		0·041		0·075		−0·043	
IQ Crichton	0·324	//	0·158		0·038		0·213	
IQ EPVT	0·184		0·059		0·186		0·161	
New CI	0·142		0·051		−0·004		0·502	///

Note
Group 1 20–40 heads n = 88
Group 2 41–60 heads n = 93
Group 3 61–95 heads n = 80
Group 4 96+ heads n = 38

In Task 2, significant class and CI differences emerge within the largest group of children (group 2, n = 129), representing 41 per cent of the sample. In this group, the middle class use nouns significantly more frequently ($r = -0{\cdot}263$, $p < 0{\cdot}002$). Groups 3 and 4 have a consistently negative r for class (i.e. in the middle-class direction), but in group 1 the r is positive, i.e. in a contrary direction to all the other groups in this task and to all four groups in Task 3. The explanation for this may be either the unequal representation of working-class and middle-class children in this group—it contains 47 working-class children but only 25 middle-class (the other 23 being 'marginal')—or the quantity of speech involved: group 1 is the lowest in quantity, with an average of only 11·4 nouns per child (standard deviation = 3·38). Spread over three series of picture cards, this means only four nouns per series, which is barely enough to name the characters, let alone construct a story around them. When the output of speech is as low in quantity as this, correlations based on a count of nouns may be quite unreliable (cf. chapter 2, p. 92), where similar considerations applied to the results for anaphoric pronouns).

The division of total speech for Task 3 (Table 3.3) shows that in all groups, middle-class children use structured nouns more frequently, the differences being significant for group 1 ($r = -0{\cdot}226$, $p = < 0{\cdot}05$), group 2 ($r = -0{\cdot}214$, $p < 0{\cdot}05$), and group 4 ($r = -0{\cdot}373$, $p < 0{\cdot}02$) which together represent 73 per cent of the children. Social class is the only variable to give consistently strong results here—Crichton is significant (in the predicted direction, i.e. high IQ) in group 1 only, and CI in group 4 only.

The subsidiary correlations which were run to determine *within-*

class differences for IQ, sex and CI give low correlations with no significant differences.

(2) **Nouns, unstructured**

This category was used by 77 per cent of the sample, and occurrences were relatively frequent (rating: 4). Unstructured nouns represent 12·6 per cent of all heads in Task 3. Both correlations and χ^2 tests will therefore be dependable, the correlations particularly so. As might be expected, there was wide variation in individual frequency of usage from child to child, some using a very large number (up to 41), others having none at all. The numerical average of 7·76 is therefore not an interpretational average, such that we could say that most children offer 7 or 8 unstructured nouns; this average is accompanied by a standard deviation of 8·94, indicating a very wide range of scores. The results are given in Table 3.4.

Table 3.4 Variable: nouns, unstructured (Task 3 only)

	Task 2		*Task 3*	
χ^2 tests	*χ^2*	*p*	*χ^2*	*p*
Class			5·47	0·02
Class (boys only)			0·90	n.s.
Class (girls only)			3·61	(< 0·10)
Sex			1·20	n.s.

	Task 2		*Task 3*		*Combined Tasks*	
Correlations	*r*	*p*	*r*	*p*	*r*	*p*
Class			−0·108			
Sex			−0·031			
IQ Crichton			−0·019			
IQ EPVT			0·070			
New CI			0·039			

The χ^2 tests show that more middle-class than working-class children use this category, and the correlations that they use it more frequently, although only NSC II is significant (r = −0·150, p = 0·009). There are no sex, IQ or CI differences. The within-class correlations fail to give any suggestive results. When total speech is divided into the four groups, groups 2, 3 and 4 all have negative (middle-class) correlations with social class and the level of significance is reached in group 3 (61–95 heads, n = 80 children) (r = −0·260, p = 0·02).

(3) **Nouns at A**

This category was used by all children in Task 3 and by 99 per cent in Task 2. Occurrences were relatively frequent (rating: 4)—nouns at A account for 11·3 per cent and 15·1 per cent of all nominal groups in Tasks 2 and 3 respectively. χ^2 tests were not possible because all except three children used the category, but the correlations will be highly reliable; they are presented in Table 3.5.

Table 3.5 Variable: nouns at Adjunct

χ^2 *tests*	*Task 2* χ^2	*p*	*Task 3* χ^2	*p*
Class				
Class (boys only)				
Class (girls only)				
Sex				

Correlations	*Task 2* r	*p*	*Task 3* r	*p*	*Combined Tasks* r	*p*
Class	−0·025		0·001		−0·007	
Sex	0·107		0·055		0·079	
IQ Crichton	0·043		0·067		0·066	
IQ EPVT	−0·061		0·018		−0·014	
New CI	0·007		0·054		0·025	

There are clearly no major differences revealed by this category, the correlations being in all cases of low value. The only exception is a correlation with sex, which is not quite significant (r = 0·107, p = 0·06), in the direction of girls. Within-class correlations show that it is working-class girls who are responsible (within the working class, r for sex = 0·207, p < 0·02; for the middle class, r = 0·088, p = n.s.). This sex difference was only apparent in Task 2.

When the sample was divided into four groups according to total output, the largest group (group 2, n = 129, representing 41 per cent of the sample) revealed a significant class-difference in the direction of the middle class (r = −0·201, p = 0·03), and a CI difference in the direction of high CI (r = 0·178, p < 0·05).

None of these differences were confirmed, however, by the results from Task 3, which were non-significant for all the major variables.

Discussion

We began by asking whether middle-class children would use more nouns of the 'structured' or the 'unstructured' type in Task 3; it was predicted that they would use more 'structured' nouns, but the outcome of the 'unstructured' nouns was uncertain, because although these are nouns and therefore relatively high in information content, they represent in this particular context a low level of complexity and are not particularly satisfactory as a response to the probe. The results indicate that, in fact, middle-class children use both kinds of noun more frequently.

There is a possibility that the middle class might have given more unstructured nouns because they were 'probed' differently by the interviewer. We found evidence (not reported in detail here) that the working class were given the probes 'what's going on/happening in the picture?' more frequently than the middle class, while the latter were given 'tell me what you can see' more frequently. It was at first thought that this last probe was responsible for the 'inventories', to which it might logically lead; but on further investigation we found no correlation between the children who were given this probe, and the frequency of unstructured nouns.

The problem of the kind of speech elicited by different probes is one which needs examining further, but so far we have no evidence that these differences in probing produced differences in the speech elicited. The reason, in this case, is probably because the question 'What's *going on/happening*?', if made when the picture was first presented, is likely to be interpreted in the more general sense ('What can you see?') unless the words *going on/happening* were made particularly salient. This could hardly be conveyed by intonation alone—it would need a specific contrast, such as 'don't give me a list of things, tell me what's going on'. Such a contrast was not made, of course. It is therefore to be expected that a certain amount of description of the 'unstructured' type would be given, because children are often asked by adults to do just this when they are shown pictures (the adult points to an object and says 'do you know what that is?'). Thus, the stimulus, in our study, of being shown a detailed picture was probably sufficient to trigger a mixture of responses irrespective of the particular question which the interviewer put.

It seems, then, that the greater use of unstructured, in addition to structured, nouns by the middle class is part of a general orientation towards nouns on the part of these children, just as the greater use of anaphoric (in addition to exophoric) pronouns by the working-class children appears to be part of a general orientation towards pronouns. Both results (i.e. for unstructured nouns and for anaphoric pronouns) were not predicted beforehand. The significance of our results for nouns is that the use of unstructured nouns does not take place at the expense of structured ones—the middle-class children use more of *both* types.

The overall correlations for 'structured' nouns (Table 3.1) were not strong enough to reach the level of significance, but the division into quantity-groups, which controls for the total speech output, shows quite clearly that most middle-class children (73 per cent) in Task 3 are using more 'structured' nouns (see Table 3.3). Thus, it is not the case that, in preferring nouns, middle-class children are using them simply to give lists of visible phenomena; they are also using them in 'structured' contexts where an alternative with a pronoun is possible. In Task 2 the class-differences for (structured) nouns are not quite so strong, but they clearly move in the same direction, and when total speech is controlled, a significant result is obtained for a large group of 129 children, representing 41 per cent of the sample. As we have seen in chapter 2, working-class children tend to take up the pronoun option more frequently; the results here suggest that this is at the expense of the noun, since they use fewer nouns. The data for pronouns and nouns thus complement each other.

The reason why the results for nouns are not, on the whole, as sharp and clear-cut as the differences among the exophoric items (see chapter 2) is because of the relatively higher frequency of nouns as a category, which means that to be statistically significant, group differences have to be very large indeed.[2] Consider the following: suppose two groups of subjects, A and B, each produce on average 25 nominal group heads consisting of nouns and exophoric pronouns. Group A has, on average, 3 exophoric pronouns and 22 nouns, whereas group B has 5 pronouns and 20 nouns. For the pronouns, the difference between 3 and 5 amounts to a difference of 67 per cent and, given a large enough sample, would be highly significant. But the corresponding adjustment to nouns, 22 from group A and 20 from group B, represents a difference of only 10 per cent and would be significant at a much lower level because of the variation in individual scores. Yet the choice of two additional exophoric pronouns and two fewer nouns can make a big difference to the communicative potential of a piece of narrative, especially if those speakers also use anaphoric pronouns in greater quantities. The cumulative effect of these pronouns is to reduce substantially the speaker's output of information.

Nouns have a high frequency of occurrence among children from all groups because they comprise a fundamental category of language. We have seen that children from some groups select pronouns in preference to nouns more frequently, but it is unthinkable that any child who has acquired a language in the normal way should select pronouns whenever the noun/pronoun choice is available. In other words we believe, following Chomsky (1965), that a vocabulary which includes a substantial number of nouns, and knowledge of the syntactic structures in which nouns can be used, is part of the *linguistic competence* of every normal child from whatever social group. What we are examining, in this study, is not the competence but the *performance* of a large sample of children in a particular speech situation. The results, however, have a bearing on a different and broader kind of competence, what Hymes calls *communicative* (as distinct from linguistic) competence (see chapter 9 for further discussion of this).

Thus, nouns are used frequently by all children in the sample, and constitute about one-third of all nominal group heads. The present study shows that among working-class children, the proportion of nouns is reduced while that of pronouns, both anaphoric and exophoric in reference, is increased. The effect of this change of emphasis is to put an extra burden on the listener, who receives a message which is less explicit verbally, and which thus depends more heavily on the context of situation for an interpretation. The underlying *causes* of this difference in orientation are to be found, it is suggested, in the different social relationships in which the two groups participate and from which they draw their experience.

Notes

[1] Henderson found that the middle-class 5-year-olds in her sample used significantly more nouns, both token (overall number) and type (*different* nouns).

[2] Nouns are the biggest single category of heads and account for about one-third of all heads. It is interesting to observe that the proportion of nouns is about the same in both tasks, once unstructured nouns have been separated out in Task 3; viz. 33·3 per cent (Task 2), and 36·8 per cent (Task 3). In Part I, the corresponding figure for nouns in Task 2 was 35·5 per cent. This appears to be the normal incidence of nouns in narrative speech; the unusually high total percentage of nouns in Task 3 is clearly due to the presence of the unstructured nouns, which arise as a peculiarity of this particular task.

Chapter 4 Modifiers

Modifiers comprise those elements of the nominal group which precede the head of the group. They may be sub-divided into the following general types, based on sequential order: Determiners, Ordinatives, Adjectives, and Nominals (or Classifiers). Adjectives may in turn be sub-modified by Intensifiers such as *very*, *too*.

Description of the categories

In the analysis of speech reported in Part I, *Determiners* were sub-divided into nine categories, most of which occurred too infrequently to give reliable results. For the subsequent analysis we therefore reduced and simplified the number of categories, while at the same time creating new categories based on our experience of the data and the further hypotheses we were testing. We now recognise, therefore, three categories of Determiner:

(i) Possessives (*my*, *our*, *his*, *their*, etc.)
(ii) *This/these*, *that/those*
(iii) Other determiners (including articles, and multi-word determiners like *all the*, *a lot of*)

The third category here is of little theoretical interest, except in so far as these determiners co-occur with nouns and may thus exhibit similar behaviour.

Category (ii) has already been considered, as one of our reference categories (chapter 2).

Possessives were re-grouped into a single category and retained as a separate group. They are distinct from articles, demonstratives and other determiners in being related to an underlying personal pronoun; thus *my* when analysed morphologically is *I* + 'Possessive', *his* is *he* + 'Possessive', etc., just as *John's* is *John* + 'Possessive'. It is interesting to note that the possessives involve reference, just as their corresponding personal pronouns do, so that in the case of third-person possessives (*his*, *her*, *its*, *their*), the reference type may be either anaphoric or exophoric with possibilities of ambiguity, as with the corresponding third-person pronouns. Thus *his brother* prompts the question '*whose brother?*' What is the referent of *his*? We may predict that these third-person possessives, if found in sufficient quantities, will exhibit the same pattern as the other exophoric categories in being a feature of working-class speech.[1]

Adjectives were sub-divided into two categories to separate *little*, *big* from all other adjectives. It is the second category, containing what we might call 'uncommon' adjectives, which will be the focus of our interest. *Little*, *big* are very frequent as modifiers but their function is different in some ways from other adjectives; they are not used contrastively (*a little boy was fishing* does not contrast with *a big boy* who was doing something else) and their information value is very small; they appear to be, in fact, little more than formulae, rather in the style of the Homeric epithet which automatically accompanies the person's name whenever the person is mentioned. In the context of our schedule, *little* was always applied to *boy* or *girl* and *big* to *fish*.

A division into 'common' and 'uncommon' adjectives was made by Bernstein in his study of adolescents (Bernstein, 1962a), but on a different basis. He found significant differences between middle and working class in the use of all adjectives, but even bigger differences in the use of 'uncommon' adjectives.

Nominals, or classifiers as they are sometimes known, include those classes of words which take a position in the structure immediately before the head. They include principally nouns, eg. *tea* in *tea party*, and participial forms (eg. *fishing*, in *fishing line*).[2] There is something of a problem in the coding of nominals, since they are not always clearly distinguishable from compound words; is *tea party*, for example, to be analysed as a single (compound) unit (noun at head), or as *tea* (nominal) + *party* (noun at H)? Categorisation of such items may be based on a variety of phonological, orthographic, grammatical or semantic criteria, each of which may yield conflicting results. The criterion we adopted was basically a semantic one: we asked how independent the nominal was. *Tea party* and *fishing rod* are typically marginal cases. If the phenomenon could be described as simply a *party*, or a *rod*, *fishing* and *tea* were regarded as nominals, i.e. the structure contains two relatively independent elements. On the other hand an *icecream* and an *airport* (for example) could not be described as a *cream* or a *port* and therefore they take the status of compound nouns. By taking this criterion we marked the use of a nominal as optional, an addition to the obligatory head of the group and one which is likely to contain a relatively high amount of information, because the nominal 'slot' is filled by lexical (rather than grammatical) items—though it must be admitted that in some instances, eg. the *fishing* of *fishing rod*, the lexical item is rather predictable and represents a low level of selection.

Intensifiers include those words like *very*, *too*, *so* which can submodify adjectives. *Very* was the commonest intensifier, but *too* and *so* were also found, as for example in 'the fish was too heavy (for him)', 'the train went so fast (that—)'.

Another category of modifier, *rankshifted nominal*, was added to account for structures like

the man's hat
the girl's dress

which can be analysed as one nominal group (*the man*) rankshifted (or 'embedded') within another (*the hat*). The structure is characterised formally by the presence of *'s*, and is obviously closely related to the possessive pronouns. The possessive noun itself normally has a referent which is animate (*the man*), though inanimate referents are quite possible and were found very occasionally in our data, eg. *the train's chimney*.

Hypotheses

The use of a noun at the head of a nominal group presents possible options from a range of modifiers which are not available when the head is a pronoun. In some instances the presence of a modifier is obligatory; for example, countable nouns in the singular form must normally be accompanied by an article or other determiner (*a/the/this cat came* is permissible; *cat came* is not). But other categories of modifier, viz. ordinatives, adjectives, nominals and intensifiers, are optional and available for selection from a wide range of possibilities. We are therefore concerned to discover whether middle-class children, who appear to use nouns more frequently and pronouns less frequently than working-class children, also take up the options within the modifier more frequently, where the options are free (i.e. for all categories except determiner). In particular we might expect differences in the use of 'uncommon' adjectives and nominals, which tend to be high in information content, i.e. they represent a choice from a wide range of possible lexical items.

Our list of modifier categories (with examples) is therefore as follows:

(1) D1 ('other' determiners)	*a* man, *the* ball, *some* people
(2) D3 (possessives)	*his* rod, *my* fish
(3) Ord. (ordinatives)	*two* boys
(4) E1 (*little*, *big*)	the *little* girl
(5) E2 (adjectives)	they're *naughty* boys, a *red* dress
(6) N (nominals)	a *fishing* line, a *tea* party
(7) I (intensifiers)	she's *very* cross
(8) r/s-nom (at M) (rankshifted nominal)	*the lady's* dress

Results

(1) **D1 (other determiners)**

This category was used by all children in the sample and occurred frequently (rating: 4). χ^2 tests of users are thus not possible here but the correlations are highly dependable.

No significant differences were found for any of the sociological variables. With social class the correlations were negative, indicating middle-class direction, but the values were not large enough to reach the level of significance. The results are therefore not presented here but are available from the data summaries, Appendix II.

(2) **D3 (possessive determiners)**

This category is used by approximately 60 per cent of the sample in both tasks. Occurrences were relatively infrequent (rating: 2). We shall therefore rely mainly on χ^2 tests for the results, which are presented in Table 4.1.

There are no class-differences in Task 2, but there is a tendency for more girls than boys to use this category ($\chi^2 = 3{\cdot}53$, $p = 0{\cdot}06$). In Task 3 this sex-difference is strong enough to be statistically significant ($\chi^2 = 5{\cdot}80$, $p < 0{\cdot}02$). Further investigation revealed that this was due entirely to a sex-difference within the working class, which is highly significant ($\chi^2 = 10{\cdot}47$, $p = 0{\cdot}002$). The working-class girls as a group thus use this category more frequently, particularly in Task 3, there being no differences between the other three groups.

No detailed investigation of the possessives has been made, but we did distinguish third-person possessives with anaphoric refer-

Table 4.1 Variable: D3, possessive determiners

χ^2 tests	Task 2 χ^2	Task 2 p	Task 3 χ^2	Task 3 p
Class	0·75	n.s.	1·19	n.s.
Class (boys only)	0·60	n.s.	0·76	n.s.
Class (girls only)	0·00	n.s.	4·82	0·03
Sex	3·53	(0·06)	5·80	< 0·02

Correlations	Task 2 r	Task 2 p	Task 3 r	Task 3 p	Combined Tasks r	Combined Tasks p
Class	0·079		0·021		0·065	
Sex	0·080		0·089		0·103	
IQ Crichton	−0·031		−0·034		−0·043	
IQ EPVT	−0·141	/	−0·095		−0·153	//
New CI	−0·142	/	−0·041		−0·136	/

ence (a man with *his* dog) from those with exophoric reference (that's *his* dog; *his* dog's running).

In both tasks, exophoric usage was rare, even among working-class children. The exophoricness, if any, was usually applied to a preceding pronoun within the same clause, for example *they* in *they're eating their dinner*. *Their* here is treated as anaphoric, referring back to *they* just mentioned; though of course if *they* is exophoric, the referent of *their* still has to be retrieved from the context of situation.

Third-person possessives were less common in Task 2; most of the occurrences of possessives were first- and second-person types, in the role-play speech, eg. ('what's X saying?') 'Did you smash my window?' 'Give me your hand.' In Task 3, most instances of possessives were third-person, and the reference type was usually anaphoric. A further investigation was carried out to establish whether *their*, the more general, undifferentiated form, occurred more frequently than the singular forms *his/her/its*. These two types were found, however, to be of approximately equal frequency. Out of 40 working-class girls who used possessives, 27 had at least one occurrence of *their*, 23 an occurrence of *his/her*; and of the 80 total instances, 37 were *his/her*, 32 were *their*, 13 were other forms of possessive. The use of singular and plural forms was therefore about equally distributed.

(3) **Ordinatives**

This category was used by 30 per cent in Task 2 and by 56 per cent in Task 3. Occurrences were relatively infrequent (rating: 2). χ^2 tests will thus be more reliable than correlations in Task 2. The results are given in Table 4.2.

Table 4.2 Variable: Ordinatives

	Task 2		*Task 3*			
χ^2 tests	χ^2	*p*	χ^2	*p*		
Class	0·22	n.s.	2·18	n.s.		
Class (boys only)	0·88	n.s.	1·23	n.s.		
Class (girls only)	0·00	n.s.	0·87	n.s.		
Sex	2·04	n.s.	0·07	n.s.		
	Task 2		*Task 3*		*Combined Tasks*	
Correlations	*r*	*p*	*r*	*p*	*r*	*p*
Class	−0·128	/	0·067		−0·032	
Sex	0·047		0·075		0·075	
IQ Crichton	0·064		−0·116	/	−0·043	
IQ EPVT	0·084		−0·130	/	−0·038	
New CI	0·059		−0·059		−0·006	

There are apparently no class-differences in the number of children using ordinatives in Task 2, but a glance at the correlations suggests that they are used more *frequently* by the middle class, even if the number of children using them is not greater. A distribution of the scores shows that most children use only one ordinative, but considerably more middle- than working-class children use two or more of these words. If we then perform another χ^2 test to compare children using 2 or more ordinatives, we find a significant class difference ($\chi^2 = 6{\cdot}36$, $p < 0{\cdot}02$) which is maintained by boys ($\chi^2 = 4{\cdot}68$, $p = 0{\cdot}03$) as well as girls ($\chi^2 = 1{\cdot}39$, p = n.s., but in the predicted direction). The number of children involved, however, is small; the test compares only 20 children with 8, out of a sample of 263 children.

These differences do not recur in Task 3, where, contrary to expectations, ordinatives appear more frequently among low IQ children ($r = -0{\cdot}116$, $p < 0{\cdot}05$). Notice that the correlations with social class in this task are positive (i.e. in the working-class direction); the χ^2 tests showed the same tendency, though the difference is not significant ($\chi^2 = 2{\cdot}18$, $p = 0{\cdot}15$). A brief investigation of the kind of ordinatives used in Task 3 showed that numerals were by far the commonest, but there were no class differences in the kind of expressions in which numerals were used. The most frequent mention was to the 'two cats on the roof', and other frequent references were to 'two (or three) people watching from the gate', 'two dogs', and 'two little girls'. *Two* was therefore the most frequent numeral. It was thought possible that the ordinatives might have been used, in Task 3, along with unstructured nouns, in phrases such as

There's two cats there
Two people over there
That's two dogs

The study showed, however, that only about a third of the ordinatives occurred in this kind of environment, and there were no class-differences in this respect.

(4) E1—the adjectives 'little', 'big'

This category was used by 47 per cent of the sample (Task 2) and by 64 per cent (Task 3). Occurrences were relatively infrequent, which indicates that the χ^2 tests will give the more dependable results. The data are given in Table 4.3.

Table 4.3 Variable: E1 (little, big)

	Task 2		*Task 3*	
χ^2 tests	χ^2	*p*	χ^2	*p*
Class	0·54	n.s.	1·43	n.s.
Class (boys only)	0·01	n.s.	0·03	n.s.
Class (girls only)	0·65	n.s.	2·42	n.s.
Sex	4·92	< 0·03	2·81	(< 0·10)

	Task 2		*Task 3*		*Combined Tasks*	
Correlations	*r*	*p*	*r*	*p*	*r*	*p*
Class	0·014		0·036		0·032	
Sex	0·139	/	0·167	//	0·183	//
IQ Crichton	0·075		0·036		0·062	
IQ EPVT	−0·089		−0·029		−0·071	
New CI	−0·069		−0·073		−0·091	

The only difference to emerge is a sex-difference, which suggests that more girls than boys use category E1. This difference is significant in Task 2, and nearly so in Task 3; and it is supported by the correlations, which show significant sex-differences for both tasks, separately and combined. When we investigate this sex-difference, however, we find that it applies within the working class only. This can be shown by χ^2 tests for sex, within each class separately, as in Table 4.4.

Table 4.4

	Task 2	*Task 3*
WC boys *v.* girls	3·96 (p < 0·05)	3·70 (p = 0·06)
MC boys *v.* girls	0·68	0·05
WC girls *v.* MC girls	0·60	2·42 (p = 0·13)

In both tasks, there is a much bigger sex-difference within the working class than within the middle class. We must note, too, in Task 3 a trend for more working-class than middle-class girls to use E1 ($\chi^2 = 2{\cdot}42$, $p = 0{\cdot}13$). The evidence suggests, then, that it is working-class girls, as a group, who use E1 more frequently than any other group.[3]

(5) **E2—all adjectives other than 'little', 'big'**

This category is used by about half the children in the sample, in both tasks. Occurrences were relatively infrequent (rating: 2). We shall therefore rely mainly on the χ^2 tests, which are presented, together with the correlations, in Table 4.5.

Table 4.5 Variable: E2 (other adjectives)

	Task 2		*Task 3*	
χ^2 tests	*χ^2*	*p*	*χ^2*	*p*
Class	18·45	0·001	3·15	(< 0·10)
Class (boys only)	9·03	0·004	3·64	(< 0·10)
Class (girls only)	8·43	0·005	0·26	n.s.
Sex	0·00	n.s.	0·01	n.s.

	Task 2		*Task 3*		*Combined Tasks*	
Correlations	*r*	*p*	*r*	*p*	*r*	*p*
Class	−0·277	///	−0·080		−0·205	///
Sex	−0·018		0·104		0·072	
IQ { Crichton	0·199	///	0·208	///	0·265	///
IQ { EPVT	0·125	/	0·116	/	0·159	//
New CI	0·171	//	0·025		0·108	

First, we observe a very large class-difference in Task 2, which is very highly significant ($\chi^2 = 18{\cdot}45$, $p < 0{\cdot}001$) and is maintained among both boys ($\chi^2 = 9{\cdot}03$, $p = 0{\cdot}004$) and girls ($\chi^2 = 8{\cdot}43$, $p = 0{\cdot}005$). These adjectives are used by 56 per cent of the middle-class children, compared with only 29 per cent of the working-class.

The correlations with social class give supporting evidence. Significant but lesser values were also obtained for IQ and the Communication Index in the predicted direction, viz. high IQ and high CI children.

The differences in Task 3 follow similar trends, but are not as strong as in Task 2. Class-differences according to the χ^2 tests are tentative ($\chi^2 = 3{\cdot}15$, $p < 0{\cdot}10$). The correlations with class are negative (i.e. towards middle class) but not significant. There are however significant correlations with both measures of IQ, especially with Crichton ($r = 0{\cdot}208$, $p < 0{\cdot}001$).

Since we have very strong class-differences in Task 2, and lesser ones, over a wider range of adjectives, in Task 3, we need to investigate what kind of adjectives are being used by the middle-class children, and what the range is in Task 3. A more detailed study of these adjectives has therefore been carried out.

Task 2, with which we shall deal first, consists of three series of picture stories, each of which concludes with a section of 'role-play' speech in response to the probe 'what's X saying' (cf. p. 58). In two of the series, the 'X' here is an adult (a lady or a man) who is required by the situation to exercise control and assert authority towards transgressors; in the first series, towards the boys who have broken the window and are running away; in the third series, towards the cat who has eaten the fish intended for someone else. The type of speech which these two situations elicit from the children is likely to be different from the responses to the other part (i.e. the narrative part) of the task; we shall refer to them as the 'social-control' situations.[4]

When the use of adjectives in Task 2 was investigated in detail, we found that instead of their being distributed evenly throughout the task in all sections, there was in fact a high concentration of adjectives in the social-control sections of speech. One adjective in particular, *naughty*, was very frequent. Thus, in the first series of cards, in reply to 'what's the lady/man saying?' we get the responses

they are/you are/you *naughty* boys

and in the third series,

He's a/you're a/you *naughty* cat

Naughty is occasionally also found in the second series (fishing), in collocation with *boy* and *fish*.

A primary division of adjectives in Task 2 must therefore separate the 'social control' type from the others. The former then include principally *naughty*; less frequently, *bad*; and one occurrence each of *silly* (a *silly* boy), *little* (you *little* fools), and *old* (*old* bully).

χ^2 tests on the number of children using the 'social control' adjectives then give the results shown in Table 4.6.

Table 4.6

	χ^2	p
Class	17·40	< 0·001
Class (boys only)	9·59	0·003
Class (girls only)	6·03	0·02
Sex	0·00	n.s.

Here, we have a very highly significant overall class difference ($p < 0{\cdot}001$) sustained both by boys ($p = 0{\cdot}003$) and girls ($p = 0{\cdot}02$), in the direction of the middle class.

The adjectives which remain when the 'social control' types have been removed are rather infrequent.[5] χ^2 tests to compare the four groups, however, still gave a significant result for boys in favour of the middle class ($\chi^2 = 3{\cdot}88$, $p = 0{\cdot}05$), and a tentative overall class difference ($\chi^2 = 3{\cdot}70$, $p = 0{\cdot}06$). In percentage terms these figures represent a difference between 21 per cent for the middle class, 12 per cent for the working class.

It is clear, then, that the great differences in the use of adjectives, as revealed by Table 4.5, are due mainly to differences in the 'social control' type, i.e. the use of *naughty* and a few other adjectives, the χ^2 test values for these being similar in magnitude to those reported initially in Table 4.5. The results for the remaining (non-social control) adjectives, on the other hand, resemble the differences in Task 3, where there is no social control situation: viz., a trend towards the middle class is discernible in both cases ($\chi^2 = 3{\cdot}70$, $p = 0{\cdot}06$, Task 2; $\chi^2 = 3{\cdot}15$, $p = 0{\cdot}08$, Task 3).

In considering the use of adjectives in Task 3 in greater depth, we formed a sub-category to separate colour-adjectives from the rest.[6] Since colour-adjectives relate only to the given material of the pictures, they are of less intrinsic interest than adjectives which go beyond the material and add dimensions of attitude (eg. *funny*, *nice*, *lovely*) or of inference (*noisy*, *windy*, *old-fashioned*). Colour-adjectives were used by relatively few children (by only 16 per cent), but those who did use them tended to mention more than one colour, or the same colour applied to more than one noun. There is a tendency for more middle-class than working-class boys to use these adjectives: $\chi^2 = 2{\cdot}86$, $p < 0{\cdot}10$; no other differences were found.

For adjectives other than those referring to colour, social class differences are found, particularly for boys. The χ^2 results are as shown in Table 4.7.

Table 4.7

	χ^2	p
Class	6·17	< 0·02
Class (boys only)	3·74	(< 0·10)
Class (girls only)	1·92	n.s.
Sex	0·07	n.s.

About half the middle-class children used one of these adjectives, compared with a third of the working-class children. This difference is significant ($\chi^2 = 6{\cdot}17$, $p < 0{\cdot}02$).

(6) **Nominals**

This category occurred rarely in Task 2; fewer than a quarter of the children used even one. It was relatively more common in Task 3, where forms like *birthday party*, *railway train/lines/station* occurred, and two-thirds of the children used the category. The results are given in Table 4.8.

No differences are found for Task 2, but the χ^2 tests for Task 3

Table 4.8 Variable: nominals (classifiers)

	Task 2		*Task 3*	
χ^2 tests	χ^2	p	χ^2	p
Class	0·42	n.s.	3·88	0·05
Class (boys only)	0·31	n.s.	0·46	n.s.
Class (girls only)	0·00	n.s.	2·93	(< 0·10)
Sex	0·00	n.s.	0·97	n.s.

	Task 2		*Task 3*		*Combined Tasks*	
Correlations	r	p	r	p	r	p
Class	−0·043		−0·050		−0·064	
Sex	−0·099		−0·072		−0·101	
IQ Crichton	0·059		0·209	///	0·209	///
IQ EPVT	0·037		0·176	//	0·176	//
New CI	−0·009		0·103		0·088	

give a significant class-difference, indicating that more middle-class children use this category. The correlations with social class confirm this, being consistently negative in sign throughout. In Task 3 there are strong correlations with IQ, suggesting that the use of nominals is determined by IQ as well as by social class.

(7) **Intensifiers**

This category was used by fewer than a quarter of the children, and occurrences were relatively infrequent (rating: 1). The results are presented in Table 4.9.

Table 4.9 Variable: intensifiers

	Task 2		*Task 3*	
χ^2 tests	χ^2	*p*	χ^2	*p*
Class	21·55	< 0·001	1·38	n.s.
Class (boys only)	3·85	0·05	1·88	n.s.
Class (girls only)	20·85	< 0·001	0·07	n.s.
Sex	4·70	0·03	0·31	n.s.

	Task 2		*Task 3*		*Combined Tasks*	
Correlations	*r*	*p*	*r*	*p*	*r*	*p*
Class	−0·303	///	−0·044		−0·203	///
Sex	0·067		0·053		0·073	
IQ Crichton	0·201	///	0·085		0·174	//
IQ EPVT	0·159	//	−0·017		0·074	
New CI	0·153	/	0·012		0·092	

Task 2 reveals a very highly significant overall class-difference ($\chi^2 = 21{\cdot}55$, $p < 0{\cdot}001$) maintained by both sexes but more particularly by girls ($\chi^2 = 20{\cdot}85$, $p < 0{\cdot}001$). The significant sex-difference ($\chi^2 = 4{\cdot}70$, $p = 0{\cdot}03$) is caused entirely by the difference between boys and girls within the middle class ($\chi^2 = 8{\cdot}10$, $p < 0{\cdot}01$), there being no difference within the working class ($\chi^2 = 0{\cdot}23$, p = n.s.). The percentages of children using intensifiers in this task are as follows:

MC girls	49
MC boys	23
WC girls	12·5
WC boys	8·5

The correlations indicate that IQ and CI are also related to the use of intensifiers but not as strongly as social class is.

The differences in Task 3 are much smaller. Both the χ^2 tests and the correlations suggest a rather more frequent use by the middle class, especially boys, but there are no significant differences. The scores for the combined tasks are strongly in favour of the middle class, presumably under the influence of the scores for Task 2.

No detailed investigation of this category has been made, but it seems likely that the big differences in the picture stories are caused mainly by the 'social control' situations, in which the middle class frequently use *naughty* (as we have seen) and a few other adjectives. They thus have the opportunity to 'intensify' with *very*, more so than working-class children, and it seems that they take up this option quite frequently, particularly the middle-class girls. Note that some of the adjectives in Task 3 do not lend themselves to intensification so readily—it is rare to find a colour-adjective thus modified, for example. In Task 3 therefore, only 20 per cent of the middle class use an intensifier and only 14 per cent of the working class.

(8) **Rankshifted nominals**

The category was used by only 8 per cent of the children in Task 2 and by 15 per cent in Task 3. Since there was no reason to expect different performances in each task, the occurrences were combined over both tasks in order to obtain a greater frequency. The χ^2 results were then as shown in Table 4.10. (The results for each task separately are not reported here, because of the infrequency of the category.)

Table 4.10

	χ^2	p
Class	0·43	n.s.
Class (boys only)	2·58	n.s.
Class (girls only)	0·03	n.s.
Sex	3·06	(< 0·10)

Working-class boys use the category least frequently (8 per cent), and there is not much difference between the other three groups (average 24 per cent). Hence we get a near-significant sex-difference (χ^2 = 3·06), which is due mainly to a sex-difference within the working class (χ^2 = 4·87, p = 0·03). The most frequent users were working-class girls (25 per cent).

Discussion

The broad prediction that middle-class speakers would take up available modifying options more frequently has been upheld, but detailed investigations of the functions of particular categories have sometimes revealed surprising and hitherto unpredicted differences. Perhaps the most interesting finding was for adjectives: first, the value of separating *little*, *big* from other adjectives was shown by the fact that the results for each of these categories moved in different directions; this would have been obscured if the two categories had been treated jointly; second, among the 'other' adjectives (E2), the big class-difference was not evenly distributed across all parts of the task but confined mainly to the social-control adjectives in one section. Thus by refining the category 'adjective' in two stages we have been able to reveal the functional differences in the use of particular types of adjective.

(i) The adjectives *little*, *big* were found to be used by more working-class girls than by any other group. This result appears to be contrary to the general prediction that middle-class speakers would use more adjectives, but we suggested that these two were different in kind from other adjectives, being restricted in their collocations and having little informative or contrastive value (*little boy*, *little girl* are virtually equivalent to *boy*, *girl* alone). *Little*, in fact, was far more common than *big* and we may therefore have been better advised to include *big* with the 'other' adjectives (i.e. with E2).

In the absence of informative and contrastive value, the function of *little* appears to be hypocoristic;[7] it has diminutive, affective connotations which are not part of the meaning of *big* or other adjectives, but which are found elsewhere in the language, for example the noun-suffixes in -y or -ie (*doggy*, *horsey*, *pussy*, *mummy*, etc.). It is interesting to find that the hypocoristic *little*, with its connotations of familiarity, affection and diminution, is used most frequently by working-class girls, particularly in the light of Bernstein's suggestion (1972, p. 491) that these girls, at least the older ones, often perform a 'mediating' social role between the parents and the other children, i.e. they have part of the task of organising, disciplining and controlling their younger brothers and sisters (see also the discussion of P2-implied, chapter 7). Such a role is not required of middle-class girls, or boys of whatever class, to nearly the same degree. Thus, the contact between working-class girls and their younger sibs is likely to perpetuate the use of hypocorisms. Boys, on the other hand, tend to avoid such forms, dropping them at an early age in favour of more 'mature' forms of expression, and this process is actively encouraged among both social classes. It is not uncommon, for example, for girls to continue addressing and referring to their parents as 'mummy' and 'daddy' even into adulthood; from boys these forms would be regarded as grossly affected.

(ii) Adjectives other than *little*, *big* gave very large differences in the direction of the middle class in Task 2, but more modest differences in the same direction in Task 3. A more detailed inspection of adjectives in Task 2 showed that most of the differences occurred in the role-play speech, middle-class children giving responses like 'you're naughty boys', 'you bad cat'. *Naughty* and *bad* were the two adjectives most frequently used. In chapter 6 we shall see that adjectives at the head of the nominal group yield similar results, again with *naughty* ('you're naughty') and a few other adjectives. The real significance of this result depends on the contrast with the type of response given by the working-class children in these social-control situations; since the linguistic categories involved are second-person pronouns at head, the discussion of this will be deferred until chapter 7.

Adjectives other than 'role-play' items gave class-differences in the direction of the middle class but on a more modest scale ($\chi^2 = 3{\cdot}70$, $p = 0{\cdot}06$), comparable with the results for adjectives in Task 3 ($\chi^2 = 3{\cdot}15$, $p = 0{\cdot}08$). But when the less interesting colour-adjectives were removed as a separate category, the class-difference increased and was significant ($\chi^2 = 6{\cdot}17$, $p < 0{\cdot}02$). There is evidence, then, that more middle-class than working-class children use those adjectives which are not given, as it were, by the data (the pictures themselves) but which require extrapolation from the data (eg. 'they're *old-fashioned* people') or are comments upon the data (adjectives of attitude like *funny*, *nice*, *lovely*).

In the sample as a whole, however, these adjectives were infrequent; we observe that the results are based not on correlations of frequency but on χ^2 tests of the number of users. We would not be justified in concluding that, for example, working-class children hardly ever use adjectives, or that their range of adjectives is greatly impoverished *vis-à-vis* the middle class, etc. In 1969 I reported big class-differences in the use of adjectives, based on preliminary findings from this data (Hawkins, 1969). I interpreted this as indicating that middle-class children used a wider range of adjectives, but the results which appeared in Task 2 were not repeated in Task 3, and if it had been the case that middle-class children had a much greater range and frequency of adjectives, why were similar results not found in both tasks? After all, there is nothing in the type of speech (descriptive *v.* narrative) which would inhibit the use of adjectives in Task 3. With the benefit of a closer investigation of adjectives we find more modest class-differences in the broader range of adjectives, and a highly-concentrated difference in the use of a small number of adjectives (especially *naughty*, *bad*) in one situation (the social-control speech of Task 2). This difference is in itself of considerable interest (see chapter 7), but the point is that we need to focus on the individual functions of sub-categories of our grammatical variables, and that in this case a claim for significant class-differences in the broad, overall category 'adjective' was not justified.

Our modest differences in the use of 'interesting' adjectives may be compared with the findings of other researchers, with which they appear to be in general agreement. Bernstein (1962a) examined 'uncommon' adjectives and found differences in favour of the middle class at a high confidence level ($p = 0{\cdot}001$). Lawton (1964) found similar differences in a sample of 15-year-olds ($p = 0{\cdot}01$); and Henderson (1970), working on the data from 5-year-old children, has found that the middle-class children use more type-adjectives, especially the high IQ children. It is likely that middle-class children possess and make use of a wider range of adjectives, just as they appear to have access to wider ranges of other lexical items such as nouns and verbs. But the class-difference is one of degree only: there are no sharp differences separating one social class from the other here.

(iii) Nominals appear to have a function similar to that of the more interesting adjectives, in so far as their information content is relatively high and their predictability correspondingly low; they thus represent the taking up of an option at points where options are available. We found that they were used hardly at all in Task 2, but in Task 3 where the range of lexical items is wider and less constrained by the nature of the data, their use increased and correlated particularly strongly with IQ. Class differences were found in the number of users ($\chi^2 = 3{\cdot}88$, $p < 0{\cdot}05$) in the direction of the middle class, but not in the correlations of frequency. These results thus support the modest differences already reported for the more interesting adjectives.

(iv) Intensifiers revealed large class-differences in Task 2, which were not maintained in Task 3. The pattern thus resembles the earlier results for adjectives; we may surmise that the intensifiers co-occur with the social-control adjectives (*very naughty*, *very bad*), and this would explain why big differences are found in Task 2 but not in Task 3. Once again, then, the difference reveals not an overall inclination on the part of the middle class to use intensifiers, but to use them in respect of a particular situation.

(v) Ordinatives correlated significantly in frequency with social class (in the predicted direction of middle class) but only in Task 2. In this instance we cannot explain this result on the basis of the role-play speech, as ordinatives appeared only in the narrative part of the task, and hardly ever in the role-play speech. A χ^2 test of speakers using two or more ordinatives gave a significant difference in favour of the middle class ($\chi^2 = 6{\cdot}36$, $p < 0{\cdot}02$), but this affected only a small proportion of the sample, viz. 20 middle-class children compared with 8 working-class children, from a total sample of 263.

Why was the difference not sustained in Task 3? The material itself may provide an answer, since the picture stories involve a small and easily countable number of characters (*three* boys playing football, *two* boys in a boat, etc.), whereas the Trotin cards portray either large numbers (of people) or single individual items (a dog, an umbrella). One could perhaps argue that ordinatives are of more importance in Task 2 because they are central to the narrative: thus '*three* boys are playing football and one of them kicks the ball through the window' is more specific than '*some* boys . . .'; whereas in Task 3 the *number* of participants is incidental to the events which are being described; but this is not a particularly powerful argument. The function of ordinatives is, in general, one which represents only a rather low level of conceptualisation; numeration tends to be learnt at an early stage in the child's acquisition of language, and there is no strong reason why class-differences of any magnitude should, in fact, be expected.

(vi) Possessive determiners (*my*, *his*, etc.) and rankshifted nominals (*the lady's* . . .) are related in function and it is interesting to note that they yield similar results, there being a tendency for both categories to be used by more working-class girls than by any other group. Rankshifted nominals were much rarer (used by 15 per cent of the sample, in Task 3) than possessive determiners (used by 60 per cent); results for the former showed a significant sex difference within the working class ($\chi^2 = 4{\cdot}87$, $p < 0{\cdot}03$), in the direction of girls; results for the latter showed a similar, but larger, sex difference within the working class ($\chi^2 = 10{\cdot}47$, $p = 0{\cdot}002$).

The reason why working-class girls, in particular, should use these forms is not clear. It might indicate that this group are more aware of the possessive relationship and exhibit a desire to attribute objects to persons, but an inspection of the functions of this category makes this explanation rather unlikely. In the first place, the so-called 'possessive' is named rather inappropriately, because the indication of 'possession' is only one of its functions. Two other common functions of this form are (1) to mark a social or kin relationship, as in *my uncle*, *her Daddy*, where there is no question of ownership (cf. 'this dog is mine', but not 'this uncle is mine'), but only of a social or kinship relationship, 'this man is uncle to me', 'that man is Daddy to her';[8] (2) with nouns denoting parts of the body, in which case 'possession' is strictly redundant and in many languages is not expressed: compare English 'in *his* hand' with French 'à *la* main'.

In some cases, use of the possessive seems to add little information, because there are virtually no meaningful contrasts; replacement by an article, or deletion, makes little difference to the meaning; compare

> they're having their dinner/they're having dinner
> a girl with her train/a girl with a train

Examples of all these types of possessive are to be found in Task 3: we have

> the lady's got her umbrella (possession)
> the girl's lost her mummy (kinship)
> they're eating their dinner (redundant)

Rankshifted nominals too may denote relationships other than possession, eg. (kinship) *the lady's husband.* Thus, to suggest that working-class girls are emphasising or more aware of *possessive* relationships would not be a satisfactory explanation of our findings, because the grammatical 'possessive' is actually used with other functions. A possible explanation for the results is this: in chapter 7 we shall see that a number of working-class girls interpreted the cards as stories and developed them into narratives. In doing so it is possible that they were concerned with the social relationships (such as kinship) between the characters depicted, producing utterances of the type 'the girl's lost *her* mummy', 'that's *their* mother and father'. Thus the use of possessives suggests an orientation not towards *possession* as such, but towards relationships between participants. The consistency of our results (the trend was apparent for D3, in both tasks, and for rankshifted nominals independently) suggests that an explanation of this kind should be sought.

Notes

1 These possessives were not included with the other reference categories because their potentialities in this direction were not appreciated until after the program had begun. A sub-division into anaphoric and exophoric was, however, made later on (see below, p. 112).

[2] The childish forms *pussy* (cat), *puffer* (train), which occurred occasionally in our data, were not counted as nominals—they were taken as part of the noun at head.

[3] There are no differences between the other three groups of children; percentages of children using *little* are: working-class boys 57 per cent, working-class girls 75 per cent, middle-class boys 58 per cent, middle-class girls 61 per cent.

[4] The children's responses to the social control situation of the first series (the boys playing football) have been investigated in detail by Turner (1972). He has developed a framework for classifying the responses, and investigates social class and other differences in the types of response offered.

[5] A list of the adjectives themselves can be seen in Appendix IV.

[6] Note: colour-adjectives are not found in Task 2 because the drawings are in black and white.

[7] Hypocorism: 'a pet name or term of endearment' (*Webster's Third International Dictionary*). Cf. Russian, which has an elaborate set of hypocoristic noun-suffixes.

[8] This point is discussed by Halliday (1966).

Chapter 5 Qualifiers

Qualifiers are the categories which occur in a position immediately following the head of the nominal group and closely associated with it. In a broad sense, qualifiers 'modify' the head and are thus similar in many respects to adjectives, nominals and other types of modifier. The qualifier slot, however, is normally filled by a set of classes different from those which occur at modifier; it includes adverbs, rankshifted groups,[1] and rankshifted clauses.

A division into types of qualifiers was made in the computer analysis, but the results were not studied systematically because of the infrequency with which each category occurred. For our extended analysis, however, with a larger sample of children, the original categories (devised by Turner—Turner and Mohan, 1970) were revised, with slight alterations.

One-word qualifiers, originally split into three types, were unified into one. The former distinctions were between the adjective-type like *nice* in *something nice*, the determiner-type like *all* or *both* in they *all*, they *both*, and an 'other'-type which included *else* as in *something else*, and *there* as in *that thing there*. The adjective-type was extremely rare (one occurrence), and we excluded most occurrences of *else* in meta-task speech ('can't think of anything *else*'). The rest seemed to be associable with each other as pronoun qualifiers (*all, both*) and exophoric qualifiers (*there*) all of which we might predict would be features of working- rather than middle-class speech.[2]

The other types of qualifier were quite different and are associated with the noun rather than with the pronoun. We have, first, *prepositional-group* qualifiers, which are rankshifted, eg.

The lady *with the hat*
Some *of the people*

and, second, *rankshifted clause* qualifiers such as

The boy *who broke the window*

and finally, rankshifted *nominal group* qualifiers like

You *naughty boys*

in which the structure is analysed as *you* at head followed by *naughty boys* as a qualifier. These three qualifier types all contain a noun within their own structure (eg. *hat*, *people*, *boys* in the examples above), and all except the last[3] may also be associated with a noun at head, thereby contrasting with *all*, *both* (the one-word qualifiers), which are generally associated with third-person pronouns.

A problem of coding arises in the case of prep.-group qualifiers, since there may occasionally be some doubt about the structural status of the prep.-group; it could be either a constituent of the clause as a whole, or a constituent of only part of the clause. For example, in

They're watching the people at the party

at the party could either be defining *the people*, in which case it is a rankshifted qualifier within the nominal group *the people at the party*, or it could be an adjunct of location operating as a constituent of the clause (cf. 'where are they watching the people?'—'at the party'). Ambiguous examples like this are sometimes determined by intonation and pausing, but not always, in which case an interpretation based on the sense of the context, rather than on any formal criterion, is necessary. Ambiguity of this kind usually arose in verbless clauses as in

a lady with two dogs

which we could treat either as two clause-elements, Z (Indeterminate) and A (Adjunct), or as one, Z, with the prepositional group rankshifted within it. Such examples as these were regarded as simple Z + A structures unless there were good reasons for not doing so.

Rankshifted clauses at Q can be sub-divided into a number of different types according to the degree of their dependency on the Head of the group. Sometimes the clause totally defines the head, eg.

(a) those are the things that shut the shop (i.e. shutters)

whereas other examples, although exhibiting a similar 'surface' structure, function differently at the 'deep' level, for example,

(b) once there was a little boy who went fishing.

In this example *who went fishing* bears a much looser, less dependent relationship to *boy*, in that it does not 'define' *boy*—there is no underlying idea of *which boy*. *Who* in this example can be replaced by *and he*, and for this reason these clauses are sometimes called 'additioning'. In (a), the relative pronoun cannot be replaced by *and they*, and the clause bears a close, defining relationship to the head-noun *things*.

A third type of construction which we analysed as rankshifted clause at Q is the *so . . . that* type, for example

he was so cross that he chased after them.

Again, the dependency of the rankshifted clause is of a different kind from the 'defining' and 'additioning' kinds mentioned above.

The types of qualifier we shall be considering are therefore as follows:

(1) Q1 (one-word qualifiers)	they *all*, they *both*
(2) r/s—p (rankshifted prep. groups)	the boys *in the boat*
(3) r/s—c (rankshifted clauses)	the man *who is waiting*
(4) r/s—n (rankshifted nominal group)	you *bad cat*

Results

(1) **One-word qualifiers**

Thirty-four per cent of the sample used this category in Task 2, and 45 per cent in Task 3. The occurrences were relatively infrequent (rating: 2). The χ^2 tests will thus be more reliable than the correlations, though the greater frequency of the category in Task 3 gives the correlations here some validity. The results are given in Table 5.1.

There are virtually no differences between any of the groups of children in Task 2, but a strong class-difference, in the direction of the working class, appears in Task 3. The difference is significant both for users ($\chi^2 = 11{\cdot}91$, $p < 0{\cdot}001$) and for frequency of instances ($r = 0{\cdot}157$, $p = 0{\cdot}007$). Percentages of children using this category are as follows:

WC boys	57
WC girls	54
MC girls	39
MC boys	28

(the difference between middle-class girls and boys is not significant, $\chi^2 = 1{\cdot}32$).

(2) **Rankshifted prep. groups**

Forty-nine per cent of the sample used this category in Task 3, but only 27 per cent did so in Task 2. Occurrences were relatively

Table 5.1 Variable: Q1

χ^2 *tests*	*Task 2* χ^2	*p*	*Task 3* χ^2	*p*
Class	0·41	n.s.	11·91	< 0·001
Class (boys only)	1·30	n.s.	9·57	0·003
Class (girls only)	0·01	n.s.	2·42	n.s.
Sex	0·41	n.s.	0·76	n.s.

Correlations	*Task 2* *r*	*p*	*Task 3* *r*	*p*	*Combined Tasks* *r*	*p*
Class	−0·050		0·157	//	0·103	
Sex	0·028		0·045		0·054	
IQ Crichton	−0·000		0·024		0·017	
IQ EPVT	−0·003		0·001		−0·002	
New CI	0·001		−0·140	/	−0·110	

infrequent (rating: 2). χ^2 tests will thus be more reliable than correlations here. The results are given in Table 5.2.

Table 5.2 Variable: r/s—p

χ^2 *tests*	*Task 2* χ^2	*p*	*Task 3* χ^2	*p*
Class	7·05	0·009	0·00	n.s.
Class (boys only)	6·30	< 0·02	0·02	n.s.
Class (girls only)	1·88	n.s.	0·00	n.s.
Sex	1·59	n.s.	0·00	n.s.

Correlations	*Task 2* *r*	*p*	*Task 3* *r*	*p*	*Combined Tasks* *r*	*p*
Class	−0·160	//	−0·034		−0·108	
Sex	0·041		0·043		0·060	
IQ Crichton	0·154	//	0·103		0·163	//
IQ EPVT	0·138	/	0·084		0·142	/
New CI	0·039		0·063		0·070	

Although fewer children used the category in Task 2, it is here that a significant class-difference is found, in the direction of the middle class ($\chi^2 = 7{\cdot}05$, $p = 0{\cdot}009$). The difference is mainly due to the boys, working-class boys producing fewer occurrences than the other groups, such that a comparison between boys and girls within the working class was nearly significant ($\chi^2 = 2{\cdot}95$, $p < 0{\cdot}10$). The correlations confirm these social class differences, and indicate IQ differences of lesser magnitude.

In Task 3, on the other hand, absolutely no differences appear, either from χ^2 or the correlations, except for a trend showing that high IQ children again use the category more frequently. It seems therefore that differences appear only in Task 2, and a more detailed investigation was made to find what kind of structures were being used there, and where the differences derived from.

Three types of r/s–p structure were recognised as sub-divisions:

(a) Ordinative (Head) followed by *of* + nominal group.

eg. $\left.\begin{array}{l}\text{One}\\ \text{some}\\ \text{all}\\ \text{two}\end{array}\right\}\text{of}\left\{\begin{array}{l}\text{them}\\ \text{the boys}\\ \text{etc.}\end{array}\right.$

We also included *first of all* with this type.

(b) A similar construction to (a), but beginning with a noun of size or quantity instead of an ordinative, eg.

(a) $\left\{\begin{array}{l}\text{bit}\\ \text{lump}\\ \text{piece}\\ \text{part}\\ \text{plate}\\ \text{pile}\end{array}\right\}\text{of}\left\{\begin{array}{l}\text{it}\\ \text{bread}\\ \text{the fish}\\ \text{etc.}\end{array}\right\}$

(c) All other constructions, eg.

the boy in the water
the end of the fishing rod
the wall of the house
the fish on the rod

Of these, type (c) was thought to be the most interesting, because of the appearance of two lexical items of relatively high information content, one at the head of the nominal group, the other at the head of the prepositional phrase. The middle-class children used more of all three types, but the difference was greatest in type (c). The χ^2 tests for social class were:

type (a), $\chi^2 = 2{\cdot}56$, $p = \text{n.s.}$
type (b), $\chi^2 = 2{\cdot}36$, $p = \text{n.s.}$
type (c), $\chi^2 = 9{\cdot}00$, $p < 0{\cdot}005$.

There is no apparent reason why the class-differences occur in Task 2 and not in Task 3, since the types just outlined do not seem to be context-specific in any way.[4] A detailed investigation of r/s–p in Task 3 has not yet been carried out, so we must regard the class-difference as tentative, since it has been established for only one of the tasks.

(3) **Rankshifted clauses**

The category was used by only 17 per cent of the children in Task 2, and by 28 per cent in Task 3. Occurrences were infrequent (rating: 1). We shall therefore consider χ^2 tests more reliable than correlations. The results are given in Table 5.3.

Table 5.3 Variable: rankshifted clauses at Q

	Task 2		*Task 3*	
χ^2 tests	χ^2	*p*	χ^2	*p*
Class	1·16	n.s.	1·15	n.s.
Class (boys only)	0·15	n.s.	1·51	n.s.
Class (girls only)	0·52	n.s.	0·73	n.s.
Sex	1·98	n.s.	0·24	n.s.

	Task 2		*Task 3*		*Combined Tasks*	
Correlations	*r*	*p*	*r*	*p*	*r*	*p*
Class	−0·127	/	−0·015		−0·076	
Sex	−0·078		0·076		0·013	
IQ Crichton	0·075		0·083		0·103	
IQ EPVT	0·018		−0·029		−0·011	
New CI	0·091		−0·021		0·030	

The χ^2 tests show no differences in the numbers who use this construction. The correlations with social class in Task 2 are significant, in the direction of the middle class, but the level of significance is not a high one, and the infrequency of the data gives the correlations themselves a rather low level of reliability.

In Task 3, no differences for any of the variables were found, either from the χ^2 tests or the correlations.

Because the frequency of these r/s–c qualifiers was so low, we considered it impracticable to make sub-classifications along the lines suggested in the introduction (p. 129), though a breakdown into separate types would obviously be desirable if the frequencies made it worthwhile. There seemed no reason, however, why the number of users over the whole schedule, for both tasks, should not be combined to give a higher incidence; this procedure was followed, but again no class or other differences were apparent.

(4) **Rankshifted nominals**

The category consists of utterances like *you naughty boys*, *you bad cat*. These occurrences are entirely confined to the social-control situations in Task 2, except for one instance which was recorded in Task 3, out of 250 children. Even in Task 2, the category was used by only 23 children (i.e. 9 per cent of the sample). There were no social class or sex differences shown by χ^2, and clearly correlations for such small numbers of users are not reliable.

Discussion

One-word qualifiers either have exophoric reference (*there*) or, more commonly, occur in association with third-person pronouns (they *all*). Our prediction that these would be used more frequently by working-class speakers was well supported by the results, which gave significant class-differences in Task 3 both for users ($\chi^2 = 11{\cdot}91$, $p < 0{\cdot}001$) and for frequency of use ($r = 0{\cdot}157$, $p = 0{\cdot}007$).

Differences comparable to these were not found in Task 2, but the reason is probably because of the type of material in the pictures. Those of Task 2 present little opportunity to use *all*, because there is no apparent concerted action in the second and third series of pictures—the action concerns *individuals* (the boy, the fish, the cat, the lady) rather than *groups* of people. Only in the first series can the 3 boys be treated as a group—'*they all* ran away', 'he told *them all* off'. Thus it seems most likely that *all* occurs in the first series only; this would explain why the vast majority of users (76 per cent of them) give only one occurrence. This being so, the restriction of the contexts in which *all* can be used is most probably responsible for the absence of class or other differences.

In Task 3, however, the situations are more varied and it is possible, indeed likely, that the large number of people who appear in each of the picture cards will be referred to collectively as *they all* or *them all*.

Whether the reference implied by *they*, *them* is anaphoric or exophoric, the use of *all* indicates that differentiation among the characters and the events is non-existent; we may compare, for example, *they're all going shopping* with *some* (*of the*) *people are going shopping*, *some* (*of the*) *people are selling things*, etc. Typical occurrences of *they all* are:

they're all going on a train
having a party
sitting down
going shopping
in the road

Our results, which show that more working- than middle-class children make this kind of reference to the characters, are thus consistent with earlier results concerning the use of pronouns; they point to the working-class children's preference for undifferentiated, non-specific references.

The other qualifiers, which all involve rankshift of some sort, are generally associated with nouns at the head of the group and thus may be expected in greater frequency from middle-class speakers on the basis of the results reported earlier (chapter 3). This expectation was not strongly upheld, however. Two of the categories, rankshifted clauses and nominals, proved very infrequent in overall quantity, and showed no significant class or other differences. The third category, rankshifted prepositional groups, was rather more frequent and yielded significant class differences in Task 2. When the examples were sub-categorised, the biggest class-difference occurred in the category which required two independent nouns of relatively high information content, eg. the *boy* in the *water*, the *end* of the *fishing rod*. More middle-class than working-class children used this category ($\chi^2 = 9{\cdot}00$, $p < 0{\cdot}005$), which gives us a significant result in the direction of our predictions. The finding must be regarded as tentative, however, since no analysis of this category has yet been carried out for Task 3.

In general, we must note the advantages of dividing qualifiers into a number of different types according to their function. It is arguable that the use of qualifiers of any kind is indicative of expansion of the nominal group beyond the essential, obligatory element (the head), and that when free options like this are available, middle-class speakers can be expected to select them more frequently, using them to expand the nominal group and give additional information; their low syntactic probability makes them features of an elaborated code. We now appreciate, on the contrary, that arguments based on purely structural considerations such as this are not as valid as arguments based on the *functions* of the grammatical elements involved. In the case of qualifiers, we find one type to be characteristic of working-class rather than middle-class speakers; clearly this is because its function relates it to third-person pronouns or exophoric reference, and functions like this override any purely structural factors such as expansion of the nominal group. On the other hand, another type of qualifier was found to be a feature of middle-class speech—those rankshifted groups which contain two high-information lexical items. Again, this is consistent with the functions of nouns in middle-class usage (see chapter 3).

On the same basis, purely structural considerations would lead us to expect the middle class to dominate the use of rankshifted clauses, on the grounds that this embedding process represents a type of structural complexity. These considerations were not supported by our results, the most likely reason being that rankshifted clauses fulfil a variety of functions, which we have not taken account of.[5] We shall probably not find meaningful differences in usage until we can examine the functions of these clauses. It is unfortunate that in our data r/s clauses were not sufficient in quantity to permit a worthwhile investigation of them.

Notes

[1] *Rankshifting* corresponds approximately to what is otherwise called 'embedding'. Normally each element (clause, group, word, etc.) operates as a constituent of the element next higher in rank; thus groups are constituents of clauses, clauses of sentences, etc. But clauses may also be embedded within the structure of another clause, groups within other groups, etc., in which case they are 'rankshifted'. The phrase, *the lady with the hat*, for example, constitutes a single nominal group with lady as the head, but contains within itself an 'embedded' or 'rankshifted', prepositional group, *with the hat*; thus we have a group within a group.

[2] *All* is the commonest one-word qualifier, usually co-occurring with *they*, *them*. Notice that although the pronoun may have anaphoric reference, the use of *they all*, *them all* implies that the speaker sees the referents as an undifferentiated group.

[3] Notice that the last, i.e. the r/s–n type, is associated with *you* and not with third-person pronouns.

[4] In the case of adjectives and intensifiers, the significant results of Task 2 which were not repeated in Task 3 were due to differences in the social-control section. Clearly this cannot be the explanation for the different pattern here (in these qualifiers), since the instances were distributed across both narrative and social-control sections of the task.

[5] Cf. also the discussion on rankshifting and complexity in chapter 6, pp. 139ff.

Chapter 6 Nominal group heads, other than nouns and pronouns

We shall now consider a group of categories which occur at the head of the nominal group, but not including nouns (discussed in chapter 3) or pronouns (discussed in chapters 2 and 7). The major categories to be considered in this chapter are *adjectives* and *rank-shifted clauses*; in addition two minor categories will be briefly dealt with, *wh-words* and *determiner/ordinatives*.

Adjectives at head, which formed a single category in the analysis reported in Part I, were subsequently re-classified into two types, a 'truly adjectival' type and a 'verbal' type. The latter consist of words derived from -en forms (past-participle forms) of verbs, and resemble passives; they have close lexical and semantic associations with verbs, which the 'true' adjectives do not have. Examples of the verbal type from our data are:

(i) The fish was eaten (meaning 'the fish was in a state of having been eaten'),
cf. The fish is half-eaten

Other common examples are:

(ii) The window is broken/smashed
(iii) Only the bones are left

The adjectival type includes those where no relationship to a verb is possible, eg.

The boys were naughty
The man was hungry

Palmer (1965, p. 68) describes our verbal type as 'past participles functioning as adjectival complements'. He compares

they were married last year (the passive form)

with

they were married when I last saw them (*be* + adjectival complement)

The two types ('true' and 'verbal') are not easy to distinguish formally; the true type may usually undergo a transformation to put the adjective in the pre-noun (modifying) position, eg. the balloon is red → the red balloon. The verbal type may often not permit this transformation, eg. (asterisks denoting an unacceptable form):

* the eaten fish, * the left bones

from

the fish is eaten the bones are left

But there are counter-examples in both directions: *afraid* appears to be a true adjective yet * *the afraid girl* is not possible; while *broken*, *open* are clearly verbal and yet they permit the transformation, as in *the broken window* and *the open door*.

The possibility of inserting *very*, *more*, *too*, etc. as sub-modifiers is usually a good criterion of the 'true' adjective type, but again one meets examples like

he was frightened

where there is an obvious relationship to a verb (frighten), but which still permit the addition of *very*, etc. Huddleston (1968, p. 50) suggests that the -ed forms which *can* be preceded by *very* (eg. *annoyed*, *frightened*) should be treated as adjectives, while those which can take adverbial elements should be regarded as embedded participial clauses, i.e. as derived from verb forms. We followed a similar analysis, counting words like *annoyed* as 'true' adjectives, and words like *married*, *eaten* as 'verbal adjectives'.

'True' adjectives are thus those adjectives at head which are not related lexically to a verb, and/or which can normally be submodified by *very*, *more*, etc. Examples of these will appear as the description progresses, but a complete list of the type-adjectives found in our corpus is given in Appendix IV.

Rankshifted clauses at head is a category which other linguists would call *nominalisation*, that is, it includes clauses which substitute for a nominal group in a larger or 'matrix' clause; thus in she saw *what had happened* the clause *what had happened* replaces X in *she saw X*, where X could be a nominal group like *the man* and fulfil the role of complement (or 'object') in that clause. We can recognise a number of different types of r/s clause at H, distinguished by the kind of relationship they hold to the 'matrix' or 'main' clause of which they form a part. Some examples of these rankshifted clauses have already been given in Part I (pp. 11–12), and in the section on wh-indirect words we shall also consider rankshifted clauses of the type

I wonder *what they're doing*
She saw *what had happened*

Rankshifted clauses frequently follow verbs of saying, thinking, knowing, seeing, etc., and it is convenient to classify them according to the type of verb they follow (perception, cognition, etc.). Another common construction is the 'that's where' type, eg.

that's *where they're playing football*
that's *where the electricity comes from*

After a verb like *see* the rankshifted clause may have a full verb, eg.

she saw *that the fish had gone*

or only a participial form, eg.

she saw *them running away*

A rankshifted clause at H frequently follows a preposition, as in

a bridge for *the trains to go through*
a house with *someone looking out*

Rankshifted clauses may be indicative of structural complexity, since they involve the 'embedding' of one clause within another to form a single, complex unit. A sentence like *she saw that something had happened* is a complex unit formed of two simple clauses, *she* (S) *saw* (P) *X* (C) and *something* (S) *had* (*or has*) (P) *happened* with a further element (*that*) brought in (optionally) as part of the process of embedding the second clause into the first. When this research project began, we worked on the hypothesis that middle-class children would use rankshifting more frequently, in so far as it is structurally more complex. Thus, Bernstein (1962, 1965) argues that one of the characteristics of a restricted code is structural predictability, in which the number of syntactic alternatives is 'often severely limited' and 'the probability of predicting the elements is greatly increased' (Bernstein, 1965). In an earlier paper (1959), he predicted that one characteristic of a restricted code would be 'short, grammatically simple sentences with verbs mainly in the active mood'. Since rankshifting is more complex and hence less predictable, it could be argued that this process would be characteristic of an elaborated code and hence found only rarely in the speech of working-class children.

More recent theoretical perspectives, however, in particular the work of Chomsky (1965) and Labov (1968), cast doubt on the possibility that some children do not have access to particular syntactic structures. Most linguists now believe that all children who have acquired a language in the normal way have access to, as part of their linguistic competence, all the basic syntactic processes which make up the language, including the process of embedding (see chapter 9 for further discussion of this). It is still possible, however, that some children do not actually use embedding in situations where it is appropriate, even if they have the competence to interpret and produce embedded sentences. But if we are to predict that working-class children use embedding less frequently than middle-class children, we need some basis, other than linguistic competence, for this prediction.

Does such a basis exist? If the use of language arises out of the form of a social relationship, is there any reason why the particular social relationships which give rise to restricted codes (i.e. relationships in which the participants identify closely with each other and share many common assumptions) should prefer simple clauses and avoid embedding? There is in fact no apparent reason why they should; the choice, simple clauses *v.* embedded clauses, is not of the same type as the choice between, for example, noun and exophoric pronoun. In the latter case, we can predict that closely shared identifications will encourage the use of exophoric pronouns because the speaker assumes that the referent is already known to the listener; in the former case, such considerations do not apply.

We can indeed, on linguistic grounds, question whether the choice, simple *v.* embedded, is a real choice at all. Take the example already mentioned,

she saw that something had happened;

is there a choice here between simple and embedded clauses? Could the meaning(s) expressed by this sentence be realised by the juxtaposition of two simple clauses? The answer is, 'no', because there is no equivalent in simple clauses (the nearest equivalent might be 'she saw it; something had happened', but this is quite different in a number of ways from the meaning of the complex sentence). Other examples show the same thing, that sentences with embedded clauses are not the equivalent of simple clauses juxtaposed; hence there is no real choice between these two modes of expression. Putting this another way, we may say that as there is no real alternative to an embedded sentence, we have no reason to predict that a speaker who is conditioned by one particular form of social relationship will use more, or fewer, embedded clauses than any other speaker. Frequency of use must thus remain an open question.

The two minor categories to be dealt with in this chapter are wh-words and determiner/ordinatives. The former were divided into two types, depending on whether the wh-word appeared in a direct question ('who did that?' in response to 'what's the lady saying?' Task 2) or in an indirect question or relative clause, eg. 'I wonder *who* did that' or 'the boy *who*'s in the water'. This latter category, which we shall call 'wh-indirect', obviously overlaps with the categories 'rankshifted clause at H' and 'rankshifted clause at Q', because wh-words often introduce such clauses. Examples of 'wh-indirect' introducing rankshifted clauses at H, are:

look *what's happened*
I wonder *who did that*
that's *what the cat did*

The following are rankshifted clauses at Q, introduced by a wh-word:

the boy *who fell in*
the people *that were on the train*

There are other clauses, however, which are introduced by a wh-indirect, but which are probably not rankshifted. Turner (1970) calls them 'additioning' clauses because they add information, rather than define a nominal group. Thus the *who*, *which*, or *that* which introduce such clauses can usually be substituted by *and he*, *and they*, *and it*, etc. Examples are:

this is a boy *that*'s caught a fish (= *and he's* caught . . .)
there was a lady *who* put that on the table (= *and she* put. . . .)

The majority of wh-indirect words introduce rankshifted clauses at H.

The direct questions (wh-direct) normally appear in the role-play speech of Task 2, since elsewhere they would have been addressed to the interviewer and hence excluded from our corpus as non-task speech. Examples of wh-direct are:

('what's the man saying?') Who's broken that window?
Who's eaten the fish?

Notice that wh-indirect is not confined to this one part of the schedule; it may occur throughout.

No predictions were made about the occurrence of wh-direct, since there is no obvious reason why one group should prefer this form. We originally expected MC children to use wh-indirect more frequently, on the basis of structural complexity (in particular, association with rankshifted clauses) but this prediction now seems unlikely in itself (see discussion of this, pp. 139ff). We may note, however, the association of wh-indirect with the pronoun *I* in sentences like 'I wonder what happened', 'I don't know who did that', etc., which we have reason to believe are a feature of middle-class speech (see chapter 7). Thus, it is possible that wh-indirect will be associated with the middle-class speakers.

Determiners/ordinatives at head were originally (in Part I) separate categories but it was decided to combine them because functionally they are very closely related. *Some* and *all*, for example, are strictly speaking, determiners while *three* is an ordinative, yet in constructions like

some/three/all of them came

the functions appear to be indistinguishable. The possessive determiners like *his*, *mine* cannot be equated with ordinatives, of course, but these were extremely rare in occurrence. The demonstrative determiners *this*, *that* (and plural forms) have already been treated separately, as reference categories (chapter 2).[1]

The commonest occurrences of determiner/ordinatives were the items *some*, *all*, *one*, *half*, followed by *of* plus another nominal group. There is thus some overlap with rankshifted prepositional groups at Q, since in a phrase like 'some of the boys', *of the boys* is analysed as a qualifier to the head-word *some* (cf. pp. 131–2, especially sub-types (a) and (b) of the rankshifted prep. groups).

The categories we are concerned with in this chapter are therefore as follows:

(1) Verbal adjectives (Ev)	the fish is *eaten*
(2) 'True' adjectives (Ea)	the lady is *cross*
(3) Rankshifted clauses	she saw *that the fish had gone*
(4) Wh-direct	*who*'s eaten the fish?
(5) Wh-indirect	he saw *what* had happened
(6) determiners/ordinatives	*some* of the boys

Results

(1) **Verbal adjectives (Ev)**

These were used by about 25 per cent of the sample, but the frequency was very low (rating: 1). No significant differences were found for any variable, either in the χ^2 tests or in the correlations, nor were any trends apparent. The relevant data may be looked up from the data summaries in Appendices II and III.

(2) **'True' adjectives (Ea)**

This category was used by 40 per cent of the children in Task 2, and by 29 per cent in Task 3. These adjectives were fairly infrequent (frequency-rating: 2) and we shall therefore find the χ^2 tests more reliable than the correlations. The results are presented in Table 6.1.

Table 6.1 Variable: Ea ('true' adjectives at head)

	Task 2		*Task 3*	
χ^2 tests	*χ^2*	*p*	*χ^2*	*p*
Class	15·20	< 0·001	1·98	n.s.
Class (boys only)	5·47	0·02	1·05	n.s.
Class (girls only)	10·40	0·002	0·42	n.s.
Sex	0·02	n.s.	1·01	n.s.

	Task 2		*Task 3*		*Combined Tasks*	
Correlations	*r*	*p*	*r*	*p*	*r*	*p*
Class	−0·287	///	0·061		−0·152	//
Sex	0·067		0·062		0·087	
IQ Crichton	0·184	//	0·036		0·140	/
IQ EPVT	0·076		−0·104		−0·017	
New CI	0·147	/	−0·015		0·087	

There is clearly a big social class difference in Task 2, in the direction of the middle class. More middle-class than working-class children use these adjectives ($\chi^2 = 15{\cdot}20$, $p < 0{\cdot}001$). The difference holds independently for boys ($\chi^2 = 5{\cdot}47$, $p < 0{\cdot}02$) and for girls ($\chi^2 = 10{\cdot}40$, $p < 0{\cdot}002$). These results are confirmed by the correlations, which are highly significant for social class. Lesser relationships with the Crichton IQ measure and the communication index are also apparent.

In Task 3, however, the pattern is quite different. No significant differences appeared, and the correlations with social class are positive, which shows there is not even a tendency towards the middle class. A more detailed examination of adjectives was clearly necessary, in order to explain the different pattern of results in each task.

When the adjectives in Task 2 were collected separately, it soon became apparent that the most frequent were the role-play items *naughty* and *cross*, and that these two words were used by far more middle- than working-class children. *Naughty* was used by only 6 working-class children (out of 139), compared with 23 out of 124 middle-class—a highly significant difference ($\chi^2 = 12{\cdot}10$, $p < 0{\cdot}001$). It was used particularly by middle-class girls, who differed significantly from working-class girls ($\chi^2 = 8{\cdot}63$, $p = 0{\cdot}005$) and exceeded even middle-class boys ($\chi^2 = 2{\cdot}71$, $p = 0{\cdot}10$).

Cross also showed a straightforward class difference, again highly significant ($\chi^2 = 30{\cdot}00$, $p < 0{\cdot}001$). It was used at least once by 34 middle-class children, compared with 4 working-class. The difference applied to boys and girls equally ($\chi^2 = 8{\cdot}93$, $p < 0{\cdot}005$, and $\chi^2 = 13{\cdot}81$, $p < 0{\cdot}001$, respectively).

There were a few adjectives which fulfilled similar functions to *naughty* and *cross*. Instead of *naughty*, *silly* and *foolish* were used once each, and instead of *cross*, *angry*, *wild*, *mad* and *annoyed* occurred, also once each. These items made no difference to the overall results.

The social class difference in Task 2 is therefore almost entirely due to the occurrence of the two words *naughty* and *cross*, and hence to the social-control situations in which they occurred. When *naughty* and *cross* were removed, the middle class still used more adjectives but there is no longer a significant difference ($\chi^2 = 0{\cdot}56$, p = n.s.). There is, however, a tendency for girls to use these remaining adjectives more than boys ($\chi^2 = 3{\cdot}52$, $p = 0{\cdot}10$) and this is independent of class.

The middle class therefore use more adjectives at head in the specific context of the social-control situations, mainly in the first and third series of the picture cards. Their responses to the probes 'what are they saying' are likely to be:

> the boys are/the cat's/he's/they're/you're (very) *naughty*

or

> the lady's/the man's/the boy's/he's/she's/I'm (very) *cross*.

The adjectives used in Task 3 can be divided, as they were for E2, into 'colour' and 'non-colour' types, and the 'non-colour' divided again into those which are modifiable by *very*, etc. or are comparative, and those which are not. The latter in this case turned out to include only *ready*, which was usually collocated with *get* in 'they're getting the tea ready', and was considered essentially verbal in type (cf. 'they're *preparing* the tea').

Not many children used colour-adjectives, but those who did were mainly working-class (9 children), not middle (2 children). The difference between the girls was significant ($\chi^2 = 4{\cdot}02$, $p = 0{\cdot}05$) because no middle-class girls used a colour-adjective at 'head'. These differences explain why the working class had a slight overall majority in adjectives at head. The non-colour adjectives excluding *ready* were used by approximately equal percentages of children, there being no significant differences anywhere. The tendency for more girls than boys to use adjectives (other than the social-control adjectives) has not been confirmed in Task 3.

(3) **Rankshifted clauses at H**

The category was used at least once by 60 per cent of the children in Task 2, and by 54 per cent in Task 3. We may therefore consider both χ^2 tests and correlations to be relevant to an interpretation of the results, which are presented in Table 6.2.

Table 6.2 Variable: rankshifted clauses at H

	Task 2		*Task 3*	
χ^2 tests	χ^2	*p*	χ^2	*p*
Class	5·69	0·02	0·08	n.s.
Class (boys only)	7·10	0·01	0·41	n.s.
Class (girls only)	0·68	n.s.	0·01	n.s.
Sex	2·69	(0·10)	0·65	n.s.

	Task 2		*Task 3*		*Combined Tasks*	
Correlations	*r*	*p*	*r*	*p*	*r*	*p*
Class	−0·190	//	−0·064		−0·161	//
Sex	0·034		0·010		0·022	
IQ Crichton	0·179	//	0·189	//	0·226	///
IQ EPVT	0·135	/	0·094		0·143	/
New CI	0·024		0·036		0·026	

There is a clear social class difference, favouring the middle class, in Task 2. The χ^2 tests show that the difference is mainly among the boys (though the girls move in the same direction), the working-class boys being the group with fewest children using rankshifted clauses. The percentages of users are:

MC girls	70
MC boys	66
WC girls	61
WC boys	41

and the difference between working-class girls and boys is significant, $\chi^2 = 4{\cdot}97$, $p < 0{\cdot}03$.

There are strong correlations with social class in Task 2, and lesser relationships with both measures of IQ. The sex-difference found in the χ^2 tests is clearly due to a difference *within* the working class, since it is not reflected in the correlations given in Table 6.2; this is confirmed by the correlations for each social class separately, in which the relationship between r/s–c and sex is highest for the working class ($r = 0{\cdot}144$, $p = 0{\cdot}09$).

The pattern of results in Task 3 is different: the χ^2 tests give no significant differences for class or sex, and there is no difference within the working class either ($\chi^2 = 0{\cdot}96$, p = n.s.). The correlations suggest a very slight trend towards the middle class, being consistently negative in sign; and there is a strong relationship with Crichton IQ scores ($r = 0{\cdot}189$, $p < 0{\cdot}002$).

(4) **Wh-direct**

This category was used quite frequently in the role-play speech of Task 2, by 51 per cent of the sample, but very rarely in the rest of the schedule. No differences were found between any of the groups, either in the χ^2 tests or in the correlations. The relevant data may be looked up in the data summaries (Appendices II and III).

(5) **Wh-indirect**

A relatively infrequent category, used by only 27 per cent of the sample. No class or other differences were found either in Task 2 or in Task 3, by χ^2 test or by correlation. The relevant data are available in the data summaries (Appendices II and III).

(6) **Determiners/ordinatives**

This category was also fairly infrequent, even though it was used by 33 per cent and 47 per cent of the sample in Tasks 2 and 3 respectively. No differences were found in either task.

Discussion

No social class or other differences were found in the use of the minor categories wh-indirect, wh-direct and determiners/ordinatives. It will be recalled that no differences were expected for the latter two, since they do not appear to fulfil functions which will obviously be associated with one social class rather than the other, or with IQ, etc. We anticipated a possible movement towards the middle class in the use of wh-indirect because of its association with complex defining clauses ('the boy *who*'s got the football') and with indirect questions involving the pronoun *I* ('I wonder *who* did that'). The frequency of occurrence of this category was however too low to make salient any potential differences.

The most significant and interesting results we obtained were those for the 'true' adjectives. The highly significant class-difference in Task 2 was found to be due almost entirely to the social-control adjectives, especially the two items *naughty* and *cross*, both of which gave highly significant results, independently. Class-differences apart from this were negligible. This difference almost exactly parallels that for the modifying adjectives reported in chapter 4, where the major class-difference was due to the use of *naughty* and a few similar adjectives. The significance of this kind of response depends of course on what the working-class children say instead of it, but we shall see that one of the categories they use more frequently is 'P2 implied', the imperative. It seems, then, that the middle class prefer to give a response which is purely verbal in nature and does not demand any action of the 'guilty party', whereas the working class may give a response which does demand such action, eg. *go away*, *get out*. These differing responses will be more fully discussed under the presentation of 'P2-implied' in the next chapter.

In Task 2, therefore, we have found class-differences in adjectives at H but these are seen to be confined mainly to the social control situations. In Task 3 more working-class children used colour-adjectives but for other adjectives there were no class-differences. These results do not coincide exactly with those for modifying adjectives (chapter 4), where distinct class-differences were revealed even after the social-control adjectives had been removed. It seems that more working-class children use colour-adjectives at H, but more middle-class children use them at M; for the non-colour adjectives, the middle class had more at M, but performed no differently from the working class, at H. We need to ask, then, why the results are different in each case. Are the two types of adjectives in fact comparable, or not? More specifically, is it possible to interchange adjectives at M with adjectives at H, and vice versa?

Many adjectives can be used in either position, but for some only one position is possible, and for others, one position is more *likely* than another in particular contexts. Thus, *naughty* can (and does) appear in both positions, and there is little difference on the functional level between a response like *you're naughty* (adjective at H) and *you're naughty boys* (adjective at M). We have found the middle class using *naughty* more frequently in both positions.

With the colour-adjectives, a functional difference can be established between the two positions of structure. Compare

(a) there's a red balloon (adj. at M)

with

(b) the balloon is red (adj. at H)

In the first of these, the focus of information, which is realised phonologically through the intonation pattern (Halliday, 1967), would in the normal or unmarked realisation fall on the noun, *balloon*;[2] in the second sentence the focus falls on *red*, thus drawing particular attention to the colour itself. This may be desirable if something else is said about *why* the balloon is red, or about the significance of the balloon's redness, but in most instances like this nothing else was said, and the sentence was thus left as an isolated statement unrelated to anything else in the description. By contrast, in sentence (a) the focus is on the noun and the colour-specification is given as additional, incidental information, so that the sentence as a whole forms an integrated part of the on-going description.

A further distinction can be drawn between these two sentences; the (b) type, but not the (a) type, is often associated with exophoric reference. Thus, unless *balloon* has already been mentioned, the *the* of sentence (b) is exophoric; it prompts the question '*what* balloon' and directs the addressee to refer to the picture. Type (b) often co-occurs with an exophoric *this/that*, with no noun specified, as in *that's red* or *that thing's red.* With type (a), the noun must of course be present. Both types of sentence can be further expanded, eg.

(c) there's a red balloon hovering over the houses
(d) the balloon hovering over the houses is red

Type (c) is more normal in its focus of information and hence much more likely to occur than type (d), which is very rare; in other words, (b)-type sentences are unlikely to be expanded.

In relating the foregoing to our results, we observe that colour-adjectives at H, which are probably associated with exophoric reference and are unlikely to be expanded, are associated with working-class speakers, whereas colour-adjectives at M, which are necessarily collocated with a noun, are features of middle-class speech. The results are thus entirely in accord with our earlier findings on exophoric usage and noun usage (chapters 2 and 3).

Many of the other adjectives which occurred in these tasks *can* occur in both structural positions (i.e. at M or at H) but are more likely to occur in one rather than the other in the particular contexts we are dealing with; *little*, for example, occurs frequently at M, almost never at H. Adjectives of evaluation, like *funny*, are also more likely at M:

there's a funny old lady

is more likely than

the old lady is funny

Some adjectives of description follow the same pattern:

the old lady

is more likely than

the lady is old

The answer to our original question is, then, that in many cases adjectives at M and at H are not comparable.[3] This is supported by the additional fact that in the actual lists of the adjectives used (see Appendix IV), few of the items correspond. There are (combining both tasks) 58 different adjectives at M, and 59 at H, but only 18 of these are the same words; i.e. there are 18 words which occur both at M and at H, but 99 words which occur at either one or the other position, not both. Thus we have a largely different set of items at M and H, fulfilling partly different functions. If the functions are different, we cannot expect social class or other differences to have the same pattern in the one set as in the other. It is therefore not surprising to find that adjectives at M revealed class-differences whereas adjectives at H did not. The necessary collocation of adjectives at M with nouns, and the trend of these adjectives towards the middle class, are consistent with our previous results for nouns reported in chapter 3.

For the category 'rankshifted clauses at H' we found significant class-differences in the direction of the middle class, but only in Task 2. The fact that differences were found in one task and not the other makes it difficult to come to any general conclusions about this category; there is no apparent reason, for example, why these clauses should show differences in one task and not the other; since they were distributed in occurrence throughout the schedule, there is no explanation in terms of social control options, such as we found for adjectives, nor are there functional differences comparable with the differences between adjectives at M and at H.

One consistent result is that these clauses are used more frequently by high IQ children in both tasks, and it was the Crichton test of active vocabulary which discriminated best. This is interesting in view of the problem of whether rankshifted clauses are indicative of complexity; the fact that children who rate highly on measures of active vocabulary tend to use these clauses more often, suggests that there may be a sense in which they reflect higher levels of syntactic organisation. It seems likely that some r/s clauses are in fact more complex than others, but so far we have no ready methods of measuring structural complexity (see chapter 9 throughout); we cannot, therefore, usefully pursue this line of inquiry.

Instead, we now require an analysis which takes account of the different sub-types of r/s clauses, some of which were mentioned earlier, in order to observe the different *functions* these clauses perform. Class and other differences cannot be given meaningful interpretations, unless we know something about the functions of the different sub-types. Our data did not supply a sufficient quantity of rankshifted clauses to make sub-classification, as a whole, a worthwhile procedure, but in the next chapter we shall have occasion to refer to one particular type, viz. those associated with the pronoun *I* (eg. I think *it's an aeroplane*). Turner and Pickvance (1971) have analysed expressions of uncertainty from similar data, which also throws light on the use of rankshifted clauses.

Notes

[1] It is worth noting that not all determiners can stand at Head; *a*, *the*, *every*, for example, cannot, but they are each related, semantically (and sometimes historically) to determiners or ordinatives which *can* stand at head: thus *a* is related to *one* (not **I want a*, but *I want one*); *the* is related to third-person pronouns (eg. *it*) or demonstratives; *every* is related to *all*, etc.

[2] In the unmarked case, the focus falls on the *last lexical item* of the clause.

[3] This is surprising in view of recent developments in transformational grammar, in which modifying adjectives are generally derived from, and hence closely related in meaning to, predicated adjectives (our 'adjectives at H'), eg. *the old lady* is derived by the application of a succession of rules from a structure like *the lady who is old*. It seems that these rules may in fact apply meaningfully only to a small set of adjectives, those which can and regularly do occur in both positions.

Chapter 7 First- and second-person pronouns

In this chapter we shall be considering all pronouns other than the third-person pronouns, which have already been dealt with as 'reference' categories in chapter 2. The major variables are the first- and second-person pronouns (P1 and P2); in addition we have one minor category, the 'indefinite' pronouns (P indef.).

Description of the categories

(i) First-person pronouns

A number of predictions and expectations concerning the use of first-person pronouns were available to us before this study began. For example, the use of the sequence *I think* was suggested as a likely feature of an elaborated code, since it marks the expression of the speaker's own opinions: 'the sequence signals difference and relates the utterance to the person. It symbolises the area of discretion . . . the egocentric basis of the interaction is raised like a flag' (Bernstein, 1962a). Bernstein found, in this study of middle- and working-class 16-year-olds discussing capital punishment, that the middle-class speakers used a higher proportion of the sequence *I think*; but he also found them using a higher frequency of the pronoun *I* in general, in relation to *you* and *they* which were characteristic of the working-class speakers. He concluded that *I* in general is a feature of an elaborated code, while absence of *I* marks a restricted code. Thus, 'if an individual takes as his reference point rigid adherence to a wide range of closely shared identifications, the area of discretion available is reduced and the differentiation of self may be constrained. . . . The relative infrequency of *I* would occur whenever the form of social relationship generated a restricted code' (*ibid.*). Elsewhere, Bernstein suggests that 'the elaborated code user comes to perceive language as a set of theoretical possibilities available *for the transmission of unique experience* (my italics). The concept of self . . . will be verbally differentiated so that it becomes in itself the object of special perceptual activity' (1965, p. 161).

On this basis we expected to find a greater use of *I* by middle-class children in our study, but the results from the original computer analysis for this category were negative; no major class-differences were apparent. When we looked at the way *I* was actually used in Tasks 2 and 3, however, we began to realise the necessity of differentiating the functions of this pronoun if we wished to obtain meaningful results. It became clear that, for example, sentences in the social-control section of Task 2 like 'you wait till I catch you' or 'I'll get you for this' contained occurrences of *I* but the *I* here could hardly be said to represent a differentiation of self, nor would such sentences be likely to form part of an elaborated code however it was defined. Differentiation of self becomes a function of *I* only when *I* is used in particular contexts, eg. with verbs of cognition (*I think*, *I know*) or of uncertainty (*I expect*, *I presume*). We concluded that it is not the grammatical category 'first-person pronoun' *in itself* which is important, but the particular ways in which such pronouns are actually used. There are going to be many instances of *I* which have very little to do with reference to one's own individual experience or the 'signalling of difference'. Hence it is quite likely that some functions of *I* will be characteristic of middle-class speakers, while other functions will be typical of working-class speakers; each social group may use first-person pronouns in quite different ways. A global observation of these pronouns would thus fail to reveal their potentially different functions and uses.

For the purpose of this study, therefore, we took account of such factors by sub-classifying pronouns on the basis of our experience with the data. It was clear that a large percentage of P1 and P2 occurred in 'direct' speech in answer to the probes 'what's X saying', i.e. in the role-play speech of Task 2. In two of the three series of cards, this speech makes available for observation the children's concepts of social control; the child was in effect asked to describe the likely (verbal) reactions of the man and the woman in the face of the boys' wrongdoing (series 1—their football had broken the window), and the reactions of the lady and boy when the cat had eaten their fish (series 3). What kind of controlling behaviour would the children ascribe to these characters? We were interested to see how the children would interpret these roles, since this would in all probability reflect the types of control used in their own family. The idea of wrongdoing is absent from the second series of cards, so the probes ('what are they saying') do not elicit social-control responses here.

Since most P1 occurred in the context of the role-play speech, a primary sub-division of the P1 category was necessary in order to distinguish the self-referent *I* with which the child refers to himself, as in

I think the boy's caught a fish

from the direct-speech P1 (*I*, *me*, *we*, *us*) as in

I'll get that cat

Obviously, the direct-speech P1 are quite different in function from the self-referent P1. The latter, consisting almost entirely of uses of the word *I*,[1] occur in structures such as:

I wonder what . . .
I hope . . .
I think . . .
I suppose . . .

Occurrences which depended on or derived from the interviewer's probes were excluded, eg.

'What can you see?'—I can see . . .
'What do you think they might be saying?'—I think they're saying . . .

In Task 3 further uses of the self-referent pronouns were found; these will be discussed when the category is considered in detail.

The direct-speech P1s will also be sub-classified more finely when the category is dealt with in detail (see Results, pp. 157ff.). Initially, however, we derive just the two P1 categories, P1 self-referent and P1-direct.

(ii) **Second-person pronouns**

Second-person pronouns did not need sub-division in quite the same way, because *you* occurred almost always in direct speech, except for the occasional *you* addressed to the inverviewer, which was normally excluded as 'meta-task' speech (see p. 59), or the generalised *you* as in

You have to be careful

It was however necessary to add the category 'P2 implied' for the 'covert subject' of imperatives, because *you* often occurred as the overt subject of an imperative, as in

'You go away'

and in order to complete the picture, we decided to count the imperatives in which *you* is not expressed, but implied, as in

'Go away', 'Swim over here'

This gives us two categories of P2, *P2-implied* and *P2-expressed.* Some instances of the latter will be similar in function to P2-implied, i.e. they will occur in conjunction with imperatives (*you go away*); other instances will have different functions, and further sub-classification will therefore be necessary (see Results, p. 161).

The three categories P1-direct, P2-expressed, P2-implied are closely associated with each other because they all occur in connection with role-play speech. They occur most frequently in Task 2 where role-play forms a specific part of the schedule, but there are as we shall see a number of occurrences of these categories in Task 3, in instances where speech was attributed to the people shown in the pictures, for example

and the man's saying 'let me have some tea'

The occurrence of *me* and *let* here (*let* is classified as P2-implied; compare P2-expressed *you let me have*) shows that direct speech is being employed within the narrative—the characters are having roles assigned to them. The motivation for role-play speech in this task comes, of course, from the child himself and not from the interviewer's probes as it does in Task 2.

Indefinite pronouns are two-morpheme words composed of the elements:

$$\left\{\begin{matrix}\text{some}\\ \text{any}\\ \text{every}\\ \text{no}\end{matrix}\right\} + \left\{\begin{matrix}\text{body}\\ \text{one}\\ \text{thing}\end{matrix}\right\} \text{eg. somebody, something, no one, etc.}$$

Occurrences of *nothing*, *anything* in the context of a refusal to the probe, eg. they're saying nothing/not saying anything, were excluded as 'meta-task' (see p. 59).

The categories of pronoun to be dealt with are therefore as follows:

(1) P1-self referent (first person, referring to speaker)
(2) P1-direct (first person in direct, i.e. role-play, speech)
(3) P2-implied (second person, latent—imperative form of verb)
(4) P2-expressed (second person, *you*)
(5) P indef. (indefinite pronouns *someone*, *something*, *anything*, etc.)

Results

(1) P1 self-referent

This category was used by only 11 per cent of the sample in Task 2, but by a larger proportion (34 per cent) in Task 3. Occurrences were relatively infrequent (rating: 2) but sufficient to give reliable correlations in Task 3. χ^2 tests will be dependable for both tasks. The results are given in Table 7.1.

Table 7.1 Variable: P1, self-referent

	Task 2		*Task 3*	
χ^2 tests	χ^2	*p*	χ^2	*p*
Class	2·96	-< 0·10)	2·54	n.s.
Class (boys only)	0·62	n.s.	1·07	n.s.
Class (girls only)	2·12	n.s.	1·17	n.s.
Sex	0·10	n.s.	0·08	n.s.

	Task 2		*Task 3*		*Combined Tasks*	
Correlations	*r*	*p*	*r*	*p*	*r*	*p*
Class	−0·105		−0·124	/	−0·142	/
Sex	−0·043		−0·064		−0·070	
IQ Crichton	0·036		0·190	//	0·165	//
IQ EPVT	−0·013		0·113	/	0·087	
New CI	0·015		0·140	/	0·117	

Task 2 reveals a tentative class-difference in users, in the direction of the middle class ($\chi^2 = 2{\cdot}96$, $p = 0{\cdot}09$); the correlation with social class supports this, being negative in sign though not strong enough to reach a level of significance. In Task 3 the χ^2 tests show no differences in users, but the correlations, which in this task are based on sufficient data to be reliable, give a significant result ($r = -0{\cdot}124$, $p = 0{\cdot}03$), in the direction of the middle class. Results were also obtained for both measures of IQ (eg. for Crichton, $r = 0{\cdot}190$, $p < 0{\cdot}002$), and for the communication index ($r = 0{\cdot}140$, $p < 0{\cdot}03$), in the direction of high IQ and high CI.

A more detailed investigation of this category was then made, and the individual occurrences were collected. It was found that a division could be made between those pronouns occurring with a 'tentative' verb like *wonder*, *expect*, *think*, *bet*, and those occurring with simpler verbs like *see*, *know*, *say*. Examples of the former have already been given: examples of the latter, from our sample, are:

I just know what the man's saying
I can tell what's biting
I know where he trodded
The same as I said in that

'Tentative' verbs imply that there is some element of uncertainty; the statement is couched in hypothetical terms, whereas the other verbs, those of perception, etc. have no such connotations—they are presented as straightforward statements of fact.

When the two types are separated, there is no difference in the use of the 'factual' type, but the 'tentative' still show a tendency towards the middle class, the number of users being too small for a significant result (χ^2 = 2·55, p = n.s.). When this distinction is applied to Task 3, however, big changes appear in the results. A third type of self-referent pronoun was also recognised in this task—the use in connection with the naming probe ('what shall we call this picture?'), sometimes in the form *let's*, eg.

Let's call it . . .
We'll call that one . . .
I want to call this picture . . .

The three types are therefore:

A 'Tentative', before *think*, *suppose*, etc.
B 'Naming', before *call*.
C 'Factual', before *see*, *know*, etc.

There appeared to be no class or sex differences in the use of types B and C but there were considerable differences for type A, in the direction of the middle class. The results are shown in Table 7.2.

Table 7.2

	χ^2	p
Class	12·60	< 0·001
Class (boys only)	6·70	0·01
Class (girls only)	4·20	0·04
Sex	1·30	n.s.

There is thus a significant class-difference both for boys and girls; more middle-class children (31 per cent with at least one occurrence) than working-class children (12 per cent) use the self-referent pronoun with verbs of 'tentativeness'.

(2) P1-direct, P2-implied, P2-expressed: Task 2

We have already noted that these three categories are all associated with the role-play speech in Task 2. We shall therefore take them as a group, but for each task separately, beginning with Task 2.

(a) *P1-direct*

This category was used by 76 per cent of the sample and occurred moderately frequently (rating: 3). Both types of test can therefore be taken as reliable. The χ^2 tests revealed no class or other differences, however, and only one correlation was significant, viz. with Crichton (r = 0·164, p = 0·004), in the direction of high IQ.

Because the uses of P1, even within these limited social control situations, were felt to be different, a more detailed analysis of them was made, and five sub-categories were established. These sub-categories are defined by functional rather than by formal linguistic criteria, though it may eventually be possible to express the one in terms of the other.[2]

The disadvantage of functional criteria is, of course, that they tend to be 'notional'. One of the aims of a linguistic discipline is to isolate these 'notions' and provide them with formal expression. But for a meaningful interpretation of one's findings, functionally based categories are essential. In this case the assignment of a response to one category or another was made according to the judgment of the author alone; to this extent the categories may not have universal validity.

The five sub-categories then are as follows (the titles 'threatening', etc. are merely convenient labels and are intended only as general, not specific guides to the distinguishing criteria):

A	Threatening	If I catch you, I'll . . .
		I'll tell the police
		I'll hit that cat
B	Helpful	I'll get you out (to boy in water)
		We'll save you (to boy in water)
C	Plea	Help me
		Get me out
		I'm hungry
		I want my dinner
D	Informative	I don't know who did it
		I went fishing and the fish pulled me in
		I think the cat did it
		I shouldn't have left the fish out

E Intention — I'll turn round
I'll come over
I'd better go and buy some more
The cat said 'I'll get on the table'

The results of this sub-division were as follows.

Type A, 'threatening', was used by more working-class children, the χ^2 tests giving the results shown in Table 7.3.

Table 7.3

	χ^2	p
Class	6·65	< 0·01
Class (boys only)	2·88	(< 0·10)
Class (girls only)	2·58	n.s.
Sex	0·22	n.s.

The overall class difference is thus highly significant beyond 0·01, and applies to boys and girls about equally; but the numbers involved are small—the percentage of children using the category are: working class 17 per cent; middle class 6 per cent.

Type B, the 'helpful' response, showed no class- or sex-differences.

Type C, the 'plea', occurred most frequently in the second series ('boy in the water'), where it was used by significantly more working-class children. The χ^2 results are shown in Table 7.4.

Table 7.4

	χ^2	p
Class	8·56	< 0·005
Class (boys only)	2·54	n.s.
Class (girls only)	5·92	0·02
Sex	0·14	n.s.

The percentages of children here are: working class 27 per cent, middle class 12 per cent.

Types D and E, the 'informative' and 'intentional', did not show overall class differences, though we might have expected the middle class to use more of these types. There is a difference, however, in both D and E, between the boys from the two social classes, and when the types are combined, the difference is significant—$\chi^2 = 4{\cdot}61$, $p < 0{\cdot}04$. Fewer working-class boys use these two types of P1 than any other group of children.

(b) *P2-implied*
This category was used by 72 per cent of the sample and occurred fairly frequently (rating: 3). The data from both correlations and χ^2 tests will therefore be reliable. The results are presented in Table 7.5.

Table 7.5 Variable: P2-implied (Task 2 only)

χ^2 *tests*	*Task 2* χ^2	*p*	*Task 3* χ^2	*p*
Class	3·30	(0·10)		
Class (boys only)	0·68	n.s.		
Class (girls only)	2·17	n.s.		
Sex	0·20	n.s.		

Correlations	*Task 2* *r*	*p*	*Task 3* *r*	*p*	*Combined Tasks* *r*	*p*
Class	0·193	///				
Sex	0·039					
IQ Crichton	−0·196	///				
IQ EPVT	−0·159	//				
New CI	−0·117					

The overall class-difference for users is nearly significant ($\chi^2 = 3{\cdot}30$, p = 0·07) in the direction of the working class. The correlations give much stronger confirmation to this tendency, being highly significant for class (r = 0·193, p < 0·001) and of similar magnitude for IQ (r = −0·196, p < 0·001) with CI maintaining a lesser relationship.

A more detailed study of these imperatives was made and a number of sub-categories were recognised, on lines similar to the sub-division of P1-direct, above. The six types were as follows:

A	Threatening	Go away Get out of it Stop banging Stop it
B	Helpful	Cheer up Come over here Swim towards the boat Don't cry
C	Plea	Help me Get me out

D	Exclamatory	Look at that fish
		See that cat
E	Prohibitive	Don't play football
		Don't swim
		Don't go fishing
F	Jussive	Go and get that ball
		Catch him
		Get him up

Again the criteria for distinguishing these categories are notional rather than formal, though we can see how types D and E are characterised by the verbs *look* and *see* in the one case, and by the negative form *don't* in the other. It is more difficult to distinguish clearly between types A and F, and B and F. The examples *catch him* and *get him up* were felt not to belong with B because they are addressed to the other boy in the boat, *not* to the boy in the water. The imperatives assigned to F and not A were thought to be 'milder' than the peremptory *go away*, *get out*; but the distinction is not a clear-cut one, and we shall thus find it necessary to combine A and F. This will give us a general, short, command-imperative, which we may contrast with the more specific types B, C, D and E.

It was later found, also, that occurrences of types A and E with *you* included, eg. *you go away* (type A) and *don't you play here* (type E), were much rarer than the imperative without *you*, and they have thus been included with types A and E here instead of being treated as separate sub-categories of P2-expressed.

Types A and F, the general command-imperatives, are both used by more working-class than middle-class children. Taking type A separately we get the results shown in Table 7.6.

Table 7.6

	χ^2	p
Class	7·65	< 0·01
Class (boys only)	2·32	n.s.
Class (girls only)	4·82	0·03
Sex	0·10	n.s.

There is an overall class-difference here which is stronger among the girls than the boys. Type F was not tested separately, but A and F combined produced χ^2 results as shown in Table 7.7.

The pattern here is similar to that for type A separately: an

Table 7.7

	χ^2	*p*
Class	14·70	< 0·001
Class (boys only)	3·08	(< 0·10)
Class (girls only)	11·65	< 0·001
Sex	0·17	n.s.

overall class-difference which is due more to a difference between girls than between boys. This is because working-class girls are the most frequent, middle-class girls the least frequent users, the percentages being as follows:

WC girls	61
WC boys	54
MC boys	37
MC girls	31

Type B, the 'helpful' utterance like *swim over here*, was not used frequently, and showed no class- or sex-differences, just as type B in P1 direct speech (*we'll save you*) also showed no differences.

Type C, the 'plea', has already been dealt with in the consideration of P1 direct, since it involves both a first-person pronoun and an imperative, as in *help me*, *get me out* (note that *help* alone was not counted at all, since its status as noun or verb is not clear—it could be expanded into either *help me* or *I need help*). We found that more working-class children, particularly girls, used the type of 'plea' which involves an imperative (pp. 158, 168).

Types D and E, the 'exclamatory' *look at that fish* and the prohibitive *don't play football*, *don't do it again*, were infrequent, and revealed no class- or sex-differences.

(c) *P2-expressed*

This category was used by a substantial proportion (70 per cent) of the sample, and was moderately frequent (rating: 3). Both types of test can therefore be expected to give dependable results. Those for the initial, overall count are given in Table 7.8. The χ^2 tests show that more middle-class children, particularly girls, use the category at least once. The correlations also suggest more frequent use by the middle class (the class correlation is negative in sign, but tentatively significant only, $p = 0{\cdot}10$), and there is a highly significant relationship with Crichton IQ.

Table 7.8 Variable: P2-expressed

χ^2 *tests*	*Task 2* χ^2	*p*	*Task 3* χ^2	*p*
Class	6·13	0·02		
Class (boys only)	0·32	n.s.		
Class (girls only)	8·04	0·005		
Sex	0·23	n.s.		

Correlations	*Task 2* *r*	*p*	*Task 3* *r*	*p*	*Combined Tasks* *r*	*p*
Class	−0·108					
Sex	0·057					
IQ Crichton	0·209	///				
IQ EPVT	0·069					
New CI	0·066					

The types of P2-expressed recognised in the detailed analysis we carried out are as follows:

Types A—E The same as for P2-implied. No occurrences were found of types C ('plea') and D ('exclamatory'). Types A and E occurred so infrequently that they were included with the corresponding types of P2-implied (see p. 160).

A[1] Threatening, but not imperative in form
You dare break my window again
How dare you break this window
You'll have to pay for it

F Interrogative
Did you break my window?
How did you fall in there?

G Appeal
You're naughty (boys)
You naughty cat

H Statement
You've smashed the window

J Thanking
Thank you (said by boy in water in response to offers of assistance).

The majority of occurrences of P2 expressed belong to types B, F and G, and we shall deal with these three types first. Type B, the 'helpful' *we'll get you out*, has already been mentioned, and shows no class- or sex-differences. Type F, the interrogative, is used by rather more middle-class children, the χ^2 results being as shown in Table 7.9.

Table 7.9

	χ^2	p
Class	3·88	0·05
Class (boys)	0·44	n.s.
Class (girls)	4·19	0·04
Sex	0·42	n.s.

The class-difference is clearly due more to the girls than to the boys, but is in any case not of a high order of significance.

Type G, the 'appeals', clearly account for the major class-difference noted for the category as a whole (see Table 7.8). The results are as shown in Table 7.10.

Table 7.10

	χ^2	p
Class	11·38	< 0·001
Class (boys)	5·02	0·025
Class (girls)	5·80	< 0·02
Sex	0·12	n.s.

The percentages of users which the χ^2 test is comparing are:

MC 30
WC 12

Thus, more middle-class children use this sub-variety of P2-expressed, and the results are highly significant among boys and girls independently. These results were, of course, predictable on the basis of our findings for adjectives at M (chapter 4) and at H (chapter 6), because these adjectives, which are a feature of middle-class speech, regularly collocate with *you* in the role-play situation, eg. *you naughty boys, you're a naughty cat*, etc.[3]

The other types of 'P2-expressed' occurred less frequently. Types A and E have already been dealt with under 'P2-implied', and type H was infrequent and showed no class- or sex-differences. Type A[1], the non-imperative threat, was used by 6 middle-class and 2 working-class children—not enough to make a significant difference; however, all the five children who used *dare* were from the middle class.

Finally, type J, *thank you*, was used by 11 middle-class children (6 boys and 5 girls), compared with none from the working class—a difference significant at 0·001 (χ^2 = 10·82).

(3) **P1-direct, P2-implied, P2-expressed: Task 3**

We suggested earlier that the use of these categories in Task 3 would imply 'role-play' speech, that is, the children would include some account of what the people in the pictures were saying as well as a description of the events. This proved to be so, with the exception of a few instances of P2-implied, which were addressed to the interviewer herself.

(a) *P1-direct (Task 3)*
The occurrence of P1-direct in Task 3 was examined in detail, and it was found that all instances were examples of 'role-play' speech. It was therefore not necessary to sub-classify, and we shall use the χ^2 tests (not the correlations, since the numbers are small) for the whole category. The results are as shown in Table 7.11.

Table 7.11

	χ^2	*p*
Class	3·02	0·08
Class (boys)	0·00	n.s.
Class (girls)	4·28	0·04
Sex	1·07	n.s.

The overall class-difference is almost significant, in the direction of the working class (p = 0·08), but this difference is due entirely to the girls, and an inspection of the numbers of children confirms that working-class girls use this category far more than the other groups. Fourteen of these girls use the category at least once, compared with 5, 4, and 3 children for each of the other groups. There is thus a clear tendency for the working-class girls to differ from the other groups.

(b) *P2-implied (Task 3)*
This category of imperatives was not entirely confined to role-play speech; some imperatives were addressed to the interviewer, for example

> Look what they're doing
> Look at that cake

These occurrences therefore formed a separate sub-category.

Ten working-class children addressed imperatives like this to the interviewer, compared with only three middle-class children. This difference is not quite significant (χ^2 = 2·67, p = 0·10).

Imperatives used in the context of role-play speech were characteristic of working-class girls. The number of children who used this category is distributed as follows:

WC girls	10
WC boys	3
MC girls	0
MC boys	2

Thus, 13 working-class compared with 2 middle-class children used imperatives in a direct speech context—a significant difference ($\chi^2 = 6{\cdot}57$, p = 0·01). The difference is attributable almost entirely to girls ($\chi^2 = 6{\cdot}58$, p = 0·01).

(c) *P2-expressed (Task 3)*
It was found necessary to make three divisions in the use of *you* in Task 3:

A	General, impersonal (= 'one')	you have to be careful you have to read that
B	Role-play	he says 'you get off that table'
C	Interviewer as addressee	you know what they're going to do?

All three types were used by only small numbers of children, type A by 10 per cent, B by 8 per cent, C by 4 per cent. Types A and C showed no class- or sex-differences, but type B was again used mainly by working-class girls—13, compared with 2, 3, and 3 from the other groups. Some of these girls were of course the same children who used the imperatives and P1s in role-play speech, so we decided to find the total number using role-play speech at all, taking all three categories into account. This gave us 18 working-class girls (24 per cent of the total) compared with 6, 6 and 4 from the other groups (average, 9 per cent). This difference was significant at the 0·005 level ($\chi^2 = 8{\cdot}70$).

(4) **P indef.**

Indefinite pronouns were used by 22 per cent of the sample in Task 2 and by 54 per cent in Task 3; they occurred relatively infrequently (rating: 2). The tests, particularly the correlations, will be more reliable for Task 3 because of the higher quantity of occurrences. Results are presented in Table 7.12.

There is a tendency for more middle-class children to use indefinites in Task 2; it is not significant by χ^2 test but the correlations do

Table 7.12 Variable: indefinite pronouns

χ^2 *tests*	*Task 2* χ^2	*p*	*Task 3* χ^2	*p*
Class	2·35	n.s.	2·36	n.s.
Class (boys only)	2·34	n.s.	5·60	$< 0·02$
Class (girls only)	0·18	n.s.	0·03	n.s.
Sex	0·01	n.s.	0·01	n.s.

Correlations	*Task 2* *r*	*p*	*Task 3* *r*	*p*	*Combined Tasks* *r*	*p*
Class	−0·128	/	−0·014		−0·070	
Sex	−0·022		0·017		0·002	
IQ Crichton	0·134	/	−0·035		0·025	
IQ EPVT	0·109		−0·018		0·034	
New CI	0·087		−0·030		0·009	

give a significant result (r = −0·128, $p < 0·03$), and show a similar relationship for the Crichton IQ measure. In Task 3 the overall measures show no significant differences but the χ^2 tests give a result in the direction of middle-class boys ($\chi^2 = 5·60$, $p = 0·02$). The overall direction of this category is thus, tentatively, towards the middle class.

A more detailed study was made to ascertain which of the indefinites occurred most, and which were responsible for the significant difference in Task 3. This revealed that *someone* (or *-body*) and *something* were by far the commonest, and that *someone* (or *-body*) was rather more frequent than *something* in Task 3. Typical constructions were:

> *someone's* getting married
> *someone*'s looking at them
> getting *something* for them to eat
> he's got *something* in his hand

Significantly more middle-class boys used *someone*, *something*, in Task 3 ($\chi^2 = 5·68$, $p < 0·02$) and there was the same tendency, though not significant, in Task 2 ($\chi^2 = 2·18$, p = n.s.).[4] There was no difference between the girls in either task, and no sex-differences.

Discussion

Our prediction regarding the category P1 self-referent, that it would be a feature of middle-class speech, was confirmed, but a more detailed analysis of the class-differences showed that they really applied to a sub-group of this category, namely to expressions of uncertainty or tentativeness such as *I expect*, *it looks like ... to me*. The class-difference was very strong in Task 3 ($\chi^2 = 12.60$, $p < 0{\cdot}001$) where most of the examples of this sub-category actually occurred, but a trend was noticed even in Task 2.

The reason why 'tentative' verbs (with associated P1 self-referent) were used more frequently in Task 3 than in Task 2 is probably due to the kind of pictorial material involved. The picture stories of Task 2 provide a firm direction for the narrative and there is little room for uncertainty, except in the probes 'what's X saying' where a reply like 'I expect she's saying ...' is possible. The picture cards in Task 3 leave much more room for uncertainty; what is happening in each picture is not obvious or determined in any way, so that the child's own interpretation can be put forward with more or less a degree of certainty: 'I expect they're going shopping', 'I think it's a balloon'. It is in this task that more middle-class speakers use such expressions.

Our results move in the predicted direction, therefore, when we take into account the particular, highly specific contexts in which first-person pronouns are used. When the occurrences with verbs of 'tentativeness' are isolated, clear social class differences emerge. It seems then that we need to link the use of the pronouns *I*, *me* to this particular kind of usage, and that these pronouns are not used more frequently by the middle class in all situations—at least, as far as the evidence we have here indicates. This 'tentative' use of *I* perhaps is best included in a consideration of the verbal group, since it is the verbs like *think*, *suppose*, *wonder*, which really express the tentative approach; on the other hand, the use of *I* in these contexts can also be regarded as an expression by the speaker of his 'unique experience', closely related in function to Bernstein's egocentric sequence *I think*, which he found to be a feature of middle-class speech. Further discussion of 'tentative' expressions in the speech of middle- and working-class children is to be found in a paper by Turner and Pickvance (1971).

The other three categories of pronoun, P1-direct, P2-implied, P2-expressed, associated in particular with the social-control speech of Task 2, gave interesting results when they were sub-classified according to their special functions, in threats, offers of help, requests for help, etc.

P1-direct was associated with working-class speakers in two functions, threats (*I'll get you for this*) and requests for help involving the imperative mood (*save me*, *get me out*). This type of threat, in which a P1 is used, is considered to be the strongest kind of threat offered in this situation, since it expresses the intention of punitive action (compare P2-implied, where the 'threats' merely demand withdrawal: *go away*, *get out*).

The category we called 'pleas', i.e. requests for help, also gave a highly significant difference in the direction of the working class ($\chi^2 = 8{\cdot}56$, $p < 0{\cdot}005$), but only when these requests were formulated in the imperative. We originally included utterances from the third series of cards ('the cat and fish') like *I'm hungry* and *I want my dinner* under the category 'plea', as well as the imperative type (*get me out*) which derives from the second series ('boy in the water'). When the former were looked at separately, we found them actually used by more middle-class than working-class speakers, though in small numbers (middle-class 12 per cent, working-class 5 per cent; $\chi^2 = 1{\cdot}53$, p = n.s.), which makes the imperative-type an even stronger feature of working-class usage. This middle-class response to the probe 'what's the boy saying' in the 'cat and fish' series contrasts with alternative possibilities such as the threats and commands which working-class speakers appear to select; here we see a small number of middle-class children choosing the option of *reporting the feelings* of the injured party (*I'm hungry*), describing how the situation affected the boy personally; the use of *I* here is comparable in function with the self-referent *I* in expressing the reaction of the individual.

P2-implied, the imperative, gave overall very highly significant results in the direction of working-class speakers. A number of sub-types were recognised, along much the same lines as the sub-types of P1-direct. Large class-differences were associated with the short action-oriented imperatives such as *go away*, *get out*, *go and get that ball*, *catch him*, *get him up*. Even those which were classified as 'pleas', eg. *get me out*, *save me*, were features of working-class rather than middle-class speech, whereas the 'pleas' which did *not* involve imperatives were, as we have already noted, more typical of the middle class. Our results are thus remarkably consistent in finding action-oriented imperatives of all kinds strongly associated with working-class speakers. On the other hand, imperatives which could be construed as offers of advice (*swim over here*) or as exclamations (*look at that fish*) or as prohibitions (*don't . . .*) revealed no class or other differences. The 'prohibitive' type is of some interest linguistically because it may serve two purposes, interpretable either as an instantaneously-applicable command (eg. *don't do that* in the sense of 'stop doing that') or as a generalised rule—*don't do it again* and *don't play football* being equivalent to *you shouldn't (ever) do it/play football* or *it's wrong to . . . .* Notice that *don't do that* can be either specific in time-reference, meaning *'stop doing what you're doing (now)'* or general in time-reference, meaning 'never do that kind of thing'. We have not enough examples of the use of prohibitives in this sample, but it would be interesting to see whether there were any class-differences in the use of the 'specific' and the 'general' type of prohibitive.

P2-expressed (the pronoun *you*) is a feature of middle- rather than working-class speech and correlates highly with the Crichton index of IQ. Sub-classification of this category showed an overwhelming middle-class preference for the type called 'appeals' which are associated with adjectives at M and at H (to be discussed below), and a lesser degree of preference for interrogative forms in which one participant asks a question of the other, eg. 'did you break my window?' 'how did you fall in?' This question-response is of interest because it clearly initiates and promotes verbal interaction between the participants, even in a situation where the questioner is the aggrieved party. The questions demand an answer, for example *it wasn't my fault* or *the fish pulled me in*, and the dialogue may go on from there. This kind of response in which the 'court' is left open for the verbal ball to go back and forth contrasts strongly with the command (like *go away*) which does not encourage any further verbal communication between the parties, but initiates some form of direct action.

A few middle-class children used *dare* in responses like *how dare you. . . .* These may be regarded as veiled threats—no specific action is proposed, nor is the addressee directed to take any specific action; in this way they contrast with the more direct threats (*I'll call the police*; *wait till I get you*) which we observed to be characteristic of working-class speakers. Veiled threats are purely verbal—an interesting example of the middle-class tendency to rely on verbal means of control not oriented towards any specific, direct action.

A general picture of broad class-differences in response to the social-control situations is now beginning to emerge. We may at this point extend our discussion to include some of the results from chapters 4 and 6, which also have a bearing on the social-control responses. There, we found highly significant differences in the use of modifying adjectives and adjectives at head. A small range of adjectives, with high frequency of usage, was involved. At M, we found only *naughty* and *bad* (plus a few others with single occurrences), at H principally *naughty* and *cross*. Correspondingly, differences appear in the use of P2-expressed, which often co-occurs with these adjectives (as in *you naughty cat*, *you're naughty*, etc.). So the typical middle-class response to the social-control probes involve an adjective. A smaller number of middle-class children respond with questions (*why did you do that?*) or with *dare* (*how dare you . . .*).

The inclusion of P2-implied as a category has enabled us to see what, by contrast, is the typical response of working-class speakers. It is clear that many of them choose an imperative form of the verb, usually with a function which can be described as action-oriented, i.e. the addressee is directed to *do* something. Another response, characteristic of working-class speakers but involving smaller numbers, is the strong form of threat using a first-person pronoun, as in *I'll call the police*. In sum, the typical linguistic patterns of control divide into two types, as follows:

Working class

1 Action-oriented imperatives (*go away*, *get out of it*, *stop doing that*) and to a lesser extent
2 Threats (*wait till I catch you*; *I'll call the police*)

Middle class

1 Attribution (*you're very naughty*; *the lady's cross*) and to a lesser extent
2 Questions (*why did you break my window?*)
3 'Dare' (*how dare you eat the fish*)
4 'Plea' without imperative [5] (*I'm hungry*, *I want my dinner*)

We may note that the kind of behaviour which these utterances seek to elicit from the addressee is different.[6] The expected response to an imperative like *go away* is physical, non-verbal action—running away; but an utterance like *you're naughty boys* demands no physical action of any type in response. What then does it seek to achieve? If there is to be any external response, it is going to be verbal in nature, not physical, and will probably take the form of an apology ('I'm sorry') or of some kind of justification ('I didn't mean to do it'), ('it wasn't my fault'). But in addition to this external, verbal response, there will almost certainly be an internal, affective response of some kind to an utterance like *'You're naughty'* or *'I'm very cross'*, which will arouse feelings of guilt; and utterances of this type, by imputing some sort of condition or attribute to a person (the condition of being naughty or cross), thus contribute towards developing an awareness of the conditions in other people which are created by one's own actions. In contrast with this, the imperatives do not impute any condition or attribute to a person at all; they simply demand some more or less immediate physical action as a response. We infer that so long as some kind of action (like running away) is taken, nothing more will be said or felt about the affair.

We are making the assumption, of course, that the children's responses to these Task 2 probes do reflect the patterns of social control which the children themselves experience within their own families or group. The situation is almost certainly not as simple as it might seem, however. It is likely that patterns of control do differ broadly from one social class to another, but also that each group, and perhaps each family, uses more than one type of social control, so that middle-class families, for example, will on occasion use action-oriented imperatives instead of, or in addition to, other forms of control. The question is whether working-class families use as wide a range of control patterns as the middle-class or whether they tend to use mainly one type, the imperatives. It is probable that imperatives constitute a primary, basic mode of control which is open to families of any social stratum. But it may be the case that middle-class families use a wider range of control patterns, varying the type according to the situation, the participants, the topic of dispute, etc., so that the children learn the appropriate responses to a variety of patterns.

The point about our results, however, is that we have found differences in response corresponding to social class differences. Since the stimulus was the same for all the children interviewed, it is difficult to see why these differential patterns should emerge, if they do not reflect patterns of control in the children's own families.

Another investigation into the social-control responses, from a different point of view, by Turner (1972) shows that a further characteristic working-class response to the probes was 'he/she's telling them off' which was used quite frequently and showed highly significant class-differences. Turner interprets this as a form of 'verbal punishment', and sees it as 'suggesting coercion and pointing to imperative control' (p. 151)—the emphasis being on the idea of punishment. It is debatable, however, whether 'telling off' can be classified as 'verbal punishment' or not. The reply 'she's telling them off' is not a direct answer to the probe-question 'what's the lady saying'; it would be an appropriate reply to the question 'what's the lady *doing*'; but as an answer to the question that was actually put, it is almost an avoidance; we are not given the lady's words, but a generalised statement about what she is *doing*. It is interesting that working-class children should interpret the question this way, in view of their other typical response, the imperatives, which are also action-oriented rather than verbally-oriented. 'Telling off' tells us nothing about what the lady (or boy, etc.) actually said; an imperative type (*go away*) could be construed as 'telling off' but so also could an adjectival type like *you naughty boys* or a form with *dare* like *you dare do that again*. The only type which probably could *not* be regarded as 'telling off' is the question, like 'why did you break my window?' 'She's telling them off' is thus a neutral, noncommittal reply in the sense that it does not tell us what strategy of social control was actually used; it interprets the original question as if '*saying*' means '*doing*'; i.e. it is actional rather than verbal in orientation.

One further point arises from our results. It appears that working-class girls use imperatives most and middle-class girls least. Two of the χ^2 tests involving imperatives showed a stronger class-difference for girls than for boys; in requests for help (*get me out*), type C of P1-direct, the class-difference for girls only is greater ($\chi^2 = 5{\cdot}92$, $p = 0{\cdot}02$) than for boys only ($\chi^2 = 2{\cdot}54$, $p = 0{\cdot}15$); and in short commands, types A and F of P2-implied (*go away, catch him*), the same pattern is evident: for girls, $\chi^2 = 11{\cdot}65$, $p < 0{\cdot}001$; for boys, $\chi^2 = 3{\cdot}08$, $p < 0{\cdot}10$. The percentages of users (see list, p. 161) give 61 per cent for working-class girls, compared with 31 per cent for middle-class girls.

This difference between working- and middle-class girls in the use of imperatives may be connected with the kind of family-role played by working-class girls. Bernstein (1972, p. 491) discusses this as follows:

> Girls, especially older girls in such families, tend to take on mothering roles. They also . . . mediate between parents and sibs. Their role then is more complex as it combines a normal sib role with that of mediator and with that of controller. . . . Thus girls are likely to be person-oriented and to have to rely on forms of control based upon linguistically elaborated meanings, rather than upon physical coercion.

It can be argued that imperatives, used to channel and direct the actions of others, constitute the primary verbal form of social control; it is therefore interesting to find that in situations where this kind of imperative can be used, more working-class girls use them than any other group. It suggests that they occupy this role of 'controller' within the family to a greater extent than girls from middle-class families.

Role-play speech in Task 3

A certain amount of direct, or 'role-play', speech, as manifested by the use of P1-direct, P2-implied, and P2-expressed, was offered as part of the description of the Trotin pictures. For each category independently, we found that working-class girls formed the dominant group of users. The consistency of this result led us to investigate the incidence of role-play speech as a whole, and we found that 24 per cent of all working-class girls offered some role-play speech, compared with an average of only 9 per cent from the other groups. This difference was strongly significant ($\chi^2 = 8{\cdot}70$, $p < 0{\cdot}005$).

The use of direct speech in this task is not occasioned by any prompting or probing on the part of the interviewer but arises spontaneously from the general description of 'what is going on' in the picture. It thus involves an imaginative interpretation of the pictures which goes beyond what is actually 'given', as it were, in the visual material. The standard response to the probe is a description of events, but in this case we have a further dimension: the characters are given roles, and what they say to each other forms part of the description.

The fact that a group of working-class girls choose to extend their descriptions into this further dimension is of some interest, since we have already noted, in chapter 4, a tendency for working-class girls to use possessive determiners (*his*, *her*, *their*, etc.) and rankshifted nominals (*Mummy's* . . .) more frequently, and we suggested that this showed a greater awareness of role-relationships (because the so-called 'possessives' often indicate a social relation rather than possession, eg. *her father*). Here then, is some confirmatory evidence of working-class girls' interest in the assignation of roles, and the social relationships between the characters visible in the pictures.

A few instances of P2-implied in Task 3 were not connected with role-play speech but were addressed to the interviewer. They were of the type *look what they're doing*, *look at that*. Ten working-class and three middle-class children used such forms; small numbers, but tentatively significant ($\chi^2 = 2{\cdot}67$, $p = 0{\cdot}10$). The direction of this result is consistent with the trend towards exophoric reference observed in chapter 2, since the imperatives here clearly possess a deictic (or 'pointing') function, as do exophoric pronouns, and in fact an exophoric reference item usually occurs in the same utterance, eg. *that*, *they* in the two examples above. Here we have, then, another small piece of evidence towards the general picture of working-class usage in this speech situation.

Indefinite pronouns

These occurred much more frequently in Task 3, where they were used by 54 per cent of the sample, than in Task 2 (22 per cent). This is probably an effect of the nature of the pictorial material, which is much less easy to identify precisely in Task 3 and hence gives rise to many instances of *someone* and *something*. When these two pronouns were investigated on their own, a tentative movement towards the middle class was noted, particularly among the boys ($\chi^2 = 5{\cdot}68$, $p < 0{\cdot}02$).

These two pronouns are like nouns in one respect, that they contrast in reference-type with exophoric pronouns; they do not require the addressee to scan the context of situation in order to locate a referent. If we take the typical examples in which these pronouns occurred in our data, viz.

(a) *someone's* getting married
(b) *someone's* looking at them
(c) getting *something* for them to eat
(d) he's got *something* in his hand

we can see that example (a) is akin to '*some people* (noun) are getting married' and contrasts with an exophoric *they* ('re getting married). Similarly, examples (b) and (c) can be related to nouns and contrasted with exophoric items, such as *he*, *that* which always provoke the underlying question 'who is *he*', 'what is *that*', etc. Indefinite pronouns like these are thus *substitute nouns* (cf. Hasan, 1968, ch. 3 on *substitution*) as is indicated by their morphology, some + one, some + thing, where *one* substitutes for a human noun, *thing* for a non-human noun. To this extent, association of these pronouns with middle-class speakers is consistent with the results for nouns in general.

In some cases, as in example (d) above, indefinite pronouns are an indication of uncertainty and thus related in function to 'tentative' verbs which we have also seen to be associated with middle-class speakers. There is a relationship between an utterance like 'he's got something in his hand' and 'I wonder what he's got in his hand' (notice *I* + tentative verb); both of them suggest uncertainty or tentativeness. This relationship could possibly extend to the other examples quoted above (eg. 'someone's getting married' with the sense of 'I wonder who's getting married') but this is likely only if the indefinite pronoun receives contrastive stress, which in the above cases it probably does not.

Indefinite pronouns thus either substitute for nouns or signal uncertainty, and in both cases may be expected to occur among middle-class speakers more frequently. Our results are thus consistent with the pattern already established in chapter 3. The reason why there is a class-difference for boys but not girls is not clear, however. It may be that because indefinites are similar in function to nouns, the two are interchangeable without much difference in meaning (*someone*, *some people*), and girls are using nouns instead of the indefinite equivalent. In this case perhaps indefinites should be included in the count of nouns, but their relative infrequency (average 1·1 occurrences per child) compared with nouns (average 22·6 per child) would make no difference to the overall results for the latter.

Notes

[1] Apart from examples like 'it looks like a balloon to *me*' which were regarded as tentative, parallel with 'I think it's a balloon'.

[2] We may mention here that it is the purpose of G. J. Turner's Ph.D. thesis to see to what extent Bernstein and Cook's (1965) social control categories may be defined using formal linguistic criteria. The social control coding frame includes such categories as 'threat of punishment', 'verbal punishment', 'command', 'personal appeal', etc. The speech of a sample of middle-class and working-class mothers and their children at 5 years and 6½ years is being examined.

[3] The percentages given above (30 per cent, 12 per cent) do not represent the full total of children giving these 'appeal' responses, because parallel constructions without *you* are also possible, eg. *naughty boys!*; *the boys/they are naughty*, etc. (notice that *you* does not co-occur with *cross*, which was a frequently-used adjective here).

[4] Cf. Table 7.12. The figures differ slightly because Table 7.12 includes users of *all* indefinite pronouns. Here we are testing for *someone*, *something* only.

[5] Originally taken as a sub-category of 'pleas'; but it is clear, on reflection, that this type really belongs as a sub-variety of (1)—it is a form of *attribution*.

[6] Cf. Bernstein's discussion of social control and family types (1972, pp. 484ff.). Bernstein differentiates between two types of appeal, the 'positional' and the 'personal'. We are here concerned with the personal.

Chapter 8 Tag clauses

'Tag' clauses have been included within a study devoted mainly to the nominal group because they incorporate a special function of pronouns. Three basic types of tag clause can be recognised.

(1) 'Mirror-image' or 'reverse-polarity' tags like *isn't it*, *aren't they*, *doesn't it*, *don't they*, etc., which occur at the end of a declarative clause, eg.

they're running away, aren't they

(2) Other 'socio-centric' sequences: in our data these included *you see*, or just *see*, both of which are normally appended to declarative clauses, eg.

they're running away, (you) see

(3) The 'ego-centric' sequence *I think*, whose distribution of occurrence is similar, eg.

they're running away, I think

Tag clauses were selected as a focus of interest by Bernstein in his empirical study (1962a) of adolescents. He distinguished what he calls 'sympathetic circularity' (SC) sequences which incorporate types 1 and 2 above, and he interpreted these as features of a restricted code, on the grounds that their function is to reinforce the social relationship between speaker and addressee(s): 'the speaker requires assurance that the message has been received . . . it is as if the speaker is saying "Check—are we together on this?" On the whole the speaker expects affirmation' (1962a, p. 233). The use of SC sequences helps 'to reduce any uncertainty which the speaker may have had when the message was first planned' (*ibid.*). The ego-centric sequence *I think*, on the other hand, has an equivalent function in an elaborated code. It 'is probably as much an indication of semantic uncertainty as the SC sequences are', but it is oriented towards the individual rather than the group because 'it invites a further *I think* on the part of the listener: . . . it signals difference and . . . symbolises the area of discretion which the form of the social relationship permits. . . . Like the SC sequences, it may indicate the strain in the social interaction but in this case the strain is taken wholly by the individual' (*ibid.*). The results of the study showed that the working-class groups used SC sequences more frequently than the middle-class groups, whereas the latter used *I think* more frequently. Lawton's (1964) replica of Bernstein's study with groups aged 12 and 15 found that 'at both ages the working-class use more socio-centric[1] sequences whereas the middle-class use the egocentric sequence *I think*. . . . The overall class difference is significant at 0·025 level of confidence.'

These results were taken as the basis for our observations; in the first place, types 1 and 2 (the 'reverse-polarity' and 'other' socio-centric sequences) were taken as a single category, which we expected to be associated with lower-class speech. At a latter stage, a division was made between the reverse-polarity type, which may be associated with any personal pronoun, and the 'other' SC sequences which involve the pronoun *you* either present (*you see, you know*) or latent (*see*).

Results

(1) **Reverse-polarity and socio-centric tags (Tags 1 + 2)**

This category was used by 22 per cent of the sample in Task 2 and by 29 per cent in Task 3. Occurrences were relatively infrequent (rating: 2). Because of the low frequencies of occurrence, the χ^2 tests will be more dependable than the correlations. The results are presented in Table 8.1.

The χ^2 tests for Task 2 show that there are no social class differences, and this is confirmed by the correlations, which are non-significant for class, IQ and CI. There is however a sex-difference, indicating that more boys than girls use this type of tag clause ($\chi^2 = 3{\cdot}92$, $p < 0{\cdot}05$). The correlations provide confirmatory evidence ($r = -0{\cdot}146$, $p = 0{\cdot}01$). Supplementary χ^2 tests to compare boys *v.* girls within each social class showed that the difference was mainly within the working class ($\chi^2 = 3{\cdot}14$, $p = 0{\cdot}08$).

In Task 3 the χ^2 tests show a significant class-difference: more working- than middle-class children use this category ($\chi^2 = 5{\cdot}68$, $p < 0{\cdot}02$), the difference being distributed equally among boys and girls. The correlations[2] give some support, with significance levels ranging between $p = 0{\cdot}10$ and $p = 0{\cdot}05$. The sex-difference noted in Task 2 is given weak support by the correlation for sex ($r = -0{\cdot}109$, $p = 0{\cdot}05$) but not by the χ^2 tests of users.

Table 8.1 Variable: Tags 1 + 2

χ^2 *tests*	*Task 2* χ^2	*p*	*Task 3* χ^2	*p*
Class	0·25	n.s.	5·68	$<$ 0·02
Class (boys only)	0·02	n.s.	2·10	n.s.
Class (girls only)	0·36	n.s.	2·78	(0·10)
Sex	3·92	0·05	0·11	n.s.

Correlations	*Task 2* *r*	*p*	*Task 3* *r*	*p*	*Combined Tasks* *r*	*p*
Class	−0·029		0·097			
Sex	−0·146	//	−0·109	/		
IQ Crichton	−0·061		0·036			
IQ EPVT	−0·052		−0·040			
New CI	0·006		−0·070			

When a more detailed investigation was made, reverse-polarity tags (type 1) were separated from other socio-centric sequences (type 2). Reverse-polarity tags were found to be much commoner: over the whole schedule, only 25 children used *you*-type SC sequences compared with 84 using reverse-polarity tags. No overall class-differences were evident among the latter, but the distribution of the 25 children using type 2 sequences was as follows:

WC children 20
MC children 5

This difference is significant (χ^2 = 7·01, p = 0·01) and it applies to boys and girls equally.

When the class-difference within Task 3 (mentioned above) was examined, we found that the difference was maintained both for type 1 and type 2 sequences, the distribution being as follows:

Rev.-pol.
WC users 37 (out of 130)
MC users 24 (out of 124) χ^2 = 2·41, p = n.s.
you-type sequences
WC users 15
MC users 4 χ^2 = 5·20, p $<$ 0·03

Notice that although the rev.-pol. difference is not statistically significant, the trend is in the same direction as the *you*-type sequences, and the rev.-pol. type is more frequent.

(2) **Ego-centric tags (Tags 3)**

This category was found to be extremely rare; it was used by 1·5 per cent of the sample in Task 2 and by 5 per cent in Task 3, and occurrences were highly infrequent (rating: 1). Because of this low frequency the figures from both tasks were combined, but no social class or other differences were apparent. The category was used by 10 middle-class and by 6 working-class children; the difference among boys (8 middle-class, 1 working-class) was almost significant ($\chi^2 = 3{\cdot}72$, $p < 0{\cdot}10$) but the numbers are too small to draw any firm conclusions.

Discussion

The results may be summarised as follows:

(i) Among the three types of tag clause recognised, reverse-polarity tags occurred with some frequency in our sample but *you*-type SC sequences and ego-centric sequences were both quite rare.

(ii) A significant class-difference for types 1 and 2 combined (the socio-centrics) was found in Task 3.

(iii) *You*-type sequences showed a significant class-difference over the whole schedule, though its users form only a small percentage (10 per cent) of the sample.

The trend of our results is thus broadly in the same direction as those found earlier by Bernstein and Lawton, but it is clear that the comparative infrequency of tag clauses reduces the significance of our findings. The difference in age between the subjects of our sample (5-year-olds) and theirs (ages 12 and 15) could be partly responsible for the difference in frequency of these tag clauses, but it is more likely to be the *situation* which is the responsible factor. In Bernstein's and Lawton's experiments the subjects discussed, as a group, a topic which was abstract and called for a high degree of generalisation—capital punishment. Both the situation (group discussion) and the topic would impose considerable encoding difficulties on the participants, and a high level of uncertainty, particularly for the working-class groups. Bernstein makes the point thus (1962a, pp. 234–5):

> the uncertainty of the appropriateness of the message, for these groups, in a discussion situation will probably be relatively great. This will add to the sociological strain inherent in producing a verbally individuated message. . . . The unspoken affirmation which the SC signal may receive, reduces the sociological strain upon the speaker. . . . As a consequence, the frequency of SC sequences [in a 'difficult' discussion] may be expected to be great.

By contrast, in our study both the situation (individual interview) and the topics imposed less strain on the participants. First, the pressures which operate in a group discussion, where the speaker has to compete with others and formulate his utterances quickly in order to keep up with the discussion, are absent in an interview, where the speaker is given unlimited time to encode his reply to a question and faces no competition from other speakers. Second, the topics in our study were specific and the material was already prescribed in visual form, which made the speaker's encoding task much easier. Thus both situation and topic imposed lesser strains on our subjects than they imposed on Bernstein's and Lawton's subjects. Our hypothesis, then, based on that of Bernstein, is that the frequency of tag clauses is a function of the degree of strain imposed on the speaker as he encodes his message: the greater the strain, the higher the incidence of tag clauses.

Within our two-task schedule we can distinguish one task from the other in degrees of encoding difficulty. Task 2 is more straightforward because the stories are outlined in detail in their visual form; even the sequence of each story is predetermined by the linear arrangement of the four cards. In Task 3, however, the material is much less constrained and it is up to the individual speaker to determine what to talk about, to decide which features of the picture card are relevant, to organise the data into some sort of sequence, etc. The speaker is faced with a much wider range of choice in this task, which thus makes encoding more difficult.

If our above hypothesis is correct, then, we should find a greater incidence of tag clauses in Task 3, since the material here presents a greater challenge to the speaker. And this is exactly what we do find; the number of socio-centric tags (types 1 and 2 combined) almost doubles (153 in Task 2; 246 in Task 3),[3] and the number of users increases from 22 per cent of the sample in Task 2 to 29 per cent in Task 3. Furthermore, it is in Task 3 that social class differences in usage begin to emerge; socio-centric tags were used by significantly more working- than middle-class children.

The pattern of results from our study and those of Bernstein and Lawton seems to suggest, therefore, that the incidence of tag clauses increases as the degree of social-psychological strain on the speaker increases, as a result of either the situation or the topic or both. With the increase in occurrence, class-differences in the use of tag clauses begin to appear: working-class speakers use more socio-centric, middle-class more egocentric, sequences. In our study we did not find a class-difference for egocentric tags (though the difference for boys only was tentatively significant), but there is evidence from elsewhere that the middle-class children do in fact have something equivalent in function to the egocentric tags: in chapter 7 we see a class-difference in the use of the pronoun *I* in conjunction with verbs of 'tentativeness', eg. *I expect*, *I wonder if*, *I think* followed by rankshifted clause (i.e. not a tag); Turner and Pickvance (1971) have made a thorough investigation of these and other 'expressions of uncertainty', and reach similar conclusions—the incidence is greater among middle-class children. Thus there seems to be a divergence of pattern according to social class: working-class speakers tend to react to uncertainty, or difficulty of encoding, with an increase in socio-centric tags; middle-class speakers with an increase in sequences involving the pronoun *I*, and other devices such as modal verbs (*may*, *might*, etc.), verbs of 'seeming' (it *seems*/-*looks* to *me*), etc. (Turner and Pickvance, 1971).

Notes

[1] The term socio-centric sequence (abbreviated SC) is used by Lawton to cover the same range of items as Bernstein's 'sympathetic circularity' sequences (also abbreviated SC).

[2] For NSC I and II, see Appendix II. The correlation with NSC I is significant, $p < 0{\cdot}05$.

[3] The total output of speech in each task is about the same: 16,715 nominal groups in Task 2, 18,415 in Task 3; thus the proportion of SC tags in Task 3 is much greater. Ego-centric tags are also more frequent in Task 3 (18 occurrences) than in Task 2 (9 occurrences); 13 children used an ego-centric tag in Task 3, compared with only 4 in Task 2. It is worth noting, also, the increase in indefinite pronouns (*someone*, *something*, etc.) in this task—from 115 occurrences in Task 2 to 336 in Task 3.

Chapter 9 Discussion and conclusions

We shall now

(1) briefly summarise the main findings;
(2) present the theoretical framework of, and background to, our study;
(3) discuss our findings in relation to this framework.

(1) A brief summary of the results

In chapter 2 third-person pronouns were divided according to reference type, and the incidence of anaphoric and exophoric reference was observed with respect to these pronouns and to a number of other grammatical categories such as demonstratives. It was predicted, and found, that the exophoric categories correlated significantly with class, more frequent usage being associated with lower social class.

A further finding, which had not been predicted, was that lower-class children also used anaphoric pronouns more frequently (but not anaphoric demonstratives, which were a middle-class phenomenon), and that the likelihood of this increased as a child's total output of speech increased. We suggested that, in Task 2, these results reflected our method of scoring pronouns as anaphoric or exophoric; in longer utterances, pronouns with a referent several clauses away were classified as anaphoric, technically (because their referent had already appeared in the text), even though their effect might be exophoric (i.e. the addressee would still have to retrieve the referent from the general context). The greater use of these quasi-exophorics by lower-class children is thus parallel with their use of 'true' exophorics.

The working-class use of anaphoric pronouns in Task 3, which is not a narrative task, is due partly, but only partly, to a group of working-class girls who interpreted some sections of the task as narrative. The most likely explanation for the high incidence of anaphorics is that it is possible, in this task, to respond without referring to the characters specifically, so that one starts with a general noun (*the people*), or an exophoric (*they*) and continues with undifferentiated *they* and *them*. This interpretation is confirmed by the high incidence of the one-word qualifier *all* (cf. *they all*, *them all*) among working-class speakers.

In general, the results show working-class children oriented towards a type of reference which is less specific and takes for granted a greater degree of common knowledge shared by speaker and addressee.

The converse of this pattern was demonstrated in chapter 3, where we found higher social class correlating with more frequent use of explicit referents, viz. nouns. For Task 3 nouns were subdivided into a 'structured' type where a true alternative to a pronoun or exophoric is given, and an 'unstructured' type where no alternative to a pronoun is likely, as for example in 'lists'. We wanted to know whether middle-class children used more nouns of the former or the latter type. In fact we found they used more of both types, suggesting a general orientation towards nouns which complements the working-class orientation towards pronouns. We must emphasise that the results do *not* indicate that working-class children (or even that *some* working-class children) use pronouns to the exclusion of nouns: the incidence of nouns was high for all children and the class-difference represents quite a small *overall* percentage, even though it is significant statistically (see discussion, chapter 3, *ad fin.*).

In chapter 4 we examined noun modifiers. On the whole it was clear that middle-class children modified nouns more frequently, using categories such as adjectives, nominals, and intensifiers. But when the major category, adjectives, was investigated more closely the class-differences were seen to be concentrated within the 'social-control' sections of Task 2 and not over the schedule as a whole, where the differences were more modest. Results from chapter 6, this time involving adjectives at H, were similar. The number of adjectives involved in the social-control speech is quite small: *naughty*, *bad*, *cross*, and a few others, used by middle-class children with high frequency. Thus, typical middle-class responses to the 'control' probes were:

you're
they're
he's } (very) naughty (boys)

the lady's
the man's
she's/he's
I'm } (very) cross

you
he's a } bad cat

The typical working-class responses to these probes emerged in chapter 7, where we found highly significant differences in the use of imperative forms such as *go away*, *get out*. Other responses to these probes, though less frequent in occurrence than the middle class's attributive adjectives or the working class's imperatives, were regularly associated with one class or the other (see table in chapter 7, p. 170); thus working-class children used first-person pronouns (P1) in threats ('I'll call the police'); middle-class children used P2 in questions ('why did you break my window?') and with 'dare' ('how dare you eat my fish?')—notice that both these responses are verbally, rather than actionally, oriented; middle-class children also used P1 to attribute states or conditions ('I'm hungry'), which again contrasts, as a response, to the imperative type.

Another sub-division of P1, viz. with verbs of uncertainty or tentativeness (*I expect*, *it looks . . . to me*), was found to be associated with middle-class speakers. We found a similar result for indefinite pronouns, especially *someone*, *something*; these pronouns are substitute nouns and can be seen as a means of expressing uncertainty (though cf. Turner, 1973). Their overall occurrence was infrequent in Task 2, where the story-outline is highly constrained, but more frequent in Task 3 where the responses were more open-ended.

In chapter 8 we found that working-class children used more socio-centric tags, particularly in Task 3. These tags are of two kinds, the reverse-polarity type, which was relatively common, and the *you see* type, which was rare. The incidence of these tags, and the significance of the class-differences, increased greatly in Task 3, which again suggests that this task presented greater encoding difficulties than Task 2, since we can regard the tag clauses as another means of expressing uncertainty or hesitation—the speaker seeks confirmation from the addressee.

There was some evidence throughout the study that working-class girls, or perhaps a sub-section of this group, performed differently from the other groups. They had a higher incidence of (1) the hypocoristic *little*, (2) the so-called 'possessive' determiners and rankshifted nominals at M, both of which can be associated with personal/social relationships (*her mother*, *the boy's father*, etc.) rather than with 'possession' of objects. (3) A relatively large group of working-class girls (24 per cent) used narrative speech within the basically descriptive Task 3, compared with only 9 per cent of the children in the other groups. (4) Action-oriented imperatives were used particularly frequently by working-class girls even though they were a feature of working-class speech generally.

Most of these differences are as much a sex-difference within the working class as a difference between working-class girls and the other groups. All of them are consistent with the role which Bernstein (1972) suggests is played by some working-class girls within the family, a role of 'mediation' and control of younger children.

Our study emphasises the importance of defining one's linguistic categories according to both functional and structural criteria rather than on structural criteria alone. Thus, elaboration of a head word by the use of modifiers and/or qualifiers is of much less significance, in itself, than the functions which such elaboration serves. In some cases, for example, qualifiers were found to be associated with exophoric pronouns or with lack of differentiation (*they all*, *them all*) and these were used more frequently by lower-class speakers, thereby contrasting with other qualifiers with different functions, which either showed no class-differences in use or were associated with middle-class speakers. Similarly, certain modifiers such as the adjective *little* were seen to have a distinct function (in this case, hypocoristic, and used most frequently by working-class girls) whereas another sub-group of adjectives also had a clearly distinct function (as exponents of social control) and were strongly associated with middle-class speakers. To treat qualifiers or adjectives as single structural categories would have obscured these important functional differences within each. Recent work by Bernstein and members of the SRU has similarly laid particular emphasis on the value of functional, as opposed to purely structural categories, for example, 'generally, we have regarded as most relevant to our research those grammatical categories which are associated with particular functions. . . . It is thought that, ultimately, functional categories will provide the best bridge between linguistic categories on the one hand and social and psychological ones on the other' (Turner and Mohan, 1970, p. 153: cf. also Turner, 1972).

One cannot, however, dispense entirely with structural criteria for classification: a judicious combination of structure and function is necessary. In our case, we began from a structural basis and then refined these categories according to function.

(2) The theoretical background

The theoretical framework of this study has undergone considerable change during the period of five years or so since its beginning. The changes have come about partly because of the results of the study itself, and partly because of two developments elsewhere, first

Chomsky's distinction between linguistic *competence* and *performance* (and Hymes's (1972) extension of the notion of competence to 'communicative competence'), and second the development of comparable studies of lower-class or Black English in the USA, which has given rise to the 'deficit/difference' controversy.

Chomsky's competence/performance distinction forced us to ask ourselves (a) whether the distinction was relevant to the work we were doing, and (b), if so, whether social class language differences corresponded to differences in competence or in performance. *Competence* in Chomsky's sense of the term (1965, p. 4) refers to the inner knowledge, which we assume the speaker (or hearer) possesses, of a set of syntactic rules which he can use to produce sentences in the language. *Performance* relates to certain limitations in the actual use of language.

> A record of natural speech will show numerous false starts, deviations from rules, changes of plan in mid-course, etc. The problem for the linguist, as well as for the child learning the language, is to determine from the data of performance the underlying system of rules that has been mastered by the speaker-hearer and that he puts to use in actual performance (Chomsky, *ibid.*).

Thus, competence cannot be observed directly—the rules have to be inferred from actual utterances. In a sense, the performance is a superficial manifestation, whereas competence represents deeper or underlying knowledge.

The question for us is this: when we observe or study differences in usage between different groups of speakers, eg. between lower- and middle-class children, are we looking for differences in competence, or in performance? Can Bernstein's restricted codes (RC) and elaborated codes (EC) be formulated in such terms? There are two possibilities: either the children in each group possess different sets of rules (competence), or they possess the same rules but apply them differently to give differences in performance. Bernstein's earlier formulations (up to 1965) of the characteristics of RC and EC have sometimes been interpreted as differences in competence, on the basis of statements like the following: 'in the case of a restricted code the number of these [syntactic] alternatives is often severely limited and the probability of predicting the elements is greatly increased' (Bernstein, 1965, p. 153); 'the lexicon [in a RC] will vary from one case to another but in all cases it is drawn from a narrow range' (*ibid.*, p. 155). One could argue, too, that one has to look for differences in competence, since performance is relatively superficial, whereas the former would have far-reaching effects and could help explain educational underachievement. On the other hand, the codes appear to be concerned with *performance*, in so far as they relate to the way language is *used* by the speaker and not to his ability (or inability) to generate particular syntactic structures. Bernstein's early accounts of code are clearly concerned with language *use*, eg. 'in the previous papers attempts have been made to find a way of analysing some of the inter-relationships between social structure, language use, and subsequent behaviour' (1962, p. 31).

The problem is that if one starts with a hypothesis that two social groups or classes differ in competence, one has great difficulty in proving this because competence cannot be observed directly from actual utterances. One cannot assume that, because a child has not been observed to use a particular syntactic structure, he does not have it within his competence; he may simply have had no occasion to use it. No matter how many utterances one observes, one still cannot conclude that there is a difference in competence, because the very next utterance might contain an example of the structure in question. Again, a single occurrence of that structure would be sufficient to eliminate it from the hypothesis, and the likely outcome from a large corpus would be a complete refutation of the hypothesis. Tests of reception or reproduction for the discovery of competence are also subject to methodological disadvantages.

It seems, then, that a formulation of RC and EC cannot be based on differences of linguistic competence in the Chomskyan sense, and indeed more recently Bernstein has explicitly stated that he is not concerned with this kind of competence as such (1972, p. 475). It seems, in fact, wise to assume that speakers from all social classes, provided they have acquired the language as a first language in the normal way, share essentially the same linguistic competence, with possible minor differences—i.e. they share the same set of underlying rules which enables them to produce sentences in that language.

If this is so, what validity does the RC/EC distinction hold? Is it possible that speakers with the same competence nevertheless have access to different codes? The answer is yes, because we have to recognise that there are other kinds of competence involved in the use of language, over and above purely linguistic competence. The two codes may thus reflect differences in these other kinds of competence (see below, p. 192).

The other major change in the theoretical issues has been the development of the deficit/difference controversy, in which the concepts of RC and EC are more or less directly implicated. A large number of scholars, mainly sociolinguists working on differences between Black and/or lower-class speakers and white middle-class speakers of English in the USA, have directly challenged the widely-held belief that lower-class children have 'less' language or are 'deficient' in language relative to their middle-class counterparts. One of the clearest statements outlining the 'deficit' hypothesis and rejecting it is William Labov's 'The logic of non-standard English' (Labov, 1969b), and I would like to summarise his arguments briefly, first because of their relevance to our study and second because his views appear to be representative of a number of scholars who reject the deficit hypothesis, eg. Wolfram (1971), Ervin-Tripp (1971), Cazden (1971), Baratz (1969), Stewart (1970) and others.

Labov takes his stand against those who argue that non-standard English is an illogical form of speech, and that Negro children from the urban ghettos receive very little verbal stimulation, cannot produce well-formed sentences, and are impoverished in their means of verbal expression. Such arguments are given in a fairly extreme form by Bereiter and Engelmann (1966, pp. 105–11), who base their 'academically-oriented pre-school program' on the hypothesis that these Negro children have virtually no language at all. They maintain that previous efforts to advance the conceptual development of these children have not been successful because the children lack the basic syntactic framework which is essential for the manipulation of concepts. The children must therefore, they believe, be first taught how to produce well-formed sentences, and they suggest (among other things) the use of language-drills which require full sentences in response to questions, eg. *the squirrel is in the tree* in response to *where is the squirrel?* Their linguistic arguments are based on two premises: (1) that Negro children say very little and cannot form connected sentences: they communicate mainly by single words and gestures; (2) that the utterances actually produced are ill-formed, ungrammatical, and above all illogical: examples given are *they mine* and *me got juice*.

This then is the basis of the 'deficit' hypothesis: children from the lowest social classes, particularly Blacks, have 'less' language, they are verbally (as well as culturally) deprived, and what language they do have is badly-formed and illogical. The significance of this position is that it is (or was) widely held by educationalists and formed the basis of major projects like 'Operation Headstart'.

Labov argues that both the premises are false. First, Negro children in fact both receive and produce a large quantity and variety of speech. The reason why this has not been apparent to investigators like Bereiter is because the children see the interview situation (and perhaps the school situation in general) as a threatening one and therefore say as little as possible. But when the right elicitation techniques are used these children are found to be highly verbal. Labov and his colleagues used Black interviewers, de-formalized the interviewer-child relationship, and used groups of subjects instead of individuals, with excellent results:

> the monosyllabic speaker who had nothing to say about anything and cannot remember what he did yesterday has disappeared. Instead we have two boys who have so much to say they keep interrupting each other. . . . And we in turn obtain the volume of speech and the rich array of grammatical devices which we need for analyzing the structure of nonstandard Negro English (1969b, p. 11).

Thus the first premise, that Negro children say little and communicate mainly by gestures or single words, is false: they were simply not motivated properly.

Second, utterances like *they mine*, *me got juice* are not illogical, nor are they ungrammatical: they exhibit regularities but follow a different set of 'rules' from those which generate sentences of standard English. In the sentence *they mine* the copula verb *be* has been deleted, but this is part of a regular process, a normal feature of the dialect. There are other sentences in which the copula would not be deleted, eg. when it occurs at the end, in a sentence like *that's what they are*. The point is that copula deletion is a regular change (and hence 'grammatical');[1] places where it may be absent can be predicted. Negro English thus follows its own set of grammatical rules, which differ in a number of important respects from those of standard English. There is certainly nothing *illogical* about copula-deletion; it is a feature of a number of languages throughout the world, for example Russian.

Third, Labov shows that utterances elicited from Black children when the right techniques are used reveal a richness of syntactic complexity: sentences with embedded clauses, dependent clauses, and comparatives, like

> when they sound on me, I say C.B.M.
> I know who can make magic
> that's who you play with
> anyway, 'Mericans is same like white people, right?

are found quite regularly. Thus there is no foundation to the premise that these children speak in monosyllables and cannot produce well-formed, complete sentences.

In sum, non-standard English is perfectly grammatical in the sense that it is regular, i.e. it can be described according to a set of rules. In most instances the rules can be put alongside an equivalent rule of standard English; the underlying systems of the two dialects are the same[2] but the realisations differ in certain ways. Here, then, we have the basis of the 'difference' hypothesis. Negro English is not 'deficient'; it is simply 'different'. This hypothesis has had a considerable effect on the direction of current linguistic and sociolinguistic research in the USA, which is concentrating on discovering what the differences are (particularly phonological and grammatical differences) and how to formulate underlying rules to describe and compare them (eg. Labov, 1969a; Labov *et al.*, 1968); there is also considerable attention to the historical *origins* of Negro English (cf. the collections of articles in Hymes (1971) and in Wolfram and Clarke (1971)).

Most linguists would, I think, accept Labov's arguments and reject the deficit hypothesis in the form suggested by Bereiter and Engelmann. But Labov's exposition raises a number of points which are open to question. First, there is potential confusion between the capabilities of a dialect (or language) and the capabilities of the individual speakers of that dialect or language. Cazden (1966) writes:

> The question of whether nonstandard dialects are deficient or just different is sometimes glossed over by the statement 'you can say anything in any language'. It may be true that any language has the resources available, in words and grammatical constructions, to encode any meaning in some way [although Hymes, 1961, offers an opposing view]. What is meant by such 'resources' is the contents of a complete dictionary [one must also add 'and grammar']. In this sense English is as good as, but not better than, French or Russian. However, when we shift from the difference between English and French to that between the speech of a middle-class child and a lower-class child, we aren't looking at the total of what is available in language as a set of symbols but only at what is actually used by certain individuals at the moment of framing an utterance. This is one distinction between language and speech, and it's a sign of confusion between the two to inject the idea that 'one language is as good as another' into the controversy over the verbal inadequacies of children in some subcultural groups.

Some of Labov's speakers may have exhibited fluency and complexity of syntax but it is still possible that other speakers do not, just as speakers of the standard dialect may vary in their command of fluency and complexity.[3]

Second, are the dialect differences to which Labov has drawn attention adequate to explain the widespread educational under-achievement, strongly associated with language 'retardation', which has been observed in so many studies, not only in the USA but also in Britain and other parts of the world? Labov argues that educational failure proceeds partly from the educational system itself and especially teachers' attitudes: teachers misinterpret non-standard English as evidence that the child is an 'illogical' and 'non-conceptual' thinker, and their attitudes towards non-standard language engender self-fulfilling prophecies of failure (see Labov, 1969b, pp. 26ff.). Teachers' attitudes are obviously an important factor, and misconceptions among them about language, grammar, 'errors', 'deviant' forms, etc. are no doubt widespread, but there are also many teachers who do not share the prejudices hinted at by Labov, and who are willing to give Negro (or lower-class) children a fair hearing. Teachers' attitudes alone cannot explain the under-performance of lower-class children.

Another factor mentioned by Labov is the influence of the peer-group, which serves to reinforce the use of non-standard forms and thus works against the teaching of standard English which the school is trying to promote; but unless one can show that the use of non-standard language is a direct cause of educational under-achievement, one has not reached the heart of the problem—and Labov does not show this. To put it another way: if the entire school system were to switch over to non-standard English, would Negro and lower-class children suddenly become spectacular educational successes? It seems very unlikely. Dialect differences, in themselves, and attitudes towards them, are insufficient to explain the observed differences in educational performance. Cazden (1970, p. 40) writes:

> The inadequacy of both the 'less language' and the 'different language' characterizations is two-fold. First, both refer only to patterns of structural form and ignore patterns of use in actual speech events. Secondly, they assume that the child learns only one way to speak which is reflected in the same fashion and to the same extent at all times. On both theoretical and practical grounds, we can no longer accept such limitations.

Cf. also Engelmann's comments on the relevance of dialect differences (1971, p. 149).

Third, Labov associates Bernstein with the 'deficit' model: thus 'the notion [that lower-class Negro children have no language at all] is first drawn from Bernstein's writings that "much of LC language consists of a kind of incidental 'emotional' accompaniment to action here and now" ' (1969, p. 4),[4] and later 'is the elaborated code of Bernstein really so "flexible, detailed and subtle" as some psychologists believe?' (*ibid.*, p. 12). The association of Bernstein with the deficit model is somewhat unjustified, since Bernstein goes to some length to emphasize that lower-class speech should *not* be regarded as deficient, but as simply different from the codes available to middle-class children. Thus, 'a RC does not necessarily affect the *amount* of speech, only its form' (1965, footnote to p. 156). 'Some children have access to no other code; their only code is a restricted one. Clearly one code is not better than another; each possesses its own aesthetic, its own possibilities' (*ibid.*, p. 164).

This point is worth pursuing a little further, however, since at many points in the 1965 article Bernstein makes statements which give the appearance that restricted codes are deficient. To the two quotes given earlier (p. 186) about the 'severely limited number of syntactic alternatives' and the 'lexicon drawn from a narrow range' may be added statements like 'on a psychological level the codes may be distinguished by the extent to which each facilitates (EC) or inhibits (RC) an orientation to symbolize intent in a verbally explicit form' (*ibid.*, p. 153). Phrases like 'a low level of vocabulary and syntactic selections', 'a limited and often rigid use of qualifiers (adjectives, adverbs etc.)' which are applied to RC, contrast with phrases like 'a complex conceptual hierarchy for the organization of experience', 'a higher level of syntactic organization and lexical selection', 'the code will facilitate the verbal transmission and elaboration of the individual's unique experience' to describe an elaborated code.

Does this mean that Bernstein is really proposing a deficit model, similar to Bereiter's? I think not. Bernstein's model *does* involve a 'deficit' but it is quite a different kind of deficit from Bereiter's. The 'verbal deprivation', 'these children have no language' approach amounts to suggesting a deficiency in linguistic competence as defined by Chomsky: the speakers do not have access to the inner knowledge of syntactic rules which is necessary to produce sentences in the language. Bernstein's deficiency would not be in linguistic competence but in some other kind of competence which involves the actual *use* of language.

What other kinds of competence are there? Hymes uses the term 'communicative competence' to add a most important sociolinguistic dimension to the notion of linguistic competence. He argues that a child learning a language masters not only a set of syntactic rules for providing sentences but also a set of sociolinguistic rules for the appropriate *use* of language in context. Imagine a child, he says, whose ability is confined to linguistic competence only. Such a child would go around uttering perfectly grammatical sentences at random, totally unrelated to any context or situation; he would almost certainly end up in a mental institution (cf. Hymes, 1972, pp. 277 ff). Thus it is just as much a part of a child's competence to know what to say, when, and to whom, as it is to be able to produce grammatical sentences. Linguistic competence is, in fact, only part of the much broader 'communicative competence' which the child acquires. Children from different social backgrounds and with different abilities may acquire either different types of competence or different degrees of the same competence.

Once the notion of competence is broadened in this way, we can see, I think, that restricted and elaborated codes represent differences in some aspects of communicative competence rather than in a narrowly linguistic competence *per se*. A restricted code is concerned with syntactic and lexical *predictability*: the speaker may have access to (i.e. competence to handle) any particular syntactic structure or lexical item but he is not likely to use a very wide range of them in any particular situation, i.e. the structures and vocabulary will be relatively predictable to an observer who is given information about the situation, the participants, the topic, the setting, etc. When an EC is being used, the syntax and vocabulary are less predictable to the observer even when the same information is given. In a RC the speaker does not make full use of the structures he actually has within his competence.[5] Thus the child who has access only to restricted codes lacks the ability to handle an elaborated code: in this sense, Bernstein *is* concerned with a 'deficit'. It is important, however, to distinguish between this and the kind of deficit Bereiter envisages. This distinction has not, I think, been sufficiently emphasised hitherto. The results of our present study will help to clarify the question further.

(3) The implications of the present study

The background to our present study has now, I think, been sufficiently sketched. We took as the basis of our hypothesis the outline of restricted and elaborated codes as presented in Bernstein (1965) together with the previously reported empirical work (Bernstein, 1962b; Lawton, 1963, 1964). In studying samples of speech from a large number of children differing in social class origins, we expected to find differences in the *frequency* with which particular syntactic patterns were used, since the codes had been defined in terms of *predictability* and the range of syntactic (and lexical) options available. We anticipated that children higher in the social scale would use patterns associated with *complexity* and with *elaboration* more frequently; these two concepts are, of course, not precisely defined but indicate such features as the use of passives, complex verbal stems, non-spatiotemporal prepositions (cf. Bernstein, 1962b); within the confines of the nominal group we expected a greater frequency of rankshifted clauses, of nouns and of 'elaborations' associable with the noun, viz. modifying adjectives, nominals, qualifiers, etc.

Our actual findings were these: first, there was no evidence that the lower-class children were 'verbally deprived' in the sense that they said very little or uttered one-word sentences, etc. The correlations of total nominal groups (which is a reliable index of the total output of speech) with all indices of social class were very low in value and showed no significant relationship,[6] i.e. the total output of speech is not affected by social class. This result is important because it shows that the working-class children were not inhibited by the presence of a middle-class interviewer as far as output of speech was concerned. The cultural divergence between Black and White in the USA, which appears to be so inhibiting for Black children as to necessitate elaborate counter-measures, thus seems to have no parallel in the situation we are studying.

Second, the conclusion was forced upon us, many times, that rather than looking for differences in syntactic categories themselves, regardless of context, we had to relate our findings to the particular situation in which the categories were being used. The frequency of adjectives was an outstanding example of this. Adjectives are indicative of elaboration of the nominal group—they represent an available option—and according to our predictions they should have been a feature of middle-class speech. We did find, in fact, that middle-class children used adjectives more frequently both at M and at H, but only in Task 2. When we investigated, it became clear that the differences were confined mainly to the three adjectives *naughty*, *bad* and *cross*, which the middle-class children were using in a particular, tightly defined situation, namely the social-control speech of Task 2. The only meaningful interpretation that could be given to this difference was in terms of what working-class children did instead, in this situation. So we observed their responses, and found that they employed an entirely different strategy of social control, centred mainly around the use of imperative forms of the verb.

Another example of this is the use of rankshifted clauses. Rankshifted clauses involve embedding, and hence a certain degree of complexity. They should therefore have appeared as a feature of middle-class speech, but only a very slight relationship, confined to one task, was observed. A closer investigation showed that only rankshifted clauses involved in expressions of uncertainty or tentativeness (*I think . . .*, *I expect . . .*, etc.) showed class-differences; in other words the incidence of rankshifted clauses is determined by the function they are performing, and has nothing to do with their complexity as such.

Our evidence is, then, superficially compatible with Labov's contention that there are no social class differences in linguistic competence. Working-class children appear to have access to as wide a range of syntactic options as middle-class children: potentially, they can produce and interpret the same set of grammatical sentences, by drawing on an underlying competence which differs very little.

Our evidence also shows that the concept of restricted and elaborated codes must be modified to take strict account of the situation, or rather of the functions to which the speech is actually put. Bernstein's earlier formulation of the codes suggested that the syntax and lexicon of an RC would be drawn from a predictably narrow range, regardless of the individual speech function; likewise, an EC would draw on a wide range, irrespective of the situation. The result of subsequent research has led to a more cautious formulation, in linguistic terms, of the two codes. Thus,

> it is clear that context is a major control upon syntactic and lexical selections, consequently, it is not easy to give general linguistic criteria for the isolation of the two codes. Derivations from the theory would be required in order to describe syntactic and lexical usage by any one speaker in a specific context (Bernstein, 1972, p. 474).

Given the need to modify the concept of code, we can go on to suggest an alternative formulation of the hypothesis by introducing the notion of verbal strategies. Thus we can make the following proposal: given a particular speech function, or context, different speakers, by virtue of differences in their social origins, or experience of role-relationships, etc., may employ different *strategies* of communication. To understand what is meant by this term, let us take a simple, hypothetical example: the particular context of answering the telephone (cf. Schegloff, 1968). Observation of a large number of subjects reveals one group of speakers (group A) whose strategy is to pick up the receiver and give their exchange and number. Another group (B) says 'Hullo. XY (First Name and Last Name) speaking.' A third group (C) gives no information of this kind but uses a conventional opening phrase such as 'are you there?'[7] or 'Speak, for thy servant heareth'. Observation of social origins and background reveals that group A have all been to private schools, group B are members of a sizeable immigrant minority and group C are lower-middle-class housewives (these three groups are not exhaustive). Let us assume that the conversations subsequent to these opening gambits reveal no group-differences in the range or frequency of syntactic structures used.

What we can see in this hypothetical example is a significant correlation between (a) strategy of communication, as manifested by a series of linguistic options, and (b) information on social or educational background. The correlation may have important consequences within the society itself; if so, its existence will probably be known by the speakers, who may all agree that the exchange plus number is the 'best' response, which should be taught in the schools, etc. But the point is that the correlation, on the linguistic side, is independent of both the linguistic competence of the speakers *and* the range or frequency of syntactic forms which they actually use (as demonstrated by their subsequent utterances); it has no consequences for what the speakers can say and habitually do say elsewhere, yet it is a linguistic phenomenon which correlates with sociological data. We can see that it is also independent of dialects such as standard and non-standard, since dialect differences are possible even within the short phrases given; group A speakers may divide into those who say 'this is Exton 4060' (standard) and those who say 'this Exton 4060' (non-standard deletion of copula); in group B we may have *speaking* (standard) *v. speakin'* (non-standard—a phonological difference); etc.

Thus, strategies of communication, in a particular context or function, may be manifest linguistically and correlate with social background, yet be independent of linguistic competence, range of syntactic and lexical options available, and dialects.[8]

In our present study we have found evidence of strategies of this kind. The results showed four major areas of social-class differences in strategy:

(i) In a situation where children were required to narrate a story from a set of pictures, the working-class children's strategy was oriented to the use of all categories of exophoric reference, and of anaphoric third-person pronouns, at the expense of nouns. The middle-class strategy was oriented towards the noun.

(ii) In a situation where children were required to describe a detailed picture, the same set of strategies appeared.

(iii) In a situation which elicited patterns of verbal social control, middle-class children used a strategy of what might be called 'appeals' of the type 'you're naughty boys', 'the lady's cross', and to a lesser extent, 'questions' ('why did you break the window?') whereas working-class children used a strategy of imperatives ('go away', 'come here') and to a lesser extent, 'direct threats' ('wait till I catch you').

(iv) Where encoding difficulty was encountered (in Task 3), middle-class children used verbs of tentativeness associated with first-person pronouns (*I expect, it seems to me*), and indefinite pronouns, where the pronoun represents a substitute noun (*someone, something*), more frequently than the working-class children, who tended to use socio-centric tags, mainly the reverse-polarity type (*isn't it, don't they*, etc.) but also the *you see* type.

Here, then, we have four situations, or contexts, in each of which we find different strategies of response, correlating with social class.

These verbal strategies, as we have called them, are in some respects similar to what Bernstein (1969) calls *speech variants*, though the precise definition of the latter term has not been clarified (see footnote 9, below). Bernstein suggests that, given a particular context, children of different backgrounds are likely to respond differently. He is arguing, in this instance, against the notion of verbal deprivation: thus, the fact that the responses may be different does not mean that one group of children are non-verbal, since they 'possess the same tacit understanding of the linguistic rule system as any children' (1969, p. 197). To illustrate the argument he uses two examples, firstly the exophoric *v.* noun realization of narrative (which we have discussed in this study); and second, differences in patterns of maternal control, where 'one mother . . . wishes to make explicit . . . certain rules and the reasons for the rules, and their consequences', while another mother 'places less emphasis on language . . ., and deals with only the particular act and does not relate this to general principles . . .' (1969, p. 195). In both examples we find people of different social background responding to the same context in different ways. Bernstein then introduces the term 'speech variant', which he defines as 'a pattern of linguistic choices which is specific to a particular context'. Clearly, the definition of 'speech variant' here, and the forementioned examples cited to illustrate it, are parallel to the definition of 'verbal strategy' and the examples which I have outlined.[9]

Bernstein goes on to argue that there is a higher-order concept of 'code', which determines the choice of a particular speech variant in a particular context; i.e. the fact that working-class children choose exophorics in one context is not unrelated to the fact that they prefer 'imperative' control in another; both are manifestations of the same underlying code, which determines these choices.

To determine whether such higher-order codes exist is a more difficult problem, for which the evidence of this study is insufficient. We can, however, examine the problem of drawing generalisations from the evidence we have so far accumulated, i.e. of generalising from one set of situations to others.[10]

I think that, in this study, we have tackled the problem of relating the results to a set of particular situations, yet at the same time we have not lost generalisability, because we can relate our linguistic findings to the sociological background of the speakers along the lines suggested by Bernstein. Take the example of the two strategies, exophorics *v.* nouns. The widespread use of exophorics assumes that the addressee shares in the speaker's knowledge of the situation to such an extent that a high degree of verbal explicitness is unnecessary. Working-class children make this assumption in a much stronger form than middle-class children, in both the situations we studied. Why do they do this? Bernstein suggests that 'the most general condition for the emergence of [a restricted] code is a social relationship based upon a common, extensive set of closely-shared identifications and expectations . . . the common cultural identity reduces the need to verbalize intent [or make it explicit]' (1965, p. 155). I am not suggesting that our evidence shows that the working-class children are confined to a set of restricted codes: my point is that the use of exophorics follows logically from the hypothesis that 'closely-shared identifications and expectations' are a stronger characteristic of working-class social relationships than of middle-class social relationships. We can either use the social background to *explain* the linguistic evidence, *or* we can use the latter to confirm a hypothesis about the former. We must be careful to avoid circularity, but if we take our linguistic evidence as partial confirmation of the sociological hypothesis, we can then make further predictions as follows: in other situations or speech functions, working-class children will tend to be less explicit in their verbal formulation; they will convey a lesser amount of explicit information.

Thus, by relating verbal strategies to social background, we are able to give the strategies a more general validity: they have predictive power for other situations or functions. Our evidence of different verbal strategies of social control may also have more general implications when it is related to social background. The fact that the children offer different strategies suggests that they themselves experience different strategies within their own families or community. This in turn has consequences for the patterns of communication between mothers and children in different social classes (Cook-Gumperz, 1973; Turner, 1972) and may have educational consequences (Bernstein, 1971, 1972).

The kind of explanation which relates differences of verbal strategy to differences in social background is, in my opinion, the only kind of explanation which is adequate. Having published, in 1969, a preview of the findings in this study,[11] I have had the advantage of hearing and reading alternative explanations for our results. Mostly these have been in terms of the situations themselves and the way the children perceive them. For example, it has been said that the working-class children, in using exophoric reference direct to the pictures themselves, are taking advantage of a situation in which the interviewer can also see the pictures, so that their strategy is, in a sense, more efficient.[12] It is certainly true that the interviewer, sitting across the table, could also see the pictures, although the pictures, of course, faced the child. The point may be valid (I believe it is not—see below, pp. 204ff.) but it still does not *explain* why the difference in strategy falls according to social class. The question of which strategy is more efficient is independent of the causes which give rise to the strategies in the first place.

Ervin-Tripp (1971) also makes the point that the interviewer could see the pictures, but suggests that the different verbal strategies result from differences in perception of the situation. Thus, the middle-class children realise that they are required to 'tell what they know'—i.e. they understand the *purpose* of the interview—whereas the working-class children are baffled. Thus

> Labov has cited examples illustrating the bewilderment of a child taken into a room by a tester and told to 'say what is in front of you' when both the tester and the child can see quite well what it is. The implication is that children may have learned that the function of such communication is to convey information. If they have not been brought up on 'known-answer' questions and taught to display their vocabulary and disregard whether the hearer knows the information, they may not understand the intent of such questions (1971, p. 50).

First, however, there is no indication in our study that the working-class children were bewildered. Bewilderment normally results in silence, but both social class groups gave a comparable output of speech. Second, the point about the middle class *displaying* their knowledge is a valid one, but again, *why* are they better able to do it? For an explanation, we must go back to their social origins and to patterns of socialisation, maternal communication, etc. which differ according to social class. In the other direction, the implications for education are obvious, because the educational system is founded on the child's ability to *display* his knowledge—he is constantly being tested and examined. Communication itself is a form of display—a display of knowledge, of opinions, of feelings, of attitudes, etc. by the speaker towards the addressee(s). Communicative competence can be thought of as the ability to make the right display in the right context. Thus, the question of display is simply another way of looking at the implications of different verbal strategies; it does not provide an *explanation* of our findings.

I have suggested, above, that an adequate explanation for the class differences in verbal strategies must be in terms of social relationships, patterns of communication and control within the family, etc. But how, specifically, might the two different strategies, exophoric *v.* nouns, arise? Two explanations may be suggested: the first based on patterns of adult usage, the second on patterns of communication between adults, particularly those within the family, and children.

First, it is possible that adult members of a working-class community use exophoric reference in a wider variety of situations and to a wider range of participants, etc. than adult members of the middle-class groups. In this case the children's greater use of exophorics is simply a reflection of typical parental patterns. This explanation would be consistent with the closer-knit structure of working-class communities, which facilitates the sharing of assumptions and of background knowledge and hence enables reference to be relatively inexplicit without destroying the basis of communication.

The difficulty of this explanation is that although the working-class communities as a whole are more tightly structured and close-knit than middle-class groups, there is no reason to suppose that the individual, nuclear working-class family is more tightly knit than the individual middle-class family; in both, shared knowledge and its consequence, inexplicit reference, can be expected to be high; but it is the individual family, rather than the wider community, which influences most strongly the speech patterns acquired by the child. On the other hand, one could argue that the speaker needs to be most explicit when shared background is lessened, so that contacts outside the immediate family assume considerable importance; working-class adults, in belonging to a close-knit wider community, undergo less pressure towards explicit reference than middle-class adults, whose extra-familial contacts are more diverse, and perhaps less well-known or at a greater social 'distance', and hence cannot be assumed to share the same extent of background information. Thus, middle-class children would frequently be exposed to relatively explicit speech patterns towards addressees from outside the family, and this would become established as 'the way of speaking to outsiders'; lower-class children, however, would hear essentially the same patterns for 'outsiders' as for members of the immediate family, since these 'outsiders' share the same set of background assumptions and are, indeed, regarded rather as extensions of the family than as 'outsiders'.

The second explanation, rather than referring to parental patterns as a *model* for the children, focusses on patterns of communication between parents (in particular—other adults to a lesser extent) and children, along the lines developed in some depth by Bernstein (1971, 1972). Bernstein indicates that different types of verbal interaction between parents and children promote different cognitive, linguistic and social orientations in the children. So far as exophoric *v.* non-exophoric reference is concerned, then, we can suggest that the differences we have found here are the result of different types of communication within the family.

We can illustrate the way different patterns of communication might operate with a specific example. Imagine a situation, for example, in which a child says 'look, mummy, he's broken that'. This utterance contains two exophoric items, *he* and *that*. One mother may accept the communication as it stands; another may reject it with a reply like 'who's broken what?', thereby forcing the child to be more explicit ('the boy next door's broken that cup'). If the mother (or any other addressee with whom the child communicates regularly) tolerates exophorics in a wide variety of situations, the child's usage of them will persist (this assumes that the child has a 'natural' inclination to use exophorics in the first place—see below); but if the addressees reject exophorics in certain situations, the child learns to discriminate the contexts (and perhaps also the participants: some addressees may be more tolerant of exophorics than others) in which they will be tolerated, from those in which they will not. If he assesses the context as one for which an exophoric reference is not appropriate (i.e. will not be accepted by the addressee), he switches to a noun (or to other more explicit forms, such as nominalisations), thereby identifying the referent. In this way, typical patterns of communication which are established between a child and his addressees may influence the type of response which the child will select in a given situation.

In order to relate this explanation to our empirical findings, we would then have to assume that in working-class families the parents (or other addressees) tend to tolerate this kind of ambiguous reference in a wider range and variety of situations than middle-class parents. Such an assumption actually fits in quite well with evidence we already have concerning the type of parent-child communication which takes place within the different social class groups, most of which suggests that lower-class parents are less inclined either to impart information to, or receive it from, their children. This evidence may be briefly reviewed.

(1) The New Communication Index, which has been used as one of the independent 'sociological' variables in our study, is based on

five indices whose aim was to discover possible differences in parent-child interaction patterns; Dorothy Henderson found highly significant class-differences in the two indices which are particularly concerned with information-oriented, or 'cognitive', communication, viz. the 'Avoidance' and 'Verbal Interaction' schedules.

In the former, the mothers were presented with eight questions which a child is likely to ask, and invited to choose from a number of responses ranging from complete evasion to 'taking the opportunity to discuss the matter with him'. Working-class mothers were found to be much more likely to avoid the question or give an evasive reply, than middle-class mothers ($p = 0{\cdot}001$). In the latter ('Verbal Interaction') schedule, the mothers were asked for their response when the child initiated a dialogue in a number of typical contexts—the responses ranging from 'tell him to stop' to 'chat with him'. The results showed that middle-class mothers were more likely to respond by chatting to the child, less likely to put him off (Henderson, 1970).

(2) In a further schedule of Henderson's study, mothers were asked for the kind of definition they would give to their children to explain the meanings of the particular words *cool*, *mix*, *dangerous*, *flexible*. The mothers were offered a choice of strategies ranging from a rather un-specific concrete example (eg. for *dangerous*: it's dangerous to play with fire) to an abstract general definition (eg. for *flexible*: something that will bend without breaking); and they were allowed to employ two strategies, eg. a general definition, followed by a concrete example. Henderson found that

> according to the mothers' reports, MC mothers relative to WC mothers
> (a) favour abstract definitions
> (b) favour *explicit* rather than implicit 'concrete' definitions
> (c) favour information-giving strategies in answer to children's questions.
> They avoid or evade answering questions much less (Henderson, 1970, pp. 327, 330).

(3) In a number of studies, Robinson and Rackstraw have shown that middle-class mothers answer their children's questions more fully: thus,

> for two *where from* and four *why* questions it was predicted and found that, relative to lower-working-class mothers, MC mothers evaded fewer questions, gave more accurate information in their answers, gave a greater amount of information, . . . and gave different types of answer to *why* questions: they were more likely

> to use appeals to higher-order categories, analogies, cause and consequences, but less likely to repeat the question as its own answer or make appeals to the simple regularity of events. *The answers of the LWC mothers could be construed as having the function of controlling rather than informing* (Robinson, 1972) (my italics).

When the study was extended from mothers to 7-year-old children, similar and additional results were found—i.e. the class-differences found for the mothers were replicated for the children (Robinson and Rackstraw, 1971, chapters 7, 8). In a recent study concerned with children's answers to questions, Robinson notes that middle-class girls[13] are 'less likely to mention places by colloquial names outside their listeners' knowledge' (1972, p. 218). The latter is a clear parallel to our findings on the use of exophorics.

There is, therefore, an accumulation of evidence to suggest that parent-child communication among the working class is less oriented towards those cognitive aspects which involve greater amounts of information, as in explanations and answers to questions. It is thus probable that working-class parents similarly have a higher level of tolerance towards the use of exophorics by their children, with the result that these children have less opportunity to discriminate between situations (and participants) in which explicit reference is essential, and those in which exophoric reference is adequate.

There is a further factor to take into consideration in this question of tolerance or rejection of exophorics: the addressee who rejects exophorics may be seen to be issuing a challenge to the child's offered mode of communication. Whether this challenge is seen as an expression of hostility[14] or not will depend to some extent on the child's previous experience of such challenges. Where they are a normal, regular feature of parent-child interaction, the child is affected in two ways: first, he adapts his own speech so that it contains fewer exophorics; he learns which sorts of situation call for explicit reference and which do not (i.e. there are always some situations where the referent is obvious and exophorics will be accepted); second, he learns that this required shift towards a cognitive (or high-information) component is *not* a shift away from the solidarity of his relationship with the addressee, i.e. that it is *not* intended as an expression of hostility. The child whose addressees are more tolerant of exophorics, however, will not only continue to use them in a wider range of situations, but may also interpret as hostility any attempt to challenge this usage.

If it is the case, then, that working-class families permit greater use of exophorics and lay particular emphasis on the controlling, rather than the informing, functions of interaction (cf. Robinson, 1972, cited above), then a working-class child entering school, and meeting demands for explicitness, may interpret these as a form of rejection. Here, then, we have another way in which the expectations of the school may conflict with the child's previous socialising experience (cf. Bernstein, 1971).

It was suggested, above, that children are predisposed in the first place to use exophorics, and will continue to use them extensively unless otherwise directed. This assumption requires some explanation; it is based on the premise that, from the child's point of view, in many situations an exophoric is more economical and involves less effort than a corresponding noun. Use of a noun involves choosing from a wide range of possibilities. With an exophoric, the burden of interpretation of the referent is shifted from the speaker to the addressee. As Joan Tough (1969, p. 12) puts it,[15]

> the child's facility in using language is tremendously increased between the ages of about two and a half and three years by the acquisition of the small closed set of pronouns. It is on the one hand an important triumph in generalization, but on the other hand it relieves him of searching for reference through the more extensive class of nouns.

Since, then, it often involves less effort on the speaker's part to use an exophoric reference, the likelihood is that once a child has mastered the use of pronouns (and other items of substitution or deixis like *this*, *that*, *here*) he will make maximum permitted use of them; the reversion to high-information items such as nouns in certain contexts can then be seen partly as the result of pressure, as it were, from outside—from addressees who, in one way or another, direct the child to use more explicit reference.

Evaluation of the verbal strategies

The question of whether one verbal strategy is 'better' than the other (eg. exophorics versus nouns) has to be answered in relation to the specific tasks the children were asked to perform.[16] The problem of whether, *in general*, exophorics are 'better', 'more efficient', etc. than nouns appears to contain a paradox; on the one hand, exophorics have a low information content and may thus be seen as less effective; on the other hand, if the referent is obvious to both speaker and addressee, identification of it by a noun is redundant and the exophoric item becomes more efficient. Everything depends, therefore, on the specific situation in which the items are to be used; if the referent is obvious to the addressee, the speaker can avoid redundancy by using an exophoric; if not, or if there is likely to be ambiguity, effective communication is achieved by specifying the referent by name; this involves more effort for the speaker but less for the addressee. The speaker has to assess each situation on its merits, and this assessment can be seen as an element of his communicative competence—his knowledge of what is appropriate to the particular situation.

Our study presented two situations in which the speaker had to choose his verbal strategy. In the first (Task 2), he was asked to tell a story based on a series of pictures. The interviewer's introduction was as follows: 'I've got some pictures that tell a story. I'm going to show them to you and I want you to tell me the story.' This seems to be a situation which calls for a relatively high information content. A story with exophoric, non-specific reference ('they're kicking that and it goes through there') is less satisfactory, as a story, than one which specifies the characters and objects ('three boys are kicking a football'). Furthermore, we found that working-class children use more anaphoric pronouns as well as the exophoric categories, so it is clear that the total amount of information which is being communicated, verbally, is less for the working-class than for the middle-class children. Similarly, in Task 3 where the children are asked to describe what is going on in the picture, the total amount of information transmitted decreases as pronoun usage increases. Both tasks are seeking information, and the introduction asks specifically that the information be transmitted verbally ('I want you to tell me the story', 'tell me what's going on in this picture').

The choice between the other verbal strategies, 'imperative' *v.* 'appeal', and 'tag clause' *v.* 'tentative', is more difficult to evaluate. Here, it is not clear that, in a particular situation or in general, one strategy is 'better' than the other—they are simply different strategies, which may be equally effective within the respective families or communities in which they are used. Some likely consequences of the 'imperative' *v.* 'appeal' modes are put forward by Bernstein (1972, pp. 490 ff). The issues raised here, of course, go beyond any purely linguistic considerations; thus, if one school, or one group of teachers within a school, rely mainly on 'appeal' types of strategy, children from families who use predominantly 'imperative' strategies will be at a disadvantage and there will be a conflict between the expectations of teacher and child, as Bernstein argues on a number of occasions (eg. 1969, pp. 196–7). On the other hand there may well be schools, especially in working-class areas, where the predominant control strategies, developed through many years of experience, are 'imperative'. In this case there will be a conflict of expectations for children normally exposed to 'appeal' types of strategy, and there may be difficulties for newly-appointed teachers with middle-class backgrounds, who will be unfamiliar with 'imperative' means of control. I would argue that we should not assume that all schools project middle-class values and employ basically middle-class means of control.

'Dialects' v. 'codes'

I mentioned earlier that verbal strategies of communication are independent of dialects such as standard and non-standard English: strategies A, B or C could be pursued in dialects X, Y or Z. This point needs to be emphasised because it has often been assumed that studies such as those of Labov and others in the USA are comparable with those of, for example, Bernstein and his associates (cf. Kochman, 1969—quoted in Cazden, 1970, p. 56).

The comparison has arisen largely because the term *social dialect* is used to include both the Labov-type and the Bernstein-type studies. The difference between strategies, or codes, on the one hand and dialects on the other can however be formulated quite simply and neatly in linguistic terms: where dialects are concerned, direct 'translation-equivalents' in each dialect are normally possible; where codes or strategies are concerned, no direct 'translation' is possible. Putting this another way, the sentence or structures of non-standard English can be related by transformational rules to equivalent sentences of standard English: rules can be devised to produce the non-standard structure from the standard, or vice versa; alternatively, both versions can be derived from an underlying structure by a set of rules which diverge at some point to yield the observed differences in surface structure.

We can see how this works in particular cases. Frequently-cited examples of non-standard forms are:

(a) deletion of possessive's: *Johnny car* (cf. standard *Johnny's car*);
(b) deletion of copula (*this mine/this is mine*);
(c) use of *it* or *they* instead of unstressed *there* (*it's a policeman/-there's a policeman*);
(d) objective for subjective form of pronoun (*her lazy/she's lazy*);
(e) multiple negatives (*we ain't never had no trouble about none of us pulling out no knife or nothing/we've never had any trouble about any of us pulling out a knife or anything*).

Notice how, in each case, a direct 'translation' from one dialect to the other is quite straightforward: given a knowledge of the rules, one can convert non-standard forms to standard *and vice versa*. The latter condition is important (see below).

Where strategies of communication are being compared, however, syntactic rules relating one to the other cannot be formulated. If one takes, for example, the observed strategies of social control, 'imperative' versus 'appeal', there are no rules which will yield *go away, get out* from *you naughty boys, the lady's cross*, or vice versa. Any attempt to derive these surface structures from underlying forms would have to begin from the underlying *speech function* (in this case, social control) rather than from underlying syntactic structures.[17] The case of the strategies *exophoric* versus *noun* is slightly different: when the sentences are formulated with fully explicit reference items (nouns) it is possible to derive, by syntactic rules, the translation-equivalent in exophorics, eg.

(a) three men are building the house

becomes

(b) they're building that

But the reciprocal relationship does not hold: given sentence (b), one cannot derive sentence (a) by syntactic rules. In some cases, therefore, a one-way relationship between strategies is possible, but strategies cannot be reciprocally determined.

Strategies can thus be distinguished from dialects on the basis of (1) reciprocality: given the form in one dialect, one can predict or derive the form in the other, and vice versa. In the case of strategies, reciprocal prediction and derivation is not possible, though one-way prediction may sometimes be possible, as in the example of nouns-to-exophorics above.

(2) Derivation (the corollary of (1)): strategies can be derived from underlying speech functions; dialects from underlying syntactic structures. These relationships may be presented diagrammatically as shown in Figure 1.

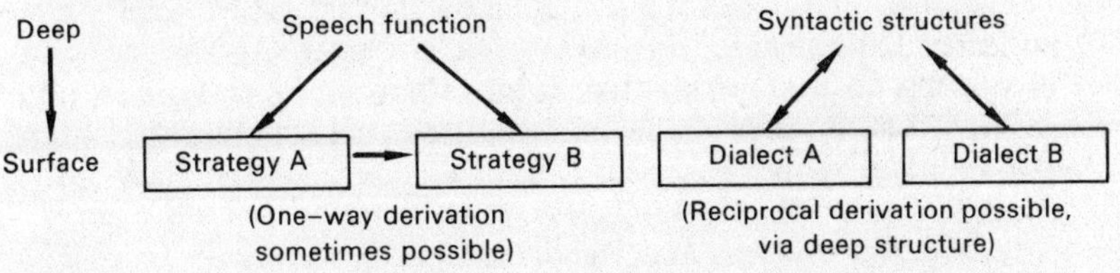

Figure 1

Once the difference between strategies and dialects is appreciated, we can perceive the ambiguity of the term *social dialect*, which has often been used to describe the field as a whole, including the theoretical and empirical work of both Bernstein and Labov (and their associates). Strictly speaking, it is Labov who is concerned with social dialect in the sense in which the term *dialect* is normally used, because Labov has shown that the kind of grammatical and phonological differences which have long been known to exist *regionally* (the traditional sense of *dialect*) can also occur *socially*, between different sub-cultural groups, within a single 'region', eg. New York City. Bernstein, on the other hand, is concerned with the functions of language in different contexts, for which the term (*social*) *dialect* is not appropriate.[18]

The role of IQ and CI in accounting for variance

Of the 'background' variables in this study, social class has received the most attention, and little has so far been said about the role of IQ and CI in the determination of linguistic choices and their effectiveness as indices of the children's performance. It remains, therefore, to consider briefly the significance of these two variables.

(1) *The communication index*

The CI normally has correlation (r) values considerably lower than those for social class, with two exceptions: CI has a higher value for anaphoric P3 in Task 2 (for CI, $p = 0{\cdot}06$; for class, p = not significant), and for nominal modifiers in Task 3 (for CI, $p = 0{\cdot}10$; for class, p = not significant), as may be verified from the correlation tables in Appendix II. In the latter instance, however, CI still does not have the highest value; it is actually IQ which accounts for most of the variance here (for Crichton, $p < 0{\cdot}001$; for EPVT, $p = 0{\cdot}002$). Hence the result for anaphoric P3 in Task 2, where CI does have the highest r value, appears isolated, particularly since it is not maintained in Task 3.

The fact that CI normally achieves lower values than class indicates that one of its aims, viz. to act as a more sensitive measure of communication within the family than social class, was not realised. The most probable explanation for this is that the index discriminates more sensitively within one area of the class spectrum, i.e. within the working class, than within the middle class, as is reported by Brandis and Henderson (1970, chapter 3, especially pp. 105 ff, 111 ff). Thus when the index is applied to the sample as a whole the relative homogeneity of the middle-class scores prevents the index from predicting language variance as effectively as social class itself does. Recent developments and modifications to the index have tried to overcome some of these problems, and to devise measures which will be sensitive across the whole spectrum of social class.

(2) *IQ*

There are two main reasons why social class has been given more attention than the other 'background' categories; first, it is clear that it accounts for more of the linguistic variance than any other category. This was one of the major findings of the computer analysis reported in Part I, and it is also evident in the results in Part II, where the correlations with class are normally higher in value than with IQ or CI (cf. the table of correlation values in Appendix II). There are, however, a few instances where the values for one of the IQ measures (usually EPVT) are higher than those for social class; these will be discussed below.

The second reason for focussing on class rather than IQ or CI differences is that the former were in evidence even when IQ and CI were held constant. Thus, in the factorial sample which was used for the computer analysis, 20 high IQ children from the middle class were matched with 20 working-class children, and 40 medium IQ children were similarly matched for class. With IQ held constant in this way we still found major differences on certain categories, particularly in the use of nouns and pronouns. Other studies using factorial designs, such as those of Henderson (in Brandis and Henderson, 1970), Turner and Pickvance (1971) and Turner (1972), made similar findings. These results are sufficient to show that IQ, or rather any underlying factor than IQ is supposed to measure, cannot be responsible on its own for the differences in the children's use of the linguistic categories. Indeed, we should argue that the factors which really determine language use are to be sought in the patterns of communication established in the home and the community, whereas IQ tests measure the effects of these deeper influences rather than some independent factor such as innate or inherited intelligence. Patterns of family communication, and social class differences between them, thus come to have greater explanatory adequacy[19] than do measures of IQ.

We can now consider the cases where IQ has higher correlation values (with some of the linguistic variables) than social class. We used two indices of IQ, the Crichton scale which is principally a test of active vocabulary, and the EPVT which measures passive vocabulary. Crichton has higher r values than class on 4 variables in Task 2 and on 9 in Task 3; EPVT has higher values than class on 5 variables in Task 2 and on 9 in Task 3, but most of these involve categories which were either too infrequent to give reliable correlations (eg. wh-indirect, rankshifted clauses at H, egocentric tags), or which required extensive re-analysis because they were found to contain widely different functions within them (eg. the first- and second-person pronouns). When we consider only the categories with 'reliable' correlations, we find that Crichton has higher r values than class in only 2 variables in Task 3 and in none in Task 2. The two variables are *structured nouns* (for Crichton, p = 0·02; for class, p = 0·07) and *nominal modifiers* (for Crichton, p < 0·001; for class, p = non-significant). EPVT on the other hand has higher values for 2 variables (P3 exophoric, and this/that at M) in Task 2 and for 3 variables (P3 exophoric, exophoric this/that at H, and nominal modifiers) in Task 3. In all these instances the IQ value is higher than any of the other 'background' variables, not just class.

It is interesting to observe here, first, that of the two IQ measures, EPVT has the highest values more often than Crichton, and second, that IQ is the strongest 'background' variable in certain categories which directly involve nouns or exophoric pronouns. These two facts are probably related, for the most likely explanation for this phenomenon is the nature of the IQ measures themselves: the tests consist of measurement of vocabulary which, in turn, means that they are measuring to a large extent the use of nouns, particularly in the case of EPVT which is a noun-oriented test where the children are asked to point to a named object in a picture. We cannot be surprised to find that the children who tend to use exophoric pronouns have low scores in the IQ tests, while those who tend to use nouns have high scores, when the tests themselves are based on noun-usage. It thus appears that IQ emerges as the measurement of an effect, rather than as the manifestation of an underlying cause; and this is why social class differences continue to appear even in those studies where IQ is held constant. One further piece of evidence may be added to this argument: it has been found that there is quite a high correlation (0·38) between the CI scores of the *mothers* and the IQ of their *children* (Brandis and Henderson, 1970, p. 99); in other words the type of communication which is promoted within the family is reflected in the performance of the children as measured by IQ tests.

Conclusion

In this study we have taken particular contexts and observed in them class-differences in strategies of communication. The statistical results showed that the different types of strategy correlate highly with indices of social class. It has been argued, in addition, that verbal strategies may be independent of other factors such as linguistic competence, grammatical complexity, and dialect differences such as standard *v.* non-standard. The need to take into consideration the underlying speech functions, rather than simply the grammatical structures themselves, has been emphasised, just as it has in other recent studies by members of the Sociological Research Unit, and in the recent theoretical models of Bernstein and Halliday.

Notes

[1] One suspects that Bereiter and Labov are using the term 'grammatical' in two quite different senses: for Bereiter, 'grammatical' means something like 'conforming to the rules of standard English'; for Labov, it means 'conforming to a set of rules'. Thus an utterance like *me got juice* is 'ungrammatical' for Bereiter but 'grammatical' for Labov. As the fairground-keeper said (in excellent non-standard English)—'you pays your money and you takes your choice'.

[2] The number of *systemic* differences between the two dialects is small and their existence is still the occasion for dispute among linguists. There is a claim, for example, that Negro English has a different system of *aspect* in the verb; in this dialect we find 'the use of *be* to indicate generality, repeated action, or existential state in sentences such as *he be with us*, *they be fooling around*' (Labov and Cohen, 1967, p. 76); but Henrie (1969) thinks that the meaning of *be* is not necessarily limited to an habitual type of activity. A further claim for a systemic difference is the following: 'another such element is *done* to indicate an intensive or perfective meaning, as in *the bullet done penetrate my body*; *I done got me a hat*. Both of these are part of an aspectual system which is plainly distinct from tense' (Labov and Cohen, *ibid.*). But notice (a) there is an equivalent in standard English for each sentence: 'the bullet *went and penetrated* my body', 'I *went and got* myself a hat'; (b) many descriptions of the standard English verb system treat the perfective and progressive forms as *aspects* rather than as the traditional *tenses* (eg. Lyons, 1968, pp. 315 ff; cf. also Palmer, 1965, p. 59); the form *went and -ed* could simply be one further aspect, though it is not usually mentioned in grammars at all. Cf. also the discussion in Wolfram (1971, pp. 108 ff) on this question of systemic differences.

[3] In spite of Cazden's timely remarks, the resources-of-the-language/resources-of-the-individual confusion is still current—see for example Baratz, 1969, pp. 95–6.

[4] This quote-within-a-quote is originally from Deutsch, Katz and Jensen (1968).

[5] To understand *why*, one has to take account of social background,

patterns of communication within the family, etc.—the sociological origins of Bernstein's codes.

[6] The values were as follows:

Task 2

Class index	*r*
SC	0·006
NSC I	0·010
NSC II	0·009

Task 3

Class index	*r*
SC	0·027
NSC I	0·058
NSC II	0·052

[7] This phrase is actually used quite widely in New Zealand. It doubtless reflects, historically, the uncertain nature of long-distance telecommunication in that country.

[8] The relationship between these strategies and communicative competence is more complex. If we can assume that all three types of response are intelligible to all speakers of the language or dialect, then they are all communicatively 'competent' to this extent; they are also 'competent' in that all are appropriate to the situation, compared with, say, an utterance like 'roses are red' which is perfectly grammatical but contextually inappropriate. But if the society recognises norms for these strategies (eg. the group A response is regarded as 'the best'), then particular responses may be judged more or less competent, eg. a group B speaker may feel he has followed the 'wrong' strategy when he finds that the caller is a member of group A.

[9] Bernstein follows his definition of 'speech variant' with some specific examples which seem, in fact, to relate to a rather different concept. It is in this sense that the definition of the term has not been sufficiently clarified (see above).

[10] The importance of taking the situation into consideration is pointed out by Cazden (1970) who argues that too many studies of language differences take no account of contextual factors. But the problem, in relating language use to particular situations, is that the findings from one situation are not necessarily generalisable to other situations, and may thus be of limited validity.

[11] This preview (Hawkins, 1969) was erroneous in some aspects (cf.

chapter 4, p. 123), though not in the general discussion of exophorics versus nouns.

[12] The 5-year-old's perception of 'efficiency' may of course be different from that of an adult. I am reminded of the highly intelligent boy of this age who refused to answer his name when the teacher called the roll. When asked why, he said, 'Well why should I? She can *see* I'm there, can't she?'

[13] The sample consisted only of girls.

[14] *Hostility* is too strong a term for what is intended, viz. the antithesis of *solidarity*.

[15] Joan Tough has investigated the speech of 3-year-old children drawn from 'favoured' and 'less-favoured' homes and finds group differences in the use of exophorics which parallel very closely the class-differences we have found.

[16] It is important to bear in mind that the question 'better for what?' has to be answered, and can be answered in different ways; eg. one strategy may yield more effective communication between speaker and listener, and hence contribute to achievement at a person-to-person level. Another strategy may be more in keeping with the goals set by the school, and hence contribute to the achievement of educational goals.

[17] A model of language which would enable verbal strategies to be derived from underlying speech functions has recently been proposed by M. A. K. Halliday (1970). He recognises a number of generalised *situation types*, i.e. the typical social contexts and behavioural settings in which language is used. Then for each situation type it is possible to identify a 'meaning potential', which is the range of semantic options available to the speaker in the context of the particular situation type. Halliday's 'meaning potential' thus appears to correspond roughly with what I have called 'verbal strategies'. Halliday in fact refers to Bernstein's work on social control and uses it to illustrate his 'semantic networks'. Turner (1972) has integrated the proposals of both Bernstein and Halliday in a study of social-control strategies used by 5- and 7-year-old children.

[18] Further differences between *code*, in Bernstein's use of the term, and *social dialect* are pointed out by Hasan (1973)—cf. particularly pp. 258, 263.

[19] In the sense in which this term is used by Chomsky (eg. 1965).

Appendix I Subsidiary tables for data presented in Part I

1 Analysis of variance, for total heads, Task 3

	d.f.	*V.*	*F.*	*p.*
Class	1	1739·1	2·39	n.s.
Sex	1	588·6	0·80	n.s.
IQ	1	43·5	0·06	n.s.
CI	1	316·0	0·43	n.s.
Class with sex	1	2173·6	2·98	n.s.
Class with IQ	1	775·0	1·06	n.s.
Class with sex with CI	1	2050·4	2·81	n.s.
Within-scores	64	729·34		

2 Ordinatives, Task 3
(a) Children with zero-scores

	Class		*Sex*		*IQ*		*CI*
Middle	20	Girls	20	High	23	High	21
Working	22	Boys	22	Medium	19	Low	21
Total	42		42		42		42

(b) Number of ordinatives

	Class		*Sex*		*IQ*		*CI*
Middle	28	Girls	37	High	30	High	30
Working	35	Boys	26	Medium	33	Low	33
Total	63		63		63		63

3 *'All modifiers' as percentage of heads, Task 3 (sums of individual percentages)*

Class		*Sex*		*IQ*		*CI*	
Middle $\Sigma =$	2188	Girls	2241	High	2221	High	2263
Working	2079	Boys	2026	Medium	2046	Low	2004
Total	4267		4267		4267		4267

4 *Adjectives, Task 3*

		Middle class	*Working class*
High CI	Girls	41	18
	Boys	37	12
	Total	78	30
Low CI	Girls	19	45
	Boys	32	24
	Total	51	69

5 *Modification, as percentage of heads, Task 3*

		Middle class High IQ	*Middle class Medium IQ*	Σ	*Working class High IQ*	*Working class Medium IQ*	Σ	
High CI	Girls	266	223		242	223		954
	Boys	239	240		233	180		892
Σ		505	463		475	403		
Low CI	Girls	274	213		217	220		924
	Boys	165	242		231	187		825
Σ		439	455		448	407		
$\Sigma\Sigma$		944	918	1862	923	810	1733	

Appendix II Summary of the correlations, Part II

These tables contain the correlation value (r) for each linguistic category with each of the major 'sociological' variables, viz. three indices of social class, two indices of IQ, the New Communication Index, and sex.

Notes

1. For social class, a positive r means working-class
   a negative r means middle-class
   For IQ, a positive r means high IQ
   a negative r means low IQ
   For NCI, a positive r means high-communicating
   a negative r means low-communicating
   For sex, a positive r means girls
   a negative r means boys
2. Statistical probabilities which are greater than 1 in 10 (10 per cent) are given alongside the r value. These probabilities are expressed as percentages, so that, for example, a probability of 1·562 means $p = 0{\cdot}01562$ in the more usual notation.
3. For Task 2, the sample size (N) is 312 children.
   For Task 3, the sample size (N) is 299 children.
4. Categories 1–20 occur at the head of the nominal group.
   Categories 21–30 occur at the modifier of the nominal group.
   Categories 31–35 occur at the qualifier of the nominal group.

Task 2

Category	SC r	SC p	NSC I r	NSC I p	NSC II r	NSC II p	Cri. r	Cri. p	EPVT r	EPVT p	NCI r	NCI p	Sex r	Sex p
1 Tot. heads	0·006		0·010		0·009		0·079		−0·087		−0·074		0·036	
2 N str.	−0·058		−0·056		−0·066		0·066		−0·037		−0·004		0·037	
3 N unstr.														
4 N at A	−0·025		−0·010		−0·020		0·043		−0·061		0·007		0·107	5·468
5 P3 anaph.	0·059		0·062		0·072		0·076		−0·082		−0·114	6·223	0·015	
6 P3 exoph.	0·223	0·023	0·195	0·085	0·210	0·042	−0·203	0·059	−0·275	0·002	−0·208	0·108	−0·102	6·895
7 Det/ord.	0·050		0·058		0·026		0·046		−0·051		0·011		0·034	
8 Ea	−0·287	0·001	−0·273	0·002	−0·272	0·002	0·184	0·145	0·076		0·147	1·624	0·067	
9 Ev	0·020		0·007		0·041		0·061		−0·041		0·039		−0·063	
10 P1 self-ref.	−0·105	6·132	−0·074		−0·054		0·036		−0·013		0·015		−0·043	
11 P1 dir. sp.	−0·001		0·027		0·027		0·164	0·403	0·044		−0·060		0·088	
12 P2 impl.	0·193	0·096	0·159	0·518	0·179	0·192	−0·196	0·084	−0·159	0·523	−0·117	5·638	0·039	
13 P2 expr.	−0·108	5·418	−0·097	8·392	−0·093	9·767	0·209	0·044	0·069		0·066		0·057	
14 P indef.	−0·128	2·230	−0·104	6·353	−0·121	3·121	0·134	1·707	0·109	5·044	0·087		−0·022	
15 S/T anaph.	−0·179	0·186	−0·169	0·311	−0·202	0·062	0·121	3·002	0·084		0·094		−0·040	
16 S/T exoph.	0·177	0·207	0·176	0·218	0·131	1·964	−0·136	1·539	−0·211	0·039	−0·193	0·209	−0·023	
17 wh-dir.	−0·035		−0·040		−0·025		−0·006		0·021		0·041		−0·019	
18 wh-indir.	−0·066		−0·051		−0·066		0·120	3·165	0·108	5·247	0·022		−0·002	

19 r/s-cl. at H	−0·190	0·110	−0·191	0·104	−0·202	0·060	0·179	0·189	0·135	1·654	0·024		0·034	
20 Advb. at H	0·156	0·605	0·151	0·765	0·176	0·218	−0·053		−0·120	3·261	−0·116	5·873	−0·011	
21 Tot. mod.	−0·081		−0·072		−0·081		0·101	7·170	−0·042		−0·023		0·052	
22 D1	−0·051		−0·039		−0·059		0·076		−0·027		−0·032		0·030	
23 D2	0·027		0·019		0·042		−0·008		−0·136	1·536	−0·038		−0·014	
24 D3	0·079		0·063		0·063		−0·031		−0·141	1·197	−0·142	2·069	0·080	
25 Ord.	−0·128	2·194	−0·104	6·341	−0·134	1·732	0·064		0·084		0·059		0·047	
26 E1	0·014		0·035		0·042		0·075		−0·089		−0·069		0·139	1·363
27 E2	−0·277	0·002	−0·290	0·001	−0·261	0·004	0·199	0·072	0·125	2·613	0·171	0·587	−0·018	
28 Nom.	−0·043		−0·043		−0·043		0·059		0·037		−0·009		−0·099	7·717
29 Intens.	−0·303	0·001	−0·287	0·001	−0·304	0·001	0·201	0·064	0·159	0·511	0·153	1·288	0·067	
30 r/s nom. (at M)	−0·090		−0·090		−0·072		0·078		0·067		0·020		0·106	5·770
31 Tot. qual.	−0·171	0·284	−0·159	0·517	−0·168	0·339	0·148	0·895	0·125	2·530	0·089		−0·012	
32 Q1	−0·050		−0·041		−0·017		−0·000		−0·003		0·001		0·028	
33 r/s-p	−0·160	0·492	−0·130	2·046	−0·207	0·048	0·154	0·639	0·138	1·433	0·039		0·041	
34 r/s-c	−0·127	2·350	−0·125	2·616	−0·104	6·334	0·075		0·018		0·091		−0·078	
35 r/s-n (at Q)	−0·017		−0·048		−0·018		0·085		0·105	6·103	0·082		−0·053	
36 Tags 1 + 2	−0·029		−0·001		−0·044		−0·061		−0·052		0·006		−0·146	0·960
37 Tags 3	0·000		−0·003		−0·025		0·061		0·004		−0·024		−0·061	

Task 3

Category	*SC*		*NSC I*		*NSC II*		*Cri.*		*EPVT*		*NCI*		*Sex*	
	r	*p*	*r*	*p*	*r*	*p*	*r*	*p*	*r*	*p*	*r*	*p*	*r*	*p*
1 Tot heads	0·027		0·058		0·052		0·066		−0·043		−0·020		0·046	
2 N str.	0·102	7·562	−0·069		−0·074		0·129	2·426	0·048		0·076		0·028	
3 N unstr.	−0·108	5·918	−0·106	6·365	−0·150	0·908	−0·019		0·070		0·039		−0·031	
4 N at A	0·001		0·048		0·022		0·067		0·018		0·054		0·055	
5 P3 anaph.	0·132	2·077	0·152	0·842	0·188	0·146	0·051		−0·110	5·525	−0·107	8·614	0·099	8·474
6 P3 exoph.	0·252	0·007	0·235	0·016	0·265	0·004	−0·146	1·135	−0·271	0·003	−0·184	0·370	0·025	
7 Det/Ord.	0·087		0·053		0·076		−0·022		−0·028		−0·006		0·083	
8 Ea	0·061		0·068		0·078		0·036		−0·104	6·982	−0·015		0·062	
9 Ev	0·067		0·086		0·068		0·059		0·002		−0·098		0·031	
10 P1 self-ref.	−0·124	2·960	−0·082		−0·057		0·190	0·134	0·113	4·795	0·140	2·501	−0·064	
11 P1 dir. sp.	0·077		0·095	9·854	0·102	7·557	0·047		−0·055		0·008		0·174	0·298
12 P2 impl.	0·161	0·554	0·157	0·649	0·157	0·670	−0·103	7·190	−0·143	1·306	−0·075		0·043	
13 P2 expr.	0·120	3·610	0·135	1·841	0·149	0·983	0·025		−0·109	5·686	−0·006		0·110	5·468
14 P indef.	−0·014		−0·008		0·008		−0·035		−0·018		−0·030		0·017	
15 S/T anaph.	0·019		0·036		0·020		0·152	0·845	0·051		0·004		−0·025	
16 S/T exoph.	0·100	7·949	0·088		0·079		−0·105	6·498	−0·155	0·710	−0·122	5·001	−0·120	3·509
17 wh-dir.	−0·034		0·012		0·011		0·014		−0·014		0·061		0·023	
18 wh-indir.	0·011		0·027		0·043		0·149	0·965	0·062		−0·016		0·042	

19 r/s-cl at H	−0·064		−0·023		−0·043		0·189	0·142	0·094	9·976	0·036		0·010	
20 Advb. at H	0·234	0·017	0·239	0·014	0·226	0·025	−0·067		−0·137	1·717	−0·223	0·065	0·033	
21 Tot. mod.	−0·032		0·006		−0·030		0·097	9·081	0·028		0·020		0·025	
22 D1	−0·063		−0·026		−0·077		0·076		0·040		0·034		−0·021	
23 D2	0·139	1·562	0·136	1·788	0·164	0·477	−0·000		−0·071		−0·027		0·044	
24 D3	0·021		0·058		0·082		−0·034		−0·095	9·630	−0·041		0·089	
25 Ord.	0·067		0·070		0·085		−0·116	4·171	−0·130	2·272	−0·059		0·075	
26 E1	0·036		0·049		0·055		0·036		−0·029		−0·073		0·167	0·409
27 E2	−0·080		−0·049		−0·054		0·208	0·056	0·116	4·251	0·025		0·104	7·000
28 Nom.	−0·050		−0·025		−0·064		0·209	0·054	0·176	0·271	0·103	9·771	−0·072	
29 Intens.	−0·044		−0·052		−0·053		0·085		−0·017		0·012		0·053	
30 r/s-nom (at M)	−0·006		0·035		0·007		0·079		0·033		−0·073		0·076	
31 Tot. qual.	0·062		0·075		0·109	5·661	0·104	6·934	0·039		−0·052		0·079	
32 Q1	0·157	0·662	0·150	0·914	0·191	0·129	0·024		0·001		−0·140	2·425	0·045	
33 r/s-p	−0·034		−0·010		0·012		0·103	7·260	0·084		0·063		0·043	
34 r/s-c	−0·015		−0·008		−0·011		0·083		−0·029		−0·021		0·076	
35 r/s-n (at Q)	0·006		0·028		0·038		0·080		0·069		0·040		0·080	
36 Tags 1 + 2	0·097	9·039	0·108	5·788	0·087		0·036		−0·040		−0·070		−0·109	5·538
37 Tags 3	−0·126	2·741	−0·131	2·213	−0·113	4·864	0·112	4·941	0·136	1·777	−0·022		−0·028	

Appendix III Basic and supplementary data, Part II

A Basic data

Notes

1 *Total users* and % *users* refer to the χ^2 sample of 263 children (Task 2) and 254 children (Task 3).

2 % *users* for each class/sex group (lower-class boys, middle-class boys, etc.) are based on the following N:

	WC boys	*MC boys*	*WC girls*	*MC girls*	*Total*
Task 2	59	65	80	59	263
Task 3	54	65	76	59	254

3 *Total occurrences* are derived from the correlations print-out and are therefore based on the larger sample of 312 children (Task 2) and 299 children (Task 3).

4 % *occurrences* are derived as follows:
Categories 2–20, i.e. 'head' categories, are percentages of total heads. Categories 22–30 (modifiers) and 32–35 (qualifiers) are percentages of a combined total, mod. + qual., so that the frequency of each type of qualifier is expressed on the same basis as each type of modifier. Thus, r/s-nom. at Q are about as frequent as r/s-nom. at M in absolute number of occurrences (36 and 30, respectively, in Task 2) but if those at Q were expressed as a percentage of total Q, they would appear to be much commoner (9·5 per cent) than those at M (0·4 per cent). Taking modifiers and qualifiers together puts them on the same basis for comparison; it makes sense linguistically, since both have similar functions.

5 *Frequency-rating*: see chapter 1, p. 70.

Task 2

	Category	*Total users*	*% users*	*% WC boys*	*% MC boys*	*% WC girls*	*% MC girls*	*Total occurrences*	*% occurrences*	*Frequency rating*
1	Tot. heads	263	100					16725		
2	N str.	263	100					5570	33·3	4
3	N unstr.									
4	N at A	260	99					1890	11·3	4
5	P3 anaph.	263	100					4702	28·1	4
6	P3 exoph.	243	92	95	89	95	90	1095	6·55	3
7	Det./ord	77	29	27	26	31	32	145	0·87	2
8	Ea	104	40	27	49	29	56	209	1·25	2
9	Ev	77	29	31	35	29	22	117	0·70	1
10	P1 self-ref.	28	11	7	12	8	17	64	0·38	1
11	P1 dir. sp.	199	76	83	72	75	73	577	3·45	3
12	P2 impl.	189	72	75	66	79	66	491	2·94	3
13	P2 expr.	183	70	64	71	61	85	484	2·89	3
14	P indef.	66	25	19	32	23	27	115	0·69	1
15	S/T anaph.	38	14	10	20	5	25	78	0·47	1
16	S/T exoph.	121	46	58	39	50	37	276	1·65	2
17	wh-dir.	133	51	58	46	45	56	225	1·35	2
18	wh-indir.	68	26	24	32	24	24	128	0·77	2

19 r/s cl.	157	60	41	66	61	70	408	2·44	2
20 Advb. at H	87	33	44	28	38	22	150	0·90	2
21 Tot. mod.							7443		
22 D1	263	100					5582	71·4	4
23 D2	161	61	70	57	66	51	510	6·52	3
24 D3	161	61	59	51	68	66	427	5·45	2
25 Ord.	78	30	20	29	34	34	166	2·12	2
26 E1	124	47	39	40	58	49	306	3·91	2
27 E2	109	41	27	55	30	56	222	2·84	2
28 Nom.	60	23	22	26	20	24	95	1·22	1
29 Intens.	59	22	8	23	13	49	105	1·34	1
30 r/s-n (at M)	20	8	2	6	10	12	30	0·38	1
31 Tot. qual.							382		
32 Q1	89	34	37	26	35	37	158	2·02	2
33 r/s-p	70	27	12	32	25	37	120	1·53	1
34 r/s-c	45	17	19	23	11	17	66	0·84	1
35 r/s-n (at Q)	23	9	8	12	9	5	36	0·46	1
36 Tags 1 + 2	58	22	29	26	15	20	153		2
37 Tags 3	4	1·5	2	3	1	0	9		1

Task 3

Category	*Total users*	*% users*	*% WC boys*	*% MC boys*	*% WC girls*	*% MC girls*	*Total occurrences*	*% occurrences*	*Frequency rating*
1 Tot. heads	254	100					18415		
2 N str.	254	100					6775	36·8	4
3 N unstr.	196	77	76	85	67	83	2320	12·6	4
4 N at A	254	100					2770	15·1	4
5 P3 anaph.	254	100					2280	12·4	4
6 P3 exoph.	230	91	96	85	93	88	1030	5·59	3
7 Det./ord.	119	47	46	45	54	41	304	1·65	2
8 Ea	75	30	31	22	36	29	172	0·93	2
9 Ev	54	21	24	17	26	17	91	0·49	1
10 P1 self-ref.	87	34	28	39	30	41	231	1·25	2
11 P1 dir. sp.	26	10	7	8	18	5	76	0·41	1
12 P2 impl.	28	11	13	6	21	2	51	0·28	1
13 P2 expr.	53	21	20	14	33	14	109	0·59	1
14 P indef.	136	54	44	68	51	49	336	1·83	2
15 S/T anaph.	46	18	19	17	20	17	70	0·38	1
16 S/T exoph.	172	68	74	72	63	63	729	3·96	3
17 wh-dir.	33	13	6	14	20	10	69	0·38	1
18 wh-indir.	70	28	28	26	29	27	131	0·71	2

19 r/s cl.	136	54	46	54	57	56	356	1·93	2
20 Advb. at H	159	63	74	57	70	49	515	2·80	3
21 Tot. mod.							12120		
22 D1	254	100					9075	70·8	4
23 D2	172	68	76	57	76	61	774	6·04	3
24 D3	143	56	43	52	72	53	376	2·93	2
25 Ord.	142	56	61	49	60	53	308	2·40	2
26 E1	162	64	57	59	75	61	492	3·84	3
27 E2	132	52	41	60	50	56	403	3·14	2
28 Nom.	166	65	65	72	55	71	526	4·10	3
29 Intens.	43	17	9	20	17	20	99	0·77	1
30 r/s-n (at M)	38	15	9	15	20	14	68	0·53	1
31 Tot. qual.							694		
32 Q1	113	45	57	28	54	39	272	2·12	2
33 r/s-p	125	49	48	51	49	49	286	2·23	2
34 r/s-c	71	28	20	31	28	32	134	1·05	2
35 r/s-n (at Q)	1	0·4	0	0	1	0	2	0·02	1
36 Tags 1 + 2	74	29	35	22	37	22	246		2
37 Tags 3	13	5	0	9	7	3	18		1

B Supplementary data

Values of χ^2 for categories not given a table in the main text. All values are non-significant. The correlation values for these categories may be seen in the correlation charts for Tasks 2 and 3.

Category and task		*Class*	*Class (boys only)*	*Class (girls only)*	*Sex*
r/s-n (at Q)	Task 2	0·00	0·16	0·24	0·52
	Task 3	0·00	0·00	0·00	0·00
Ev ('verbal' adj.)	Task 2	0·00	0·15	0·49	1·30
	Task 3	2·23	0·54	1·23	0·06
wh-direct	Task 2	0·01	1·21	1·22	0·00
	Task 3	0·82	1·41	1·65	1·03
wh-indir.	Task 2	0·49	0·74	0·00	0·49
	Task 3	0·37	0·94	1·01	0·26
Det./Ord.	Task 2	0·00	0·01	0·01	0·58
	Task 3	0·32	0·15	1·84	0·22
Pl dir. sp.	Task 2	0·93	1·47	0·01	0·23

Appendix IV List of adjectives

Adjectives at M
(Listed alphabetically)
bad
biggest
blonde
bumpy
clever
crowded
dangerous
different (comp.)
dirty
empty
fancy
fast
fat
funny
good, better, best
great
heavy
high
horrible
horrid
hot
juicy
little
long
lovely
low
nasty
naughty
new
nice
noisy
old (= aged)
old (hypocoristic, as in *silly old fool*)
old-fashioned

Adjectives at H
(Listed alphabetically)
afraid
angry
annoyed
big
blind
blonde
busy
careful
cold
cross
daft
dangerous
deep
disappointed
dry
empty
fair (= just)
fed up
fine
foolish
frightened
full
funny
furry
good
happy
hard (= difficult)
heavy
high
hot
hungry
kind
late
lazy

plump
pretty
real
reckless
round
same
scared
short
silly
silver
slow
small
special
spotted
sticky
strong
sunny
tiny
white
wild
windy
wrong
Colour-adjectives
black
blue
brown
green
mauve
purple
red
stripey/striped
white
yellow

lovely
mad
miserable
naughty
nice
nosey
quiet
raw
round
sad
scared
sick
silly
small
sorry
strong
sure
surprised
tight
unhappy
warm
wet
wide
wild
wobbly
Colour-adjectives
black
blue
brown
green
mauve
red
white
yellow

Verbal adjectives (*Ev*)

blocked up
broken
built up
busted
caught
coloured
closed
crashed
crowded
cut
dashed
done (= broken)

invited
laid (of table)
laid out
left (out, over)
locked
locked in, out
lost
made
married
mended
open
parked

drawn
dressed up
drownded
eaten (up)
finished
fixed on
flooded
glued
gone
shut
smashed
squashed
stuck (= unable to move)
stuck (= attached)
tied (up)
undressed
written

Bibliography

BARATZ, J. (1969) 'Teaching reading in a Negro school', in Baratz, J. and Shuy, R. W. (eds), *Teaching Black Children to Read*, Center for Applied Linguistics.

BEREITER, C. (1965) 'Academic instruction and pre-school children', in Corbin, R. and Crosby, M. (eds), *Language Programs for the Disadvantaged*, NCTE, Champaign, Ill.

BEREITER, C. *et al.* (1966) 'An academically-oriented pre-school for culturally deprived children', in Hechinger, F. (ed.), *Preschool Education Today*, Doubleday.

BERNSTEIN, B. (1959) 'A public language: some sociological implications of linguistic form', *British Journal of Sociology*, X, 311.

BERNSTEIN, B. (1961) 'Social class and linguistic development: a theory of social learning', in Halsey, A. H., Floud, J. and Anderson, C. A. (eds), *Education, Economy and Society*, Free Press.

BERNSTEIN, B. (1962a) 'Social class, linguistic codes and grammatical elements', *Language and Speech*, 5, 221.

BERNSTEIN, B. (1962b) 'Linguistic codes, hesitation phenomena and intelligence', *Language and Speech*, 5, 31–46.

BERNSTEIN, B. (1965) 'A socio-linguistic approach to social learning', in Gould, J. (ed.), *Penguin Social Science Survey*, Penguin.

BERNSTEIN, B. (1969) 'A critique of the concept of compensatory education', in Bernstein, B. (ed.), *Class, Codes and Control*, vol. 1, Routledge & Kegan Paul, 1971.

BERNSTEIN, B. (1971) 'Social class, language and socialization', in T. A. Sebeok (ed.), *Current Trends in Linguistics*, vol. 12, Mouton.

BERNSTEIN, B. (1972) 'A socio-linguistic approach to socialization', in Hymes, D. and Gumperz, J. (eds), *Directions in Sociolinguistics*, Holt, Rinehart & Winston.

BERNSTEIN, B. and COOK, J. (1965) 'A coding manual for social control', SRU mimeograph. See also Cook-Gumperz (1973).

BERNSTEIN, B. and HENDERSON, D. (1969) 'Social class difference in the relevance of language to socialization', *Sociology*, 3, 1–20.

BRANDIS, W. and HENDERSON, D. (1970) *Social Class, Language and Communication*, Routledge & Kegan Paul.

CAZDEN, C. B. (1966) 'Sub-cultural differences in child language: an inter-disciplinary review', *Merrill-Palmer Quarterly*, 12, 185.

CAZDEN, C. B. (1970) 'The situation: a neglected source of social-class differences in language use', *Journal of Social Issues*, 26, 2.

CAZDEN, C. B. (1971) 'Approaches to social dialects in early childhood education', in *Sociolinguistics: a Cross-disciplinary Perspective*, Center for Applied Linguistics.

CHOMSKY, N. (1965) *Aspects of the Theory of Syntax*, MIT Press.

COOK-GUMPERZ, J. (1973) *Social Control and Socialization*, Routledge & Kegan Paul.

DEUTSCH, M., KATZ, I. and JENSEN, A. R. (eds) (1968) *Social Class, Race and Psychological Development*, Holt, Rinehart & Winston.

ENGELMANN, S. (1971) 'The inadequacies of the linguistic approach', in *Sociolinguistics: a Cross-disciplinary Perspective*, Center for Applied Linguistics.

ERVIN-TRIPP, S. (1971) 'Social dialects in developmental sociolinguistics', in *Sociolinguistics: a Cross-disciplinary Perspective*, Center for Applied Linguistics.

HALLIDAY, M. A. K. (1966) 'Grammar, Society and the Noun', inaugural address, University College, London.

HALLIDAY, M. A. K. (1967) *Intonation and Grammar in British English*, Mouton.

HALLIDAY, M. A. K. (1970) *Introduction to System-structure Theory of Language*, Holt, Reinhart & Winston.

HASAN, R. (1968) *Grammatical Cohesion in Spoken and Written English*, Longmans.

HASAN, R. (1973) 'Code, register and social dialect', in Bernstein, B. (ed.), *Class, Codes and Control*, vol. 2, Routledge & Kegan Paul.

HAWKINS, P. R. (1969) 'Social class, the nominal group and reference', *Language and Speech*, 12, 125.

HENDERSON, D. (1970) 'Contextual specificity, discretion, and cognitive socialization: with special reference to language', *Sociology*, 4, 3, 311.

HENRIE, S. N. (1969) 'A study of verb phrases used by 5-year-old non-standard Negro English speaking children', unpublished Ph.D. thesis, University of California, Berkeley.

HUDDLESTON, R. D. *et al.* (1968) *Sentence and Clause in Scientific English*, Communication Research Centre, University College, London.

HUDSON, R. A. (1971) *English Complex Sentences—an Introduction to Systemic Grammar*, North Holland.

HYMES, D. (1971) (ed.) *Pidginization and Creolization of Languages*, Cambridge University Press.

HYMES, D. (1972) 'On communicative competence', in Pride, J. B. and Holmes, J. (eds), *Sociolinguistics*, Penguin.

KOCHMAN, T. (1969) 'Social factors in the consideration of teaching standard English', *Florida FL Reporter*, 7, 1.

LABOV, W. (1969a) 'Contraction, deletion, and inherent variation of the English copula', *Language*, 45, 715.

LABOV, W. (1969b) 'The logic of non-standard English', in Alatis, J. (ed.), *Report of the 20th Annual RTM*, Georgetown University Press.

LABOV, W. and COHEN, P. (1967) 'Systematic relations of standard and non-standard rules in the grammars of Negro speakers', *Project Literary Reports*, 8, Cornell University Press.

LABOV, W. *et al.* (1968) *A Study of Non-standard English of Negro and Puerto Rican Speakers in New York City. Final Report*, Cooperative Research Project 3288, Office of Education.

LAWTON, D. (1963) 'Social-class differences in language development', *Language and Speech*, 6, pt 3.

LAWTON, D. (1964) 'Social-class language differences in group discussions', *Language and Speech*, 7, pt 3.

LAWTON, D. (1968) *Social Class, Language and Education*, Routledge & Kegan Paul.

LINDQUIST, E. F. (1940) *Statistical Analysis in Educational Research*, Houghton Mifflin.

LYONS, J. (1968) *Introduction to Theoretical Linguistics*, Cambridge University Press.

MORONEY, M. J. (1956) *Facts from Figures*, 3rd revised edition, Penguin.

PALMER, F. R. (1965) *A Linguistic Study of the English Verb*, Longmans.

ROBINSON, W. P. (1965) 'The elaborated code in working-class language', *Language and Speech*, 8, 243.

ROBINSON, W. P. (1972) 'Where do children's answers come from?', in Bernstein, B. (ed.), *Class, Codes, and Control*, vol. 2, Routledge & Kegan Paul.

ROBINSON, W. P. and RACKSTRAW, S. J. (1967) 'Variation in mothers' answers to children's questions', *Sociology*, 1, 259.

ROBINSON, W. P. and RACKSTRAW, S. J. (1971) *A Question of Answers*, Routledge & Kegan Paul.

SCHEGLOFF, E. A. (1968) 'Sequencing in conversational openings', *American Anthropologist*, 70, 6.

STEWART, W. A. (1970) 'Linguistic-cultural differences and American education', *Florida FL Reporter*, 7, no. 1.

TOUGH, J. (1969) 'Language and environment: an interim report', University of Leeds, stencilled.

TURNER, G. J. (1972) 'Social class and children's language of control at age 5 and age 7', in Bernstein, B. (ed.), *Class, Codes and Control*, vol. 2, Routledge & Kegan Paul.

TURNER, G. J. (1973) 'Social class, age and uncertainty', in Adlam, D. S. (ed.), *Code in Context*, Routledge & Kegan Paul, forthcoming.

TURNER, G. J. and MOHAN, B. A. (1970) *A Linguistic Description and Computer Program for Children's Speech*, Routledge & Kegan Paul.

TURNER, G. J. and PICKVANCE, R. E. (1971) Social class difference in the expression of uncertainty in 5-year-old children', *Language and Speech*, 14, 303.

WOLFRAM, W. (1971) 'Social dialects from a linguistic perspective', in *Sociolinguistics: a Cross-disciplinary Perspective*, Center for Applied Linguistics.

WOLFRAM, W. and CLARKE, N. H. (eds) (1971) *Black-White Speech Relationships*, Center for Applied Linguistics.

Index

Routledge Social Science Series

Routledge & Kegan Paul London and Boston
68–74 Carter Lane London EC4V 5EL
9 Park Street Boston Mass 02108

Contents

Authors wishing to submit manuscripts for any series in this catalogue should send them to the Social Science Editor, Routledge & Kegan Paul Ltd, 68–74 Carter Lane, London EC4V 5EL

●*Books so marked are available in paperback*
All books are in Metric Demy 8vo format (216 × 138mm approx.)

International Library of Sociology

General Editor John Rex

GENERAL SOCIOLOGY

Barnsley, J. H. The Social Reality of Ethics. *464 pp.*
Belshaw, Cyril. The Conditions of Social Performance. *An Exploratory Theory. 144 pp.*
Brown, Robert. Explanation in Social Science. *208 pp.*
● Rules and Laws in Sociology. *192 pp.*
Bruford, W. H. Chekhov and His Russia. *A Sociological Study. 244 pp.*
Cain, Maureen E. Society and the Policeman's Role. *326 pp.*
Gibson, Quentin. The Logic of Social Enquiry. *240 pp.*
Glucksmann, M. Structuralist Analysis in Contemporary Social Thought. *212 pp.*
Gurvitch, Georges. Sociology of Law. *Preface by Roscoe Pound. 264 pp.*
Hodge, H. A. Wilhelm Dilthey. *An Introduction. 184 pp.*
Homans, George C. Sentiments and Activities. *336 pp.*
Johnson, Harry M. Sociology: *a Systematic Introduction. Foreword by Robert K. Merton. 710 pp.*
Mannheim, Karl. Essays on Sociology and Social Psychology. *Edited by Paul Keckskemeti. With Editorial Note by Adolph Lowe. 344 pp.*
Systematic Sociology: *An Introduction to the Study of Society. Edited by J. S. Erös and Professor W. A. C. Stewart. 220 pp.*
Martindale, Don. The Nature and Types of Sociological Theory. *292 pp.*
●**Maus, Heinz.** A Short History of Sociology. *234 pp.*
Mey, Harald. Field-Theory. *A Study of its Application in the Social Sciences. 352 pp.*
Myrdal, Gunnar. Value in Social Theory: *A Collection of Essays on Methodology. Edited by Paul Streeten. 332 pp.*
Ogburn, William F., and **Nimkoff, Meyer F.** A Handbook of Sociology. *Preface by Karl Mannheim. 656 pp. 46 figures. 35 tables.*
Parsons, Talcott, and **Smelser, Neil J.** Economy and Society: *A Study in the Integration of Economic and Social Theory. 362 pp.*
●**Rex, John.** Key Problems of Sociological Theory. *220 pp.*
Discovering Sociology. *278 pp.*
Sociology and the Demystification of the Modern World. *282 pp.*
●**Rex, John** (Ed.) Approaches to Sociology. *Contributions by Peter Abell, Frank Bechhofer, Basil Bernstein, Ronald Fletcher, David Frisby, Miriam Glucksmann, Peter Lassman, Herminio Martins, John Rex, Roland Robertson, John Westergaard and Jock Young. 302 pp.*
Rigby, A. Alternative Realities. *352 pp.*
Roche, M. Phenomenology, Language and the Social Sciences. *374 pp.*
Sahay, A. Sociological Analysis. *220 pp.*
Urry, John. Reference Groups and the Theory of Revolution. *244 pp.*
Weinberg, E. Development of Sociology in the Soviet Union. *173 pp.*

FOREIGN CLASSICS OF SOCIOLOGY

●**Durkheim, Emile.** Suicide. *A Study in Sociology. Edited and with an Introduction by George Simpson. 404 pp.*

Professional Ethics and Civic Morals. *Translated by Cornelia Brookfield. 288 pp.*

●**Gerth, H. H.,** and **Mills, C. Wright.** From Max Weber: *Essays in Sociology. 502 pp.*

●**Tönnies, Ferdinand.** Community and Association. (*Gemeinschaft und Gesellschaft.*) *Translated and Supplemented by Charles P. Loomis. Foreword by Pitirim A. Sorokin. 334 pp.*

SOCIAL STRUCTURE

Andreski, Stanislav. Military Organization and Society. *Foreword by Professor A. R. Radcliffe-Brown. 226 pp. 1 folder.*

Coontz, Sydney H. Population Theories and the Economic Interpretation. *202 pp.*

Coser, Lewis. The Functions of Social Conflict. *204 pp.*

Dickie-Clark, H. F. Marginal Situation: *A Sociological Study of a Coloured Group. 240 pp. 11 tables.*

Glaser, Barney, and **Strauss, Anselm L.** Status Passage. *A Formal Theory. 208 pp.*

Glass, D. V. (Ed.) Social Mobility in Britain. *Contributions by J. Berent, T. Bottomore, R. C. Chambers, J. Floud, D. V. Glass, J. R. Hall, H. T. Himmelweit, R. K. Kelsall, F. M. Martin, C. A. Moser, R. Mukherjee, and W. Ziegel. 420 pp.*

Jones, Garth N. Planned Organizational Change: *An Exploratory Study Using an Empirical Approach. 268 pp.*

Kelsall, R. K. Higher Civil Servants in Britain: *From 1870 to the Present Day. 268 pp. 31 tables.*

König, René. The Community. *232 pp. Illustrated.*

●**Lawton, Denis.** Social Class, Language and Education. *192 pp.*

McLeish, John. The Theory of Social Change: *Four Views Considered. 128 pp.*

Marsh, David C. The Changing Social Structure of England and Wales, 1871-1961. *288 pp.*

Mouzelis, Nicos. Organization and Bureaucracy. *An Analysis of Modern Theories. 240 pp.*

Mulkay, M. J. Functionalism, Exchange and Theoretical Strategy. *272 pp.*

Ossowski, Stanislaw. Class Structure in the Social Consciousness. *210 pp.*

Podgórecki, Adam. Law and Society. *About 300 pp.*

SOCIOLOGY AND POLITICS

Acton, T. A. Gypsy Politics and Social Change. *316 pp.*

Hechter, Michael. Internal Colonialism. *The Celtic Fringe in British National Development, 1536–1966. About 350 pp.*

Hertz, Frederick. Nationality in History and Politics: *A Psychology and Sociology of National Sentiment and Nationalism. 432 pp.*

Kornhauser, William. The Politics of Mass Society. *272 pp. 20 tables.*

Laidler, Harry W. History of Socialism. *Social-Economic Movements: An Historical and Comparative Survey of Socialism, Communism, Co-operation, Utopianism; and other Systems of Reform and Reconstruction. 992 pp.*

Lasswell, H. D. Analysis of Political Behaviour. *324 pp.*

Mannheim, Karl. Freedom, Power and Democratic Planning. *Edited by Hans Gerth and Ernest K. Bramstedt. 424 pp.*

Mansur, Fatma. Process of Independence. *Foreword by A. H. Hanson. 208 pp.*

Martin, David A. Pacifism: *an Historical and Sociological Study. 262 pp.*

Myrdal, Gunnar. The Political Element in the Development of Economic Theory. *Translated from the German by Paul Streeten. 282 pp.*

Wootton, Graham. Workers, Unions and the State. *188 pp.*

FOREIGN AFFAIRS: THEIR SOCIAL, POLITICAL AND ECONOMIC FOUNDATIONS

Mayer, J. P. Political Thought in France from the Revolution to the Fifth Republic. *164 pp.*

CRIMINOLOGY

Ancel, Marc. Social Defence: *A Modern Approach to Criminal Problems. Foreword by Leon Radzinowicz. 240 pp.*

Cain, Maureen E. Society and the Policeman's Role. *326 pp.*

Cloward, Richard A., and **Ohlin, Lloyd E.** Delinquency and Opportunity: *A Theory of Delinquent Gangs. 248 pp.*

Downes, David M. The Delinquent Solution. *A Study in Subcultural Theory. 296 pp.*

Dunlop, A. B., and **McCabe, S.** Young Men in Detention Centres. *192 pp.*

Friedlander, Kate. The Psycho-Analytical Approach to Juvenile Delinquency: *Theory, Case Studies, Treatment. 320 pp.*

Glueck, Sheldon, and **Eleanor.** Family Environment and Delinquency. *With the statistical assistance of Rose W. Kneznek. 340 pp.*

Lopez-Rey, Manuel. Crime. *An Analytical Appraisal. 288 pp.*

Mannheim, Hermann. Comparative Criminology: *a Text Book. Two volumes. 442 pp. and 380 pp.*

Morris, Terence. The Criminal Area: *A Study in Social Ecology. Foreword by Hermann Mannheim. 232 pp. 25 tables. 4 maps.*

Rock, Paul. Making People Pay. *338 pp.*

● **Taylor, Ian, Walton, Paul,** and **Young, Jock.** The New Criminology. *For a Social Theory of Deviance. 325 pp.*

SOCIAL PSYCHOLOGY

Bagley, Christopher. The Social Psychology of the Epileptic Child. *320 pp.*

Barbu, Zevedei. Problems of Historical Psychology. *248 pp.*

Blackburn, Julian. Psychology and the Social Pattern. *184 pp.*

●**Brittan, Arthur.** Meanings and Situations. *224 pp.*

Carroll, J. Break-Out from the Crystal Palace. *200 pp.*

●**Fleming, C. M.** Adolescence: Its Social Psychology. *With an Introduction to recent findings from the fields of Anthropology, Physiology, Medicine, Psychometrics and Sociometry. 288 pp.*

● The Social Psychology of Education: *An Introduction and Guide to Its Study. 136 pp.*

Homans, George C. The Human Group. *Foreword by Bernard DeVoto. Introduction by Robert K. Merton. 526 pp.*

● Social Behaviour: *its Elementary Forms. 416 pp.*

●**Klein, Josephine.** The Study of Groups. *226 pp. 31 figures. 5 tables.*

Linton, Ralph. The Cultural Background of Personality. *132 pp.*

●**Mayo, Elton.** The Social Problems of an Industrial Civilization. *With an appendix on the Political Problem. 180 pp.*

Ottaway, A. K. C. Learning Through Group Experience. *176 pp.*

Ridder, J. C. de. The Personality of the Urban African in South Africa. *A Thermatic Apperception Test Study. 196 pp. 12 plates.*

●**Rose, Arnold M.** (Ed.) Human Behaviour and Social Processes: *an Interactionist Approach. Contributions by Arnold M. Rose, Ralph H. Turner, Anselm Strauss, Everett C. Hughes, E. Franklin Frazier, Howard S. Becker, et al. 696 pp.*

Smelser, Neil J. Theory of Collective Behaviour. *448 pp.*

Stephenson, Geoffrey M. The Development of Conscience. *128 pp.*

Young, Kimball. Handbook of Social Psychology. *658 pp. 16 figures. 10 tables.*

SOCIOLOGY OF THE FAMILY

Banks, J. A. Prosperity and Parenthood: *A Study of Family Planning among The Victorian Middle Classes. 262 pp.*

Bell, Colin R. Middle Class Families: *Social and Geographical Mobility. 224 pp.*

Burton, Lindy. Vulnerable Children. *272 pp.*

Gavron, Hannah. The Captive Wife: *Conflicts of Household Mothers. 190 pp.*

George, Victor, and **Wilding, Paul.** Motherless Families. *220 pp.*

Klein, Josephine. Samples from English Cultures.

1. Three Preliminary Studies and Aspects of Adult Life in England. *447 pp.*
2. Child-Rearing Practices and Index. *247 pp.*

Klein, Viola. Britain's Married Women Workers. *180 pp.*

The Feminine Character. *History of an Ideology. 244 pp.*

McWhinnie, Alexina M. Adopted Children. *How They Grow Up. 304 pp.*

● **Myrdal, Alva,** and **Klein, Viola.** Women's Two Roles: *Home and Work. 238 pp. 27 tables.*

Parsons, Talcott, and **Bales, Robert F.** Family: Socialization and Interaction Process. *In collaboration with James Olds, Morris Zelditch and Philip E. Slater. 456 pp. 50 figures and tables.*

SOCIAL SERVICES

Bastide, Roger. The Sociology of Mental Disorder. *Translated from the French by Jean McNeil. 260 pp.*

Carlebach, Julius. Caring For Children in Trouble. *266 pp.*

Forder, R. A. (Ed.) Penelope Hall's Social Services of England and Wales. *352 pp.*

George, Victor. Foster Care. *Theory and Practice. 234 pp.*

Social Security: *Beveridge and After. 258 pp.*

George, V., and **Wilding, P.** Motherless Families. *248 pp.*

● **Goetschius, George W.** Working with Community Groups. *256 pp.*

Goetschius, George W., and **Tash, Joan.** Working with Unattached Youth. *416 pp.*

Hall, M. P., and **Howes, I. V.** The Church in Social Work. *A Study of Moral Welfare Work undertaken by the Church of England. 320 pp.*

Heywood, Jean S. Children in Care: *the Development of the Service for the Deprived Child. 264 pp.*

Hoenig, J., and **Hamilton, Marian W.** The De-Segregation of the Mentally Ill. *284 pp.*

Jones, Kathleen. Mental Health and Social Policy, 1845-1959. *264 pp.*

King, Roy D., Raynes, Norma V., and **Tizard, Jack.** Patterns of Residential Care. *356 pp.*

Leigh, John. Young People and Leisure. *256 pp.*

Morris, Mary. Voluntary Work and the Welfare State. *300 pp.*

Morris, Pauline. Put Away: *A Sociological Study of Institutions for the Mentally Retarded. 364 pp.*

Nokes, P. L. The Professional Task in Welfare Practice. *152 pp.*

Timms, Noel. Psychiatric Social Work in Great Britain (1939-1962). *280 pp.*

● Social Casework: *Principles and Practice. 256 pp.*

Young, A. F. Social Services in British Industry. *272 pp.*

Young, A. F., and **Ashton, E. T.** British Social Work in the Nineteenth Century. *288 pp.*

SOCIOLOGY OF EDUCATION

Banks, Olive. Parity and Prestige in English Secondary Education: a Study in Educational Sociology. *272 pp.*

Bentwich, Joseph. Education in Israel. *224 pp. 8 pp. plates.*

● **Blyth, W. A. L.** English Primary Education. *A Sociological Description.*

1. Schools. *232 pp.*
2. Background. *168 pp.*

Collier, K. G. The Social Purposes of Education: *Personal and Social Values in Education. 268 pp.*

Dale, R. R., and **Griffith, S.** Down Stream: *Failure in the Grammar School. 108 pp.*

Dore, R. P. Education in Tokugawa Japan. *356 pp. 9 pp. plates.*

Evans, K. M. Sociometry and Education. *158 pp.*

●**Ford, Julienne.** Social Class and the Comprehensive School. *192 pp.*

Foster, P. J. Education and Social Change in Ghana. *336 pp. 3 maps.*

Fraser, W. R. Education and Society in Modern France. *150 pp.*

Grace, Gerald R. Role Conflict and the Teacher. *About 200 pp.*

Hans, Nicholas. New Trends in Education in the Eighteenth Century. *278 pp. 19 tables.*

● Comparative Education: *A Study of Educational Factors and Traditions. 360 pp.*

Hargreaves, David. Interpersonal Relations and Education. *432 pp.*

● Social Relations in a Secondary School. *240 pp.*

Holmes, Brian. Problems in Education. *A Comparative Approach. 336 pp.*

King, Ronald. Values and Involvement in a Grammar School. *164 pp.*

School Organization and Pupil Involvement. *A Study of Secondary Schools.*

●**Mannheim, Karl,** and **Stewart, W. A. C.** An Introduction to the Sociology of Education. *206 pp.*

Morris, Raymond N. The Sixth Form and College Entrance. *231 pp.*

●**Musgrove, F.** Youth and the Social Order. *176 pp.*

●**Ottaway, A. K. C.** Education and Society: An Introduction to the Sociology of Education. *With an Introduction by W. O. Lester Smith. 212 pp.*

Peers, Robert. Adult Education: *A Comparative Study. 398 pp.*

Pritchard, D. G. Education and the Handicapped: *1760 to 1960. 258 pp.*

Richardson, Helen. Adolescent Girls in Approved Schools. *308 pp.*

Stratta, Erica. The Education of Borstal Boys. *A Study of their Educational Experiences prior to, and during, Borstal Training. 256 pp.*

Taylor, P. H., Reid, W. A., and **Holley, B. J.** The English Sixth Form. *A Case Study in Curriculum Research. 200 pp.*

SOCIOLOGY OF CULTURE

Eppel, E. M., and **M.** Adolescents and Morality: *A Study of some Moral Values and Dilemmas of Working Adolescents in the Context of a changing Climate of Opinion. Foreword by W. J. H. Sprott. 268 pp. 39 tables.*

●**Fromm, Erich.** The Fear of Freedom. *286 pp.*

● The Sane Society. *400 pp.*

Mannheim, Karl. Essays on the Sociology of Culture. *Edited by Ernst Mannheim in co-operation with Paul Kecskemeti. Editorial Note by Adolph Lowe. 280 pp.*

Weber, Alfred. Farewell to European History: *or The Conquest of Nihilism. Translated from the German by R. F. C. Hull. 224 pp.*

SOCIOLOGY OF RELIGION

Argyle, Michael and **Beit-Hallahmi, Benjamin.** The Social Psychology of Religion. *About 256 pp.*
Nelson, G. K. Spiritualism and Society. *313 pp.*
Stark, Werner. The Sociology of Religion. *A Study of Christendom.*
Volume I. *Established Religion. 248 pp.*
Volume II. *Sectarian Religion. 368 pp.*
Volume III. *The Universal Church. 464 pp.*
Volume IV. *Types of Religious Man. 352 pp.*
Volume V. *Types of Religious Culture. 464 pp.*
Turner, B. S. Weber and Islam. *216 pp.*
Watt, W. Montgomery. Islam and the Integration of Society. *320 pp.*

SOCIOLOGY OF ART AND LITERATURE

Jarvie, Ian C. Towards a Sociology of the Cinema. *A Comparative Essay on the Structure and Functioning of a Major Entertainment Industry. 405 pp.*
Rust, Frances S. Dance in Society. *An Analysis of the Relationships between the Social Dance and Society in England from the Middle Ages to the Present Day. 256 pp. 8 pp. of plates.*
Schücking, L. L. The Sociology of Literary Taste. *112 pp.*
Wolff, Janet. Hermeneutic Philosophy and the Sociology of Art. *About 200 pp.*

SOCIOLOGY OF KNOWLEDGE

Diesing, P. Patterns of Discovery in the Social Sciences. *262 pp.*
●**Douglas, J. D.** (Ed.) Understanding Everyday Life. *370 pp.*
●**Hamilton, P.** Knowledge and Social Structure. *174 pp.*
Jarvie, I. C. Concepts and Society. *232 pp.*
Mannheim, Karl. Essays on the Sociology of Knowledge. *Edited by Paul Kecskemeti. Editorial Note by Adolph Lowe. 353 pp.*
Remmling, Gunter W. (Ed.) Towards the Sociology of Knowledge. *Origin and Development of a Sociological Thought Style. 463 pp.*
Stark, Werner. The Sociology of Knowledge: *An Essay in Aid of a Deeper Understanding of the History of Ideas. 384 pp.*

URBAN SOCIOLOGY

Ashworth, William. The Genesis of Modern British Town Planning: *A Study in Economic and Social History of the Nineteenth and Twentieth Centuries. 288 pp.*
Cullingworth, J. B. Housing Needs and Planning Policy: *A Restatement of the Problems of Housing Need and 'Overspill' in England and Wales. 232 pp. 44 tables. 8 maps.*

Dickinson, Robert E. City and Region: *A Geographical Interpretation 608 pp. 125 figures.*

The West European City: *A Geographical Interpretation. 600 pp. 129 maps. 29 plates.*

● The City Region in Western Europe. *320 pp. Maps.*

Humphreys, Alexander J. New Dubliners: *Urbanization and the Irish Family. Foreword by George C. Homans. 304 pp.*

Jackson, Brian. Working Class Community: *Some General Notions raised by a Series of Studies in Northern England. 192 pp.*

Jennings, Hilda. Societies in the Making: *a Study of Development and Re-development within a County Borough. Foreword by D. A. Clark. 286 pp.*

●**Mann, P. H.** An Approach to Urban Sociology. *240 pp.*

Morris, R. N., and **Mogey, J.** The Sociology of Housing. *Studies at Berinsfield. 232 pp. 4 pp. plates.*

Rosser, C., and **Harris, C.** The Family and Social Change. *A Study of Family and Kinship in a South Wales Town. 352 pp. 8 maps.*

RURAL SOCIOLOGY

Chambers, R. J. H. Settlement Schemes in Tropical Africa: *A Selective Study. 268 pp.*

Haswell, M. R. The Economics of Development in Village India. *120 pp.*

Littlejohn, James. Westrigg: *the Sociology of a Cheviot Parish. 172 pp. 5 figures.*

Mayer, Adrian C. Peasants in the Pacific. *A Study of Fiji Indian Rural Society. 248 pp. 20 plates.*

Williams, W. M. The Sociology of an English Village: *Gosforth. 272 pp. 12 figures. 13 tables.*

SOCIOLOGY OF INDUSTRY AND DISTRIBUTION

Anderson, Nels. Work and Leisure. *280 pp.*

●**Blau, Peter M.,** and **Scott, W. Richard.** Formal Organizations: *a Comparative approach. Introduction and Additional Bibliography by J. H. Smith. 326 pp.*

Eldridge, J. E. T. Industrial Disputes. *Essays in the Sociology of Industrial Relations. 288 pp.*

Hetzler, Stanley. Applied Measures for Promoting Technological Growth. *352 pp.*

Technological Growth and Social Change. *Achieving Modernization. 269 pp.*

Hollowell, Peter G. The Lorry Driver. *272 pp.*

Jefferys, Margot, *with the assistance of Winifred Moss.* Mobility in the Labour Market: *Employment Changes in Battersea and Dagenham. Preface by Barbara Wootton. 186 pp. 51 tables.*

Millerson, Geoffrey. The Qualifying Associations: *a Study in Professionalization. 320 pp.*

Smelser, Neil J. Social Change in the Industrial Revolution: *An Application of Theory to the Lancashire Cotton Industry, 1770-1840. 468 pp. 12 figures. 14 tables.*

Williams, Gertrude. Recruitment to Skilled Trades. *240 pp.*

Young, A. F. Industrial Injuries Insurance: *an Examination of British Policy. 192 pp.*

DOCUMENTARY

Schlesinger, Rudolf (Ed.) Changing Attitudes in Soviet Russia.

2. The Nationalities Problem and Soviet Administration. *Selected Readings on the Development of Soviet Nationalities Policies. Introduced by the editor. Translated by W. W. Gottlieb. 324 pp.*

ANTHROPOLOGY

Ammar, Hamed. Growing up in an Egyptian Village: *Silwa, Province of Aswan. 336 pp.*

Brandel-Syrier, Mia. Reeftown Elite. *A Study of Social Mobility in a Modern African Community on the Reef. 376 pp.*

Crook, David, and **Isabel.** Revolution in a Chinese Village: *Ten Mile Inn. 230 pp. 8 plates. 1 map.*

Dickie-Clark, H. F. The Marginal Situation. *A Sociological Study of a Coloured Group. 236 pp.*

Dube, S. C. Indian Village. *Foreword by Morris Edward Opler. 276 pp. 4 plates.*

India's Changing Villages: *Human Factors in Community Development. 260 pp. 8 plates. 1 map.*

Firth, Raymond. Malay Fishermen. *Their Peasant Economy. 420 pp. 17 pp. plates.*

Firth, R., Hubert, J., and **Forge, A.** Families and their Relatives. *Kinship in a Middle-Class Sector of London: An Anthropological Study. 456 pp.*

Gulliver, P. H. Social Control in an African Society: a Study of the Arusha, Agricultural Masai of Northern Tanganyika. *320 pp. 8 plates. 10 figures.*

Family Herds. *288 pp.*

Ishwaran, K. Shivapur. *A South Indian Village. 216 pp.*

Tradition and Economy in Village India: *An Interactionist Approach. Foreword by Conrad Arensburg. 176 pp.*

Jarvie, Ian C. The Revolution in Anthropology. *268 pp.*

Jarvie, Ian C., and **Agassi, Joseph.** Hong Kong. *A Society in Transition. 396 pp. Illustrated with plates and maps.*

Little, Kenneth L. Mende of Sierra Leone. *308 pp. and folder.*

Negroes in Britain. *With a New Introduction and Contemporary Study by Leonard Bloom. 320 pp.*

Lowie, Robert H. Social Organization. *494 pp.*
Mayer, Adrian C. Caste and Kinship in Central India: *A Village and its Region. 328 pp. 16 plates. 15 figures. 16 tables.*
Peasants in the Pacific. *A Study of Fiji Indian Rural Society. 248 pp.*
Smith, Raymond T. The Negro Family in British Guiana: *Family Structure and Social Status in the Villages. With a Foreword by Meyer Fortes. 314 pp. 8 plates. 1 figure. 4 maps.*

SOCIOLOGY AND PHILOSOPHY

Barnsley, John H. The Social Reality of Ethics. *A Comparative Analysis of Moral Codes. 448 pp.*
Diesing, Paul. Patterns of Discovery in the Social Sciences. *362 pp.*
●**Douglas, Jack D.** (Ed.) Understanding Everyday Life. *Toward the Reconstruction of Sociological Knowledge. Contributions by Alan F. Blum. Aaron W. Cicourel, Norman K. Denzin, Jack D. Douglas, John Heeren, Peter McHugh, Peter K. Manning, Melvin Power, Matthew Speier, Roy Turner, D. Lawrence Wieder, Thomas P. Wilson and Don H. Zimmerman. 370 pp.*
Jarvie, Ian C. Concepts and Society. *216 pp.*
Pelz, Werner. The Scope of Understanding in Sociology. *Towards a more radical reorientation in the social humanistic sciences. 283 pp.*
Roche, Maurice. Phenomenology, Language and the Social Sciences. *371 pp.*
Sahay, Arun. Sociological Analysis. *212 pp.*
Sklair, Leslie. The Sociology of Progress. *320 pp.*

International Library of Anthropology

General Editor Adam Kuper

Brown, Paula. The Chimbu. *A Study of Change in the New Guinea Highlands. 151 pp.*
Lloyd, P. C. Power and Independence. *Urban Africans' Perception of Social Inequality. 264 pp.*
Pettigrew, Joyce. Robber Noblemen. *A Study of the Political System of the Sikh Jats. 284 pp.*
Van Den Berghe, Pierre L. Power and Privilege at an African University. *278 pp.*

International Library of Social Policy

General Editor Kathleen Jones

Bayley, M. Mental Handicap and Community Care. *426 pp.*
Butler, J. R. Family Doctors and Public Policy. *208 pp.*
Holman, Robert. Trading in Children. *A Study of Private Fostering. 355 pp.*

Jones, Kathleen. History of the Mental Health Service. *428 pp.*
Thomas, J. E. The English Prison Officer since 1850: *A Study in Conflict. 258 pp.*
Woodward, J. To Do the Sick No Harm. *A Study of the British Voluntary Hospital System to 1875. About 220 pp.*

International Library of Welfare and Philosophy

General Editors Noel Timms and David Watson

● **Plant, Raymond.** Community and Ideology. *104 pp.*

Primary Socialization, Language and Education

General Editor Basil Bernstein

Bernstein, Basil. Class, Codes and Control. *2 volumes.*
1. *Theoretical Studies Towards a Sociology of Language. 254 pp.*
2. *Applied Studies Towards a Sociology of Language. About 400 pp.*

Brandis, W., and **Bernstein, B.** Selection and Control. *176 pp.*
Brandis, Walter, and **Henderson, Dorothy.** Social Class, Language and Communication. *288 pp.*
Cook-Gumperz, Jenny. Social Control and Socialization. *A Study of Class Differences in the Language of Maternal Control. 290 pp.*
● **Gahagan, D. M.,** and **G. A.** Talk Reform. *Exploration in Language for Infant School Children. 160 pp.*
Robinson, W. P., and **Rackstraw, Susan D. A.** A Question of Answers. *2 volumes. 192 pp. and 180 pp.*
Turner, Geoffrey J., and **Mohan, Bernard A.** A Linguistic Description and Computer Programme for Children's Speech. *208 pp.*

Reports of the Institute of Community Studies

Cartwright, Ann. Human Relations and Hospital Care. *272 pp.*
● Parents and Family Planning Services. *306 pp.*
Patients and their Doctors. *A Study of General Practice. 304 pp.*
● **Jackson, Brian.** Streaming: *an Education System in Miniature. 168 pp.*
Jackson, Brian, and **Marsden, Dennis.** Education and the Working Class: *Some General Themes raised by a Study of 88 Working-class Children in a Northern Industrial City. 268 pp. 2 folders.*
Marris, Peter. The Experience of Higher Education. *232 pp. 27 tables.*
Loss and Change. *192 pp.*

Marris, Peter, and **Rein, Martin.** Dilemmas of Social Reform. *Poverty and Community Action in the United States. 256 pp.*

Marris, Peter, and **Somerset, Anthony.** African Businessmen. *A Study of Entrepreneurship and Development in Kenya. 256 pp.*

Mills, Richard. Young Outsiders: *a Study in Alternative Communities. 216 pp.*

Runciman, W. G. Relative Deprivation and Social Justice. *A Study of Attitudes to Social Inequality in Twentieth-Century England. 352 pp.*

Willmott, Peter. Adolescent Boys in East London. *230 pp.*

Willmott, Peter, and **Young, Michael.** Family and Class in a London Suburb. *202 pp. 47 tables.*

Young, Michael. Innovation and Research in Education. *192 pp.*

●**Young, Michael,** and **McGeeney, Patrick.** Learning Begins at Home. *A Study of a Junior School and its Parents. 128 pp.*

Young, Michael, and **Willmott, Peter.** Family and Kinship in East London. *Foreword by Richard M. Titmuss. 252 pp. 39 tables.*

The Symmetrical Family. *410 pp.*

Reports of the Institute for Social Studies in Medical Care

Cartwright, Ann, Hockey, Lisbeth, and **Anderson, John L.** Life Before Death. *310 pp.*

Dunnell, Karen, and **Cartwright, Ann.** Medicine Takers, Prescribers and Hoarders. *190 pp.*

Medicine, Illness and Society

General Editor W. M. Williams

Robinson, David. The Process of Becoming Ill. *142 pp.*

Stacey, Margaret, *et al.* Hospitals, Children and Their Families. *The Report of a Pilot Study. 202 pp.*

Monographs in Social Theory

General Editor Arthur Brittan

●**Barnes, B.** Scientific Knowledge and Sociological Theory. *About 200 pp.*

Bauman, Zygmunt. Culture as Praxis. *204 pp.*

●**Dixon, Keith.** Sociological Theory. *Pretence and Possibility. 142 pp.*

●**Smith, Anthony D.** The Concept of Social Change. *A Critique of the Functionalist Theory of Social Change. 208 pp.*

Routledge Social Science Journals

The British Journal of Sociology. *Edited by Terence P. Morris. Vol. 1, No. 1, March 1950 and Quarterly. Roy. 8vo. Back numbers available.* ***An international journal with articles on all aspects of sociology.***

Economy and Society. *Vol. 1, No. 1. February 1972 and Quarterly. Metric Roy. 8vo. A journal for all social scientists covering sociology, philosophy, anthropology, economics and history. Back numbers available.*

Year Book of Social Policy in Britain, The. *Edited by Kathleen Jones. 1971. Published annually.*

Printed in Great Britain by Unwin Brothers Limited
The Gresham Press Old Woking Surrey
A member of the Staples Printing Group